China's Belt and Road Initiative

Pradumna B. Rana • Xianbai Ji

China's Belt and Road Initiative

Impacts on Asia and Policy Agenda

palgrave
macmillan

Pradumna B. Rana
S. Rajaratnam School of
International Studies
Nanyang Technological University
Singapore, Singapore

Xianbai Ji
S. Rajaratnam School of
International Studies
Nanyang Technological University
Singapore, Singapore

ISBN 978-981-15-5170-3 ISBN 978-981-15-5171-0 (eBook)
https://doi.org/10.1007/978-981-15-5171-0

This Palgrave Macmillan imprint is published by the registered company Springer Nature Singapore Pte Ltd.
The registered company address is: 152 Beach Road, #21-01/04 Gateway East, Singapore 189721, Singapore

Foreword

The BRI has catapulted China to a prominent position in advancing connectivity across the Asian, European, and African continents mirroring the old Silk Road of the bygone era. From the perspective of stakeholder countries, however, the BRI infrastructure campaign presents both benefits as well as risks.

The BRI has the potential to bring huge amounts of investments and loans to developing Asian countries that suffer from infrastructure funding shortages. China and BRI participating countries are also opening up the market-place thereby allowing people to transact businesses across territories which they could not do previously. On the other hand, there is no free lunch. China may expect some kind of favourable treatment by the beneficiaries of the BRI and expand its geopolitical clout across Asia. Large-scale BRI infrastructure projects will also have significant fiscal, labour, and environmental sustainability implications that must be addressed collaboratively by China and its BRI partners.

In the usual Chinese style, the BRI vision was announced with few details and was difficult to understand at first. Issues are becoming clearer now and at the Second BRI Forum in April 2019, President Xi Jinping pledged to reform the BRI including placing emphasis on 'high quality' green and clean projects that would be inclusive, market-driven, and sustainable.

This book reviews the evolution of the BRI vision, alerts Asian countries to a menu of alternative infrastructure funding opportunities presented by other major powers, empirically estimates the potential macroeconomic impacts of the BRI corridors, surveys Asian opinion leaders on various aspects of the BRI, and carries out regional case studies on the BRI's economic and geopolitical impacts on Southeast Asia, South Asia, and Central Asia.

The authors, one of whom has many years of experience at the Asian Development Bank, conclude that the BRI is a potential force for good, but in order for that to happen both China and BRI stakeholder countries need to implement a number of policy reforms. Accordingly, the authors propose a comprehensive set of reforms. I believe that with the implementation of these reforms, there is a greater chance that an improved BRI 2.0 will be mutually beneficial and give rise to win–win situations as originally envisaged by Beijing. The book is, therefore, timely and useful.

Besides policy-makers, this book is also a valuable resource to academia, think tanks, development institutions, students, and even the general public as a welcome contribution to the growing literature on Asian economic development, China's foreign economic policy, and regional integration.

Singapore is an important commercial, financial, and transport hub and it could usefully contribute to and benefit from the BRI. The country is located strategically along the Maritime Silk Road and at the tip of the overland China-Indochina Peninsula Economic Corridor that connects China with mainland Southeast Asia. Given its experience on infrastructure financing and economic development, Singapore is particularly well positioned to play a match-making role to offer ideas and suggestions to improve the BRI. Singapore can convene meetings of interested investors and mobilise funds for the construction of BRI-related projects.

I also see opportunities for Singapore to help build technical and human capacity, train labour force, and maintain logistical order in collaboration with China and other BRI stakeholder countries. For example, in January 2019, China Council for the Promotion of International Trade and Singapore International Mediation Centre signed an MOU for jointly establishing a multilateral mediators' panel to settle commercial disputes arising from the BRI.

Ambassador Ong Keng Yong
Executive Deputy Chairman
S. Rajaratnam School of International Studies
Nanyang Technological University
Singapore

Preface

The central thesis of an earlier book edited by Pradumna B. Rana, entitled *Renaissance of Asia: Evolving Relations between South Asia and East Asia*, was that Asia's emergence, integration, and the irresistible shift of economic power from the West to the East are not without precedence. If one looks back at the economic history of Asia one should really be talking about Asia's 're-emergence', 'Asia's re-integration', or the 'Renaissance of Asia'. This is because even in the previous eras of globalisation, a prosperous Asia was regionally integrated and globally connected.

One key factor that has been driving 'Asia's re-emergence' and 'Asia's re-integration' and converting 'Maritime Asia' into 'Continental Asia' is the proliferation of efforts to promote cross-border infrastructure development and transport connectivity in Asia. Among these efforts China's Belt and Road Initiative (BRI), which retraces the old Silk Roads, is in a class of its own in terms of ambition, scale, and scope. Parallel initiatives championed by Japan, the United States, and the European Union and various Asian sub-regional initiatives like the ASEAN Masterplan for Connectivity, the Greater Mekong Sub-regional programme, and the Central Asian Regional Economic Cooperation Program have also proliferated. Of course, the BRI, labelled by President Xi as the 'project of the century' also has enormous geopolitical and strategic dimensions.

The Academic Research Fund Tier 1 (AcRF Tier 1) grant RG80/18 that we won together with Associate Professor Chia Wai-Mun for a Study to Analyse the Economic and Strategic Impacts of the Belt and Road Initiative provided an opportunity for detailed research on the subject of the BRI and other connectivity issues and initiatives in Asia. We are therefore grateful to the Ministry of Education in Singapore for the generous research grant. The research also recieved support from the Collaborative Innovation Center for New-type Urbanization and Social Governance of Jiangsu Province with Soochow University, China. When we embarked on the journey we had no idea that we would land up with a book.

The book is policy-oriented. It will be useful to policy-makers in countries that have already participated in the BRI or planning to do so sometime in the future. The book will also be useful to academics, think tank staff, and company executives who are interested in Asia's Renaissance.

This book owes much to many. We are grateful for the support and encouragement of Ambassador Ong Keng Yong, Dean Ralf Emmers, Dean Joseph Liow and Dean Chen Jinhua. We would also like to thank the Centre of Multilateralism Studies (CMS) of S. Rajaratnam School of International Studies (RSIS) where we are based and CMS staff Alan Chong, Phidel Vineles, and other colleagues.

Thanks are also due to Sreeya Mukherjee for her excellent research support and for going over drafts of the book. Li Changtai and Avani Giri have also contributed to this book in important ways.

For the behind-the-scenes help at the Palgrave Macmillan, we are grateful to Ruth Jenner, Lavanya Devgun and Arumugam Hemalatha for their kind help and assistance.

Finally, we both are grateful to our families for their continued support without which the book could not have been prepared.

Singapore, Singapore

Pradumna B. Rana
Xianbai Ji

Contents

About the Authors

Pradumna B. Rana is an associate professor at the Centre for Multilateralism Studies, S. Rajaratnam School of International Studies, Nanyang Technological University (NTU), Singapore. He is an international economist with expertise in the areas of international macroeconomics, trade, and development issues focusing on Asia. He was the senior director of the Asian Development Bank's Office of Regional Economic Integration which spearheaded ADB's support for Asian economic integration. Prior to that, he held various senior positions at the ADB for many years. He has teaching and research experience at NTU, National University of Singapore, and the Tribhuvan University, Nepal. He obtained his PhD from Vanderbilt University where he was a Fulbright Scholar and a master's in economics from Michigan State University and Tribhuvan University where he was a gold medalist. He has written widely in the areas of Asian economic development and integration, financial crises, and economic policy reforms in transition economies. These include 16 authored or edited books, over 25 chapters in books, and over 50 articles in international scholarly journals. His recently co-authored books are *Jumpstarting South Asia: Revisiting Economic Reforms and Look East Policies, South Asia: Rising to the Challenge of Globalisation*, and *Asia and the Global Economic Crisis: Challenges in a Financially Integrated World* (Palgrave Macmillan). His recently co-edited books are *Pan-Asian Integration: Linking East and South Asia* (Palgrave Macmillan) and *National Strategies for Regional Integration: South and East Asian Case Studies.* He has written widely in internationally reputed journals such as the *Journal of International Economics, The Review of Economic and*

Statistics, Journal of Development Economics, World Development, International Trade Journal, Journal of Asian Economics, Singapore Economic Review, East Asian Economic Review, Global Governance, and Global Policy.

Xianbai Ji is a research fellow with the International Political Economy Programme at S. Rajaratnam School of International Studies (RSIS), Nanyang Technological University, Singapore. He works on international economic relations, trade diplomacy, and regional integration mainly in Asia and Europe. He has been affiliated with the European Union Centre in Singapore as associate fellow (since 2014), and with the Australian National University as Europa visiting fellow (in 2017). He has written for *Asia Europe Journal*, *Singapore Economic Review*, *Pacific Focus*, and *East Asian Economic Review* and with leading think tanks such as Council on Foreign Relations, German Institute for International and Security Affairs (SWP), and Australian Institute of International Affairs. He is also a current affairs columnist for China Global Television Network (CGTN). He received his PhD from RSIS in 2019 as a prestigious Nanyang President's Graduate Scholar.

Abbreviations and Acronyms

ADB	Asian Development Bank
AEC	ASEAN Economic Community
AEP	Act East Policy
AfDB	African Development Bank
AIIB	Asian Infrastructure Investment Bank
APEC	Asia-Pacific Economic Cooperation
ASCN	ASEAN Smart Cities Network
ASEAN	Association of Southeast Asian Nations
ASEM	Asia-Europe Meeting
Asia EDGE	Enhancing Development and Growth through Energy Initiative
BBIN	Bangladesh, Bhutan, India, Nepal
BCIM	Bangladesh-China-India-Myanmar Economic Corridor
BIMSTEC	Bay of Bengal Initiative for Multi-Sectoral Technical and Economic Cooperation
BRF	Belt and Road Forum for International Cooperation
BRI	Belt and Road Initiative
BUILD Act	Better Utilization of Investments Leading to Development Act
BSA	Bilateral swap agreement
CAF	Development Bank of Latin America
CAR	Central Asian republic
CCAWA	China-Central Asia-West Asia Economic Corridor
CCI	China-Singapore (Chongqing) Demonstration Initiative on Strategic Connectivity
CDB	China Development Bank
CEA	EU Strategy on Connecting Europe and Asia
CICPEC	China-Indochina Peninsula Economic Corridor
CLMV	Cambodia, Laos, Myanmar, and Vietnam

CLT	China-Laos-Thailand high-speed railway
CMEC	China-Myanmar Economic Corridor
CMR	China-Mongolia-Russia Economic Corridor
CPEC	China-Pakistan Economic Corridor
DAC	OECD Development Assistance Committee
DCCP	Digital Connectivity and Cybersecurity Partnership
DFC	US International Development Finance Corporation
DSR	Digital Silk Road
CGE	Computable general equilibrium
CPEC	China-Pakistan Economic Corridor
EAS	East Asia Summit
EBRD	European Bank for Reconstruction and Development
ECRL	East Coast Rail Link
EEC	Eastern Economic Corridor of Thailand
EIB	European Investment Bank
EPQI	Enhanced Partnership for Quality Infrastructure
EU	European Union
Exim Bank	Export-Import Bank
FDI	Foreign direct investment
FOIP	Free and Open Indo-Pacific
FTA	Free trade agreement
G20	Group of 20
GDP	Gross domestic product
GMEC	Ganga-Mekong Economic Corridor
GTAP	Global Trade Analysis Project
HSR	High-speed railway
IA	Impact Assessment
IADB	Inter-American Development Bank
IAI	Initiative for ASEAN Integration
ICT	Information and communications technology
IFAD	International Fund for Agricultural Development
IIATC	India-Iran-Afghanistan Transit Corridor
IMF	International Monetary Fund
INSTC	International North-South Transport Corridor
ITAN	Infrastructure Transaction and Assistance Network
JBIC	Japan Bank for International Cooperation
JICA	Japan International Cooperation Agency
KMMT	Kaladan Multi-modal Transit Transport Corridor
LAC	Latin America and the Caribbean
LSG	Leading Small Group for Promoting the Belt and Road Initiative
MCC	Millennium Challenge Corporation
MCDF	Multilateral Cooperation Centre for Development Finance

MDB	Multilateral development bank
MIEC	Mekong-India Economic Corridor
MOU	Memorandum of Understanding
MPAC	Master Plan on ASEAN Connectivity
MSR	Maritime Silk Road
NDB	New Development Bank
NDRC	National Development and Reform Commission
NELB	New Eurasian Land Bridge
NEXI	Nippon Export and Investment Insurance
NGO	Non-governmental organisation
O&M	Operation and maintenance
ODA	Official development assistance
OECD	Organisation for Economic Co-operation and Development
OPIC	Overseas Private Investment Corporation
PPGD	Public and publicly guaranteed debt
SAARC	South Asian Association for Regional Cooperation
SAGQ	South Asian Growth Quadrangle
SASEC	South Asia Sub-regional Economic Cooperation
SCO	Shanghai Cooperation Organisation
SCS	South China Sea
SEZ	Special economic zone
SLCLIZ	Sri Lanka-China Logistics and Industrial Zone
SKRL	Singapore-Kunming Rail Link
SME	Small and medium-sized enterprise
SREB	Silk Road Economic Belt
SRF	Silk Road Fund
SSEZ	Sihanoukville Special Economic Zone
TCOB	Two Corridors, One Belt
TFA	WTO Trade Facilitation Agreement
THEC	Trans-Himalayan Economic Corridor
THMCN	Trans-Himalayan Multi-dimensional Connectivity Network
UN	United Nations
UNCTAD	United Nations Conference on Trade and Development
US	United States
WEF	World Economic Forum
WTO	World Trade Organisation

List of Figures

List of Tables

CHAPTER 1

China's Belt and Road Initiative: Introduction and Overview

1 Introduction

In September 2013 on a state visit to Kazakhstan, Chinese President Xi Jinping encouraged China and Central Asia to jointly build a Silk Road Economic Belt (SREB) to turn their 'good political relations, geographical proximity and economic complementarity into drivers of practical cooperation and sustained growth' (Xi 2013). Less than a month later, addressing the Indonesian Parliament, Xi spoke of developing the 21st Century Maritime Silk Road (MSR) that can transform oceans from a barrier to exchange into a bond of friendship. Initially grouped together as the 'One Belt, One Road', the SREB and MSR are now collectively referred to as the 'Belt and Road Initiative' (BRI). The founding premise of the BRI, as promulgated by Beijing, is to promote economic prosperity, mutual learning, and world peace through enhanced physical, financial, and human connectivity across the Asian, European, and African continents and their adjacent seas. Labelled by President Xi as 'a project of the century', the BRI has captured the world's imagination instantly and become China's landmark foreign and economic policy initiative (Rolland 2017).

Since the beginning, China has proclaimed the BRI to be a business proposition that will result in win-win situations[1] for all participants, given the world's massive appetite for infrastructure financing. The latest estimate by the Asian Development Bank (ADB) notes that Asia alone needs to invest approximately $26 trillion between 2016 and 2030 to meet its

P. B. Rana, X. Ji, *China's Belt and Road Initiative*,
https://doi.org/10.1007/978-981-15-5171-0_1

infrastructure shortfall (ADB 2017). The Global Infrastructure Outlook, a Group of 20 initiative prepared with Oxford Economics (2017), puts Asia's annual infrastructure financing gap at $275 billion. This compares with roughly $18.5 billion in annual lending by the World Bank to Asia and another $29 billion by ADB in 2017. There is clearly a gap in the market. While the BRI by itself will not be able to fill this gap, it has kick-started a new cycle of infrastructure spending in Asia and beyond.

China's announcement of the BRI was followed by Japan, the United States and Europe, individually or cooperatively, stepping up infrastructure investment and development efforts in the Indo-Pacific and the Eurasian regions. As such, the World Bank (2019) suggests that the BRI can substantially improve trade, foreign investment, and living conditions for citizens in the participating countries as well as the global economy at large.

However, the BRI presents many risks such as debtor countries not being able to service BRI-related debt and potential damages to environment due to mega-scale BRI projects. Also, in the usual Chinese style, the BRI vision was announced with few details and the concept sounded vague and difficult to understand. Mass and chaotic campaigns followed where everyone pitched in with frenzied enthusiasm to meet their superiors' wishes. Such efforts, in some cases, have led to low-quality and mismatched projects, duplication, conflicts of interest and corruption (Ang 2018). Another salient accusation is that Beijing deliberately pursues malicious 'debt trap diplomacy' to project undue political influence over sovereign nations that borrow from China under the BRI.[2] The United States has been particularly critical of the BRI's allegedly neo-colonial connotation, with Vice President Mike Pence (2018) lashing out at China for constructing a 'constricting belt' and a 'one-way road' that would drown BRI countries in a 'sea of debt'. Prominent Asian holdouts such as India likewise assert that the BRI is a web of influence activity, driven by the impulse of reconstructing a Sino-centric world order rather than a responsible aspiration of providing global public goods using Chinese funds (Chellaney 2018).

Wherever one stands in this debate, we see the BRI as a China-led international economic cooperation campaign directed at achieving improved connectivity, regional cooperation, and economic development on a trans-continental scale. Thus, the BRI has great potential to benefit many lower- and middle-income developing countries that are not adequately served by existing infrastructure and strapped for new investment.

But for all that, China's multi-faceted motives behind the BRI must be understood and the multitude of risks and downsides associated with BRI projects addressed. Already written into the constitution of the Communist Party of China in 2017, the BRI is here to stay and is likely to become *the* defining global economic agenda item for the decades to come. Therefore, whether the BRI emerges as a 'bonanza' or a 'nightmare' for recipient countries, as Lim (2018) puts it, in the end depends on the policy actions taken by China as well as by BRI participating countries to maximise the benefits and minimise the risks of BRI projects. For the purported win-win potential to come into fruition, China has to come up with new policies and guidelines for the BRI to respond to warranted criticisms in shoring up the BRI's legitimacy and developmental impact. At the Second Belt and Road Forum (BRF) in 2019, President Xi acknowledged various constructive criticisms and pledged to reform the BRI. Fine tuning and quality control are to be done with emphasis placed on 'high quality' projects (Xi 2019). BRI participating countries, for their part, also need to reach an internal consensus on how to engage with China and then adopt policy reforms to create conducive national conditions for making the best use of BRI funds.

In this context, this policy-oriented book studies and investigates the BRI's impact on Asia and outlines a policy agenda for both China and regional BRI participating countries to work towards an improved BRI 2.0. Specific objectives of the book are to: (1) review the evolving BRI vision, scope, institutions, and progress that has been made on BRI cooperation; (2) conduct a comprehensive assessment of the economic and geopolitical dimensions of the BRI; (3) provide empirical evidence on how BRI countries could benefit from greater transport connectivity and trade openness; (4) identify the major benefits and risks of the BRI from the perspective of countries in Southeast Asia, South Asia and Central Asia; and (5) offer actionable policy recommendations to make the BRI a win-win venture. In terms of methodology, we employ a mixed-method research strategy that incorporates (1) computable general equilibrium (CGE) modelling, (2) perception survey, and (3) desk research and regional case studies.

The BRI is still a work-in-progress. Despite a stated focus on Afro-Eurasia, the BRI is an inclusive concept with geographical malleability, meaning any country that wishes to support the BRI is considered to be a part of it. As a result, China has refrained from issuing an official map of participating countries and is pro-actively reaching out to countries that have not yet signed up to it. Therefore, for the purpose of this book, we consider any country that has signed a BRI memorandum of understanding (MOU) or joint statement with China as a BRI participating (or stakeholder) country. As of October 2019, 137 countries had signed at least one BRI agreement with China, 47 of which are from the Asia-Pacific region (Fig. 1.1). China has also not fully fleshed out the exact criteria for defining what constitutes a BRI project. Hence, in this book, all China-related infrastructure and development projects in Asian BRI countries after 2013 are considered as BRI projects. Estimates of Chinese financing under the auspices of the BRI range from $575 billion to 8 trillion (Hillman 2018). The wide range is a reflection of the amorphous nature of the BRI and the limited data availability.

2 Origins of the BRI

The BRI concept has a deep historical root. It drew inspiration from the overland and maritime silk roads of the bygone era (Rimmer 2018). Active since more than two-thousand years ago, the historical land-based silk road had two main routes. The northern route stretched from Chang'an (present-day Xi'an) westward to the Mediterranean through great central Eurasian cities of Samarkand, Bukhara, and Tehran. Along this trading route, luxurious goods such as Chinese silk, lacquerware, porcelain, and medicinal herbs; European glassware and coal; Persian dates, saffron, and pistachio nuts; Indian paper, sandalwood, and cotton; and Central Asia's musical instruments, jade, almonds, indigo, and frankincense were

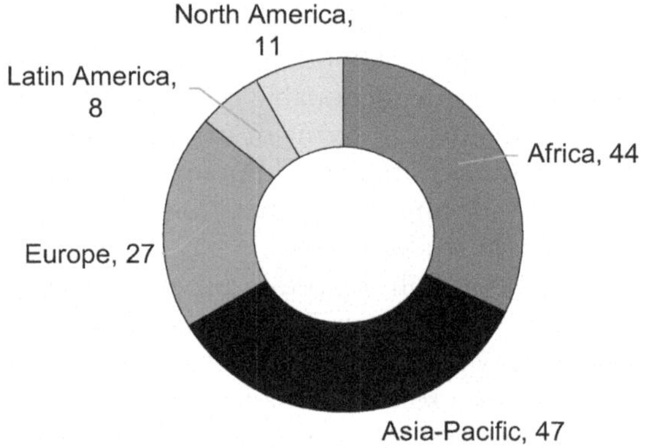

Fig. 1.1 Continental breakdown of BRI participating countries (as of October 2019). Source: Belt and Road Portal

transported to different destinations by laden camels and traded at border markets. And where merchants went, envoys, courtiers, intellectuals, pilgrims, and craftsmen alike followed suit, spreading religions, cultures, and technologies across the connected civilisations. To the south of the northern trans-continental route lay an intra-continental southwestern silk road (Rana and Chia 2017). This road began in Yunnan, passed through Myanmar, India, Nepal, and Tibet and looped back to Yunnan. These two terrestrial silk road routes heralded the first phase of globalisation where trade ceased to be a local affair and started to become global in nature (Vanham 2019).

The land-based silk roads reached their peak during China's Tang Dynasty. From the seventh century, Islamic traders based in the Arabian heartland began dominating the Mediterranean and the Indian Ocean trade. Spice displaced silk as the main commodity being traded, earning the route a name of 'spice road'. In the fifteenth century, this spice road also fell into disfavour when the breakup of the Mongol Empire and the bloody successions of dynasties and empires in China and Europe almost blocked off all east-west commercial traffic. But in the meantime, maritime navigation and ship-building technologies leaped forward, making for the ascendency of the ancient maritime silk road at the dawn of the second phase of globalisation. The Ming Dynasty dispatched Admiral Zheng He on seven epic treasure voyages to the Western Seas (Indian Ocean) between 1405 and 1433. Generations of Portuguese, Spanish, Dutch, and English explorers also opened direct maritime trading routes between Western Europe and East Asia. Seaborne trade flourished subsequently, as not only light-weight luxurious goods, but also bulky and heavy items were traded. Afterwards peaceful exchanges between the East and the West were suffocated by colonialism, the two World Wars and the Cold War. The heyday of the land and maritime silk roads coincided with a historical period in which Asia (mainly China and India) accounted for the largest share of the gross domestic product (GDP) of humanity (Maddison 2007). The demise of the silk roads, as maintained by the Chinese historiography, was associated with China's perceived civilisational downturn and centuries of national humiliation. As it re-emerges as a preponderant great power on the world stage, China under President Xi has decided to embark on an ambitious journey to resurrect the ancient silk roads through its modern-day incarnation to reclaim China's rightful greatness (Ferdinand 2016; Callahan 2016).

Besides the deep-seated historic underpinning, the BRI can be understood as the more direct outgrowth of two erstwhile Chinese state-building campaigns launched towards the end of the twentieth century (Yeh and Wharton 2016). One is the Western Development Strategy (WDS) put forward in 1999. In congruence with the BRI, the WDS was focused on constructing economic infrastructures in inner western provinces so that interior China could catch up with the economic success on the Chinese eastern seaboard. The other policy, also adopted in 1999, is the 'Going Global' (GG) campaign to facilitate China's international economic expansion amidst a booming world economy. While this pair of national policies yielded only mixed results, they nevertheless equipped China with valuable skill sets and first-hand experiences in relation to transacting in unfamiliar regulatory environments and executing infrastructure projects in harsh natural terrains in and beyond China's borders. When taking office as the new Party chief, Xi built upon those qualities and fused the WDS and GG into a single organising global economic agenda in the form of the BRI.

It should also be noted that, at the time of the BRI's pronouncement, China was facing difficult situations, both at home and abroad. Domestically, the rapid economic growth brought about by an export-oriented development model was slowing down due in part to rising labour cost and China moving up the value chain. Then nascent efforts to transit to a domestic consumption-driven economic model were abruptly knocked off course by exogenous economic crises originating in the West. Even worse, the Four-Trillion-Yuan stimulus package enacted in November 2008 at the height of the Global Financial Crisis backfired, leaving China with economic quagmires of capital glut, industrial over-capacity and over-stretch of state-owned enterprises. Indeed, President Xi listed redressing over-capacity as a top priority for supply-side economic restructuring at the first Central Economic Work Conference he chaired in December 2012. Externally, China faced a string of geopolitical headwinds. The Obama administration 'rebalanced' to the Asia-Pacific with vengeance to contain China's growing regional clout. Sino-Japanese relations descended to historical lows because of Japan's war-time legacy and territorial disputes over the Diaoyu/Senkaku island. Concurrently, China's relations with some southern neighbours deteriorated with the Philippines taking China to the court at The Hague over the legality of China's territorial claim in the South China Sea. Hedging against geopolitical pressure at its front door, Wang Jisi, Dean of Peking University's School of International Studies, in 2012 advocated China 'marching westwards' (Wang 2014) into its continental backyard. By so doing, as his reasoning went, China could expand diplomatic manoeuvring space while avoiding an open confrontation on its eastern flank. Chinese authorities acted on Wang's strategic thinking, as well as on the domestic economic imperative of finding new outlets for excess capacity (Huang 2016), when proclaiming the BRI a year later.

The scope, priorities and geographical reach of the BRI were spelled out in a policy document entitled 'Vision and Actions on Jointly Building the Silk Road Economic Belt and the 21st Century Maritime Silk Road' issued jointly by China's National Development and Reform Commission (NDRC), Ministry of Foreign Affairs and Ministry of Commerce in March 2015. The next section summarises this vision.

3 BRI Vision

The BRI is in fact an umbrella initiative or a 'Christmas tree' (Clover and Hornby 2015), knitting together a diverse array of China-led pro-connectivity, pro-development and pro-integration activities. Its overarching vision of promoting connectivity across the breadth of the Afro-Eurasian supercontinent is anchored on five thematic policy objectives:

1. Policy coordination which calls for BRI countries to synchronise national development strategies in favour of regional integration and to provide joint policy support to BRI projects.
2. Infrastructure connectivity is the priority area of cooperation under the BRI. China strives to develop an integrated infrastructure network connecting all sub-regions, core cities, economic centres and industrial parks along the Belt and the Road to drive inter-connected economic growth. Types of infrastructure to be constructed include transport (e.g., road, rail, sea ports, air, and pipelines), industrial facilities (e.g., industrial estates and parks), environment, energy (e.g., power plants and transmission lines), digital, social and urban infrastructure. As to sequencing, the initial focus is to build infrastructure for transport, energy resources and telecommunications, followed by investments in manufacturing and trade, mining, international finance, culture, media, and tourism (Deloitte 2018).
3. Unimpeded trade is to create free trade areas and mutual investment zones, enhance customs cooperation and capacity, try out new forms of international commerce, build up industrial and supply chain cooperation, and assist in one another's trade law enforcement endeavours.

4. Financial integration will mobilise multilateral, national, and unconventional sources of infrastructure investment into financing BRI projects while strengthening financial cooperation and connectivity across BRI countries. China also attaches importance to expanding the scope and scale of bilateral currency swaps, trade settlement in local currencies, banking sector liberalisation, regional bond market development, and cross-border financial regulatory alignment.
5. People-to-people bond plays an important role under the BRI. It seeks to cultivate a conducive social, public, and intellectual context to ensure that the benefits of BRI cooperation are widely and fairly distributed among the populations. The line-up of activities include cultural and academic exchange, media cooperation, entrepreneurship training, joint bidding for international sports events, collaboration on scientific and technological research, policy dialogues between parliaments, political parties, think tanks and non-governmental organisations from BRI countries.

Appendix 1 provides a brief summary of progress thus far across the five areas of cooperation.

The BRI's geographical span is ambitious and open-ended. It officially features six land economic corridors as part of the SREB (see Fig. 1.2).

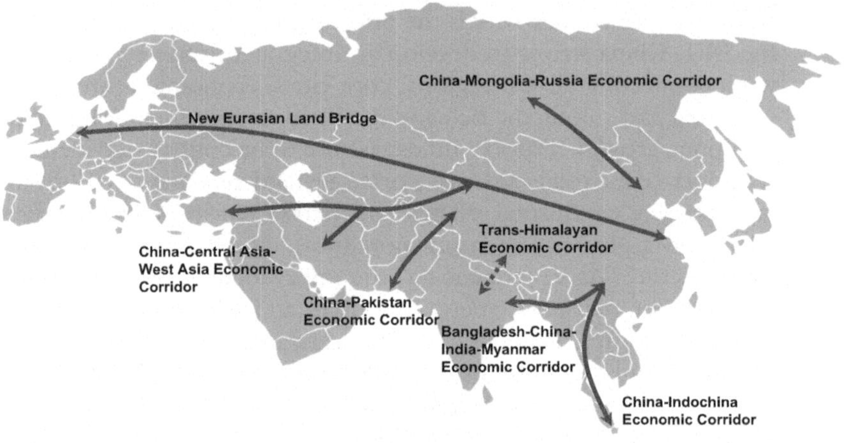

Fig. 1.2 Land-based BRI corridors.
Source: Authors' conceptualisation

Most of them go through China's traditional frontiers like Xinjiang and Tibet.

The New Eurasian Land Bridge (NELB) is an international railway line connecting China's port city of Lianyungang and Rotterdam of the Netherlands. Between the two coastal bridgeheads, the NELB runs through China, Kazakhstan, Russia, Belarus, Poland, Germany, and the Netherlands. Along this and other routes, trains from China to Europe have risen from three a week to over 25. An industrial zone cum distribution centre is being built in Khorgos with $600 million of investment (The Economist 2020). The China-Mongolia-Russia Economic Corridor is a trilateral arrangement of building trans-national infrastructure networks. It realises policy cooperation between China (rejuvenating the old industrial bases in Northeast China), Russia (advancing the development of the Far East) and Mongolia (addressing its land-locked economic disadvantage). The China-Central Asia-West Asia Economic Corridor extends the BRI to West Asia through Central Asia, lowering the logistical barriers across the Caspian, Black and Mediterranean Seas. The geo-economic logic underpinning this corridor is to make available a larger quantity of Caspian and Iranian energy for Chinese consumption while affording China an alternative trading route with Europe through Turkey that completely bypasses Russia.

China-Indochina Economic Corridor connects China's Yunnan and Guangxi provinces with the contiguous mainland Southeast Asian nations. It broadly overlaps with the United Nations' Trans-Asian Railway Network, the Association of Southeast Asian Nations' connectivity masterplan and ADB's Greater Mekong Sub-region Economic Cooperation scheme. The China-Pakistan Economic Corridor (CPEC) is a comprehensive cooperative initiative encompassing railway, road, energy, industrial parks and social and urban development dimensions. CPEC opens a short passage for China to access the Indian Ocean, but the planning of it to pass through the disputed area of Kashmir contested between India and China has turned CPEC into a geopolitically controversial endeavour. Because of India's resultant firm opposition to CPEC and to the BRI as a whole, the Bangladesh-China-India-Myanmar (BCIM) Economic Corridor of the BRI is unlikely to take off the ground. The BCIM corridor aspires to improve transport connectivity between Kunming, Mandalay, Dhaka, and Kolkata. Its origin can be traced back to the 1999 Kunming Initiative. In the face of India's antipathy, China is presently developing a China-Myanmar Economic Corridor with a view to extending it to

Bangladesh and India when geopolitical circumstances are more permissive. The same dynamics has played out on a seventh overland corridor loosely associated with the BRI, the Trans-Himalayan Economic Corridor (THEC) from China to Nepal and India. Various Chinese officials including Wei Wei (2014), a former Chinese ambassador to India, have been talking enthusiastically about this route. Nepal sees the THEC as an opportunity to transform itself to a land-bridge between China and India. Given India's anti-BRI policy, during President Xi's visit to Kathmandu in October 2019, it was decided to a build a bilateral corridor called the Trans-Himalayan Multi-dimensional Connectivity Network (or the China-Nepal Trans-Himalayan Economic Corridor) as an interim measure.

The MSR, the BRI's maritime arm, is geared towards the development of ports, aiming to diversify shipping lines and expand shipping capacity through seaports financing, construction and operation. It comprises four blue economic passages, the most prominent of which is the route running from China's Fujian province to the Mediterranean Europe through South China Sea, Indian Ocean and the Suez Canal. This route largely takes shape around Zheng He's expedition trips to the West. The second MSR corridor also begins from coastal China and goes south to Indonesia, New Zealand and the Pacific islands. Failure to get Australia on board is regrettable in this regard, but this branch of the MSR matches well with Indonesia's 'Global Maritime Fulcrum' strategy and New Zealand's long-term yearning for greater economic integration with East Asia. The third MSR corridor branches out to American countries, taking a trans-Pacific focus. In 2018, President Xi in his congratulatory letter to the China-Latin American and Caribbean (LAC) Countries Forum, designated this route as the 'Trans-Pacific Maritime Silk Road'. A fourth blue passage was conceptualised in 2018 with the publication of China's inaugural Arctic policy white paper which unveiled a Polar Silk Road (PSR). The PSR is to take advantage of the seasonal accessibility of the Arctic Ocean to open a new trading route between China and Europe. Together, the MSR will give rise to five ocean-based, self-contained economic circles: the Trans-Pacific Economic Circle, the South China Sea Economic Circle, the Indian Ocean Economic Circle, the Mediterranean Economic Circle, and the Trans-Arctic Economic Circle.

The BRI is beyond just physical infrastructure development and has also found its way into the digital space. There is a plan to build a Digital Silk Road (DSR) supported by cross-border optical cable connection, satellite connectivity, and digital innovation. Normatively, China justifies the development of the DSR on the notions of 'digital human rights'. China claims that Internet access and information inter-connectivity are essential for addressing the digital and technological divide within BRI countries. The DSR since 2018 has come into sharper focus with China and the United States locked in a systemic contest for tech influence. As Washington played on the regional wariness about China's alleged digital hegemony and exportation of 'surveillance state' authoritarian governance model, the development of the DSR has been limited, mainly in the realms of e-commerce, mobile payment, gaming services and smart city projects.

Another component of the BRI that has become prominent since early 2020 amid the COVID-19 pandemic, is the 'Health Silk Road'. First conceived in 2016, the construction of the 'Health Silk Road' was institutionalised with the signing of the MOU with the World Health Organisation and the issuance of the 'Beijing Communiqué of the Belt and Road Health Cooperation' in 2017. During the last few years, China has enhanced its health cooperation with Asia-Pacific countries along the Belt and Road routes on the control and prevention of infectious diseases and other public health emergencies. With the outbreak of COVID-19 pandemic in 2020, China is supplying many countries affected by the virus with surgical masks, ventilators, personal protective suits and other healthcare items by making use of BRI transport infrastructure. Asia Times (2020) notes that (as of 2 April 2020) there were at least 89 countries from Africa, Latin America, Europe, and Southeast Asia that had received urgently needed medical and humanitarian support from China. While the pandemic has slowed the construction of the physical BRI infrastructure projects, China has intensified 'medical diplomacy' to demonstrate its commitment to safeguarding global health security.

As such, China is recasting itself as a responsible stakeholder of what President Xi calls 'a community of common health for mankind' and claiming the de facto leadership of practical global health cooperation. By the same token, the DSR has also received a timely boost from the coronavirus contagion. Social distancing measures and wholesale community lockdowns have shifted the balance between digital economy and retail commerce in the former's favour, significantly benefiting the DSR for which cross-border e-commerce is the mainstay. In addition, many countries have doubled down on various China-inspired digital solutions to combat COVID-19. China's use of a colour-coded app for monitoring individuals' health, contacts and movement is a case in point. Notwithstanding criticisms surrounding civic liberty, the app is being replicated by other badly afflicted countries. Singapore rolled out a similar app, 'TraceTogether', in March 2020 while American tech giants Apple and Google announced a plan to turn smart phones into opt-in contact tracing devices. The latest developments suggest that the Health Silk Road and DSRs may have strengthened China's soft power. But once supply chains reconnect and global health issues are resolved, China and BRI participating countries will once again re-start the 'Physical BRI' to build transport networks, industrial parks and power plants.

4 Coordination and Financing Mechanisms

The apex steering committee and executive agency for the BRI within China is the Leading Small Group (LSG) for Promoting the Belt and Road Initiative headed by Vice Premier Han Zheng, the second-in-charge of China's state system. The BRI LSG issues broad policy guidelines on BRI implementation and meets regularly with high-ranking officials from financial, economic, industry, trade, foreign policy, and international development ministries. The Chinese military is emphatically not present at the BRI LSG meetings (Manuel 2019), contradicting the popular portrayal of the BRI as an expansionist geostrategic undertaking. The day-to-day work of the LSG is carried out by the Office of the Leading Small Group for Promoting the Belt and Road Initiative located at the premises of the NDRC. A Belt and Road Promotion Centre was established in 2017 within the NDRC for purposes of strategic planning. In March 2018, during a government reshuffle, a new China International Development Cooperation Agency was established with a mandate of managing the aid component of the BRI.

Internationally, the platform for coordinating BRI cooperation and consensus-building is the biannual BRF for International Cooperation, also colloquially known as the 'BRI Summit'. The BRF seeks to 'pool more consensus, identify cooperation directions, push forward the implementation of projects, and improve supporting systems' (Xinhua 2017). The multi-day forum typically features an opening ceremony, a high-level plenary session, a leaders' roundtable and a number of parallel thematic forums. The events conclude with the issuance of a joint communique and a list of deliverables setting out the detailed cooperation agenda for the next two years. The 2017 BRF was attended by 32 heads of state, government, and international organisations whereas the 2019 forum had 38 foreign leaders in attendance. The absence of top-level delegations from the United States, the European Union (EU), Japan, and India, however, has raised questions over the BRF's global standing and geopolitical representation.

Another important international coordination mechanism is the one between China's Ministry of Finance and several multilateral development banks (MDBs) led by the World Bank. This partnership was formalised through an MOU signed in 2017. The Global Infrastructure Facility and the Global Connectivity Alliance were established pursuant to the MOU to provide project preparation funds, and transaction structure advice to help accelerate project readiness.

Regarding the financing structure of the BRI, Beijing strives for a multi-pillar financial system that could channel a mix of public, private, and blended capital into BRI infrastructure projects (Fig. 1.3). First, China seeks to partner with global institutions such as the World Bank, the International Monetary Fund (IMF) and the International Fund for Agricultural Development (IFAD) on BRI cooperation and project funding. However, so far, the World Bank and IMF have not officially co-financed any BRI projects with China. Instead, they have provided technical advice and capacity building programmes to BRI participating countries to facilitate their BRI project preparation and implementation. It is only the IFAD that has co-financed agriculture-related BRI infrastructure with China through the China-IFAD South-South and Triangular Cooperation Facility.

The BRI's second financing pillar involves major regional MDBs in Africa, Asia, Europe, and the Americas. The BRI's MDB partners include not only traditional development donors such as ADB and the European Investment Bank but also new China-backed MDBs like the Asian Infrastructure Investment Bank (AIIB) and the BRICS New Development Bank (NDB). By 2018, China and regional MDBs had co-financed over 100 programmes in some 70 countries. But because these regional MDBs have other members besides China, they cannot be used to exclusively finance BRI projects. Chinese financial institutions have, therefore, joined their foreign counterparts to form international banking consortiums (or bilateral funds) to back BRI projects, hence the third pillar of the BRI financing structure. Major consortiums of this type include China-Central and Eastern European Countries Financial Holding (€10 billion), China-Eurasian Economic Cooperation Fund ($5 billion), China-Africa Fund for Industrial Cooperation ($10 billion), China-LAC Cooperation Fund ($10 billion), China-LAC Fund for Industrial Cooperation ($10 billion),

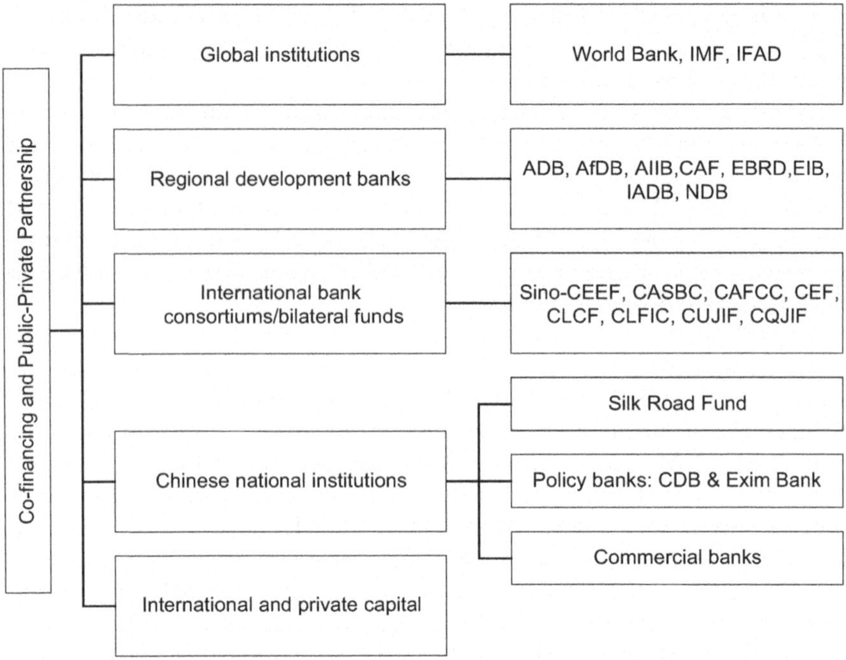

Fig. 1.3 Envisioned multi-pillar financing structure of the BRI.
Note: *ADB* Asian Development Bank, *AfDB* African Development Bank, *AIIB* Asian Infrastructure Investment Bank, *CAF* Development Bank of Latin America, *CAFCC* China-African Financial Cooperation Consortium, *CAFIC* China-African Fund for Industrial Cooperation, *CASBC* China-Arab States Bank Consortium, *CEF* China-Eurasian Economic Cooperation Fund, *CLCF* China-LAC Cooperation Fund, *CLFIC* China-LAC Fund for Industrial Cooperation, *CQJIF* China-Qatar Joint Investment Fund, *CUJIF* China-UAE Joint Investment Fund, *EBRD* European Bank for Reconstruction and Development, *EIB* European Investment Bank, *IADB* Inter-American Development Bank, *IFAD* International Fund for Agricultural Development, *IMF* International Monetary Fund, *NDB* New Development Bank, *Sino-CEEF* China-Central and Eastern European Countries Financial Holding
Source: Authors' illustration

China-Arab States Bank Consortium ($3 billion), and China's bilateral funds with United Arab Emirates ($10 billion) and Qatar ($10 billion) (He 2019). The fourth pillar of BRI financing consists of China's state-owned commercial and policy banks like China Development Bank (CDB), Export-Import (Exim) Bank of China, and the Silk Road Fund (SRF). The fifth financing pillar of the BRI is co-financing with private sources of capital. To that effect, at the 2019 BRF, China convened an inaugural BRI CEO Conference to showcase investment opportunities in BRI projects.

Notwithstanding this policy intent, in reality it is the fourth pillar that has been most extensively used thus far to finance BRI projects. According to the United States-China Economic and Security Review Commission (2018), the AIIB, NDB, and SRF play only a marginal role, collectively contributing only 1.6 per cent of total BRI funding by 2016. In contrast, major Chinese commercial banks and policy banks shouldered the brunt of BRI financing by contributing 52.1 per cent and 46.3 per cent, respectively. This pattern of Chinese banks dominating BRI projects is corroborated by multiple sources. Deloitte (2018) estimates that by the end of 2016, Chinese state-owned commercial banks provided more than half of BRI financing (51%), followed by the CDB (38%), Exim Bank (8%), and SRF, AIIB, and NDB (1% each). He (2019) also suggests that by 2018 Chinese capital accounted for 85 per cent of BRI funding with the rest supplied by private equity and bond financing (13%) and MDBs (2%).

5 Economic Relations Between China and Asian Sub-regions

Given this book's focus on three Asian sub-regions of East and Southeast Asia, South Asia and Central Asia,[3] it is instructive to provide a bird's-eye view on their economic relations with China both before and after the BRI was launched in 2013.

China's merchandise trade with Asian BRI countries was rising steadily prior to Xi's announcement of the BRI in 2013 but plateaued thereafter, as global trade as a whole faced strong headwinds (Fig. 1.4). In 2017, two-way trade reached $897 billion, up more than threefold from $263 billion in 2005. For 2017, East and Southeast Asia accounted for the largest portion of China's trade with Asia (91%), followed by South Asia excluding India (5%) and Central Asia (4%). In the first half of 2019, ASEAN surpassed the United States as China's second-largest trading partner next only to the EU. A year later in the first half of 2020, ASEAN became China's largest trading partner. But in terms of growth rate, South Asia stands out. China-South Asia trade expanded rapidly from $8 billion in 2005 to $42 billion in 2017 at a compound annual growth rate (CAGR) of 13.7 per cent. This compares to the CAGR for East and Southeast Asia and Central Asia of 9.7 per cent and 11.7 per cent, respectively over the same period.

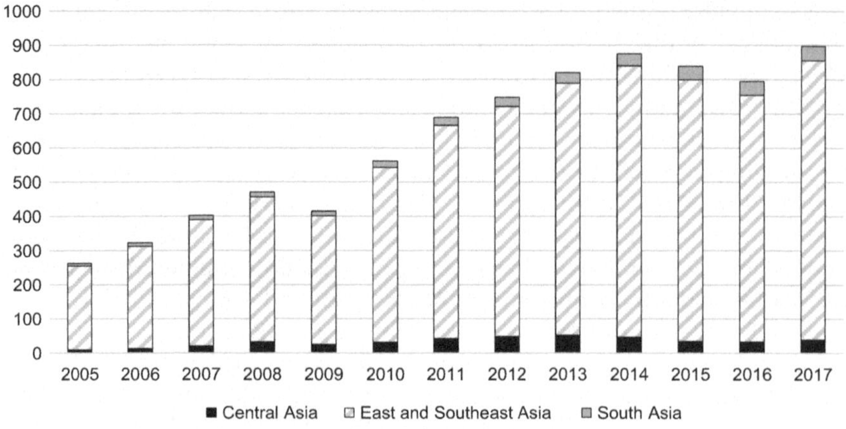

Fig. 1.4 China's total two-way trade with Asian BRI sub-regions ($ billion). Source: World Integrated Trade Solution statistics

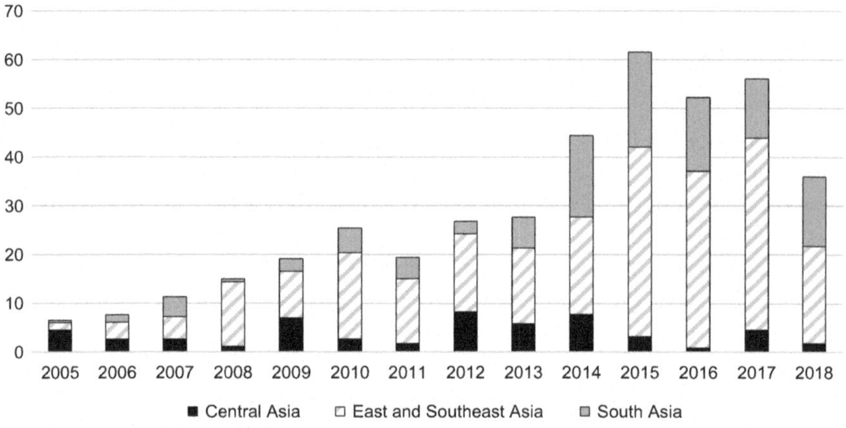

Fig. 1.5 China's investment and construction contracts in Asian BRI sub-regions ($ billion).
Source: China Global Investment Tracker database

The value of China's investment and construction contracts, which is a proxy for Chinese BRI investments, in the three Asian sub-regions is shown in Fig. 1.5. The data show that China's BRI investment in the three sub-regions increased from 2013 to 2015 but has fallen since then to about $35 billion in 2018. This trend reflects China's overall shift from a 'freehand brushwork' approach that prioritised investment quantity to a 'meticulous painting' approach that emphasises investment and project quality.

East and Southeast Asia, which accounts for the largest share of China's trade with Asia, is also the largest recipient of Chinese investments into the BRI era. Cumulatively from 2013 through 2018, East and Southeast Asia received Chinese investment and construction contracts to the tune of $179 billion. These investments and contracts have largely been in Malaysia ($35 billion) and Singapore ($30 billion). The surge in Chinese investment in Laos is also notable. By industry, energy ($57 billion) and transport and logistics ($40 billion) have secured the lion's share of Chinese capital and contract inflows, followed by real estate ($30 billion). Meanwhile, South Asia is also a bright spot in this picture. Total Chinese investment and contracts in South Asian BRI countries topped $84 billion between 2013 and 2018. Pakistan has received the highest proportion of Chinese funds and contracts, thanks to the advancement of CPEC. As is the case with East and Southeast Asia, Chinese investors and contractors show preference for energy ($43 billion) and transport and logistics ($28 billion) sectors. China's investment footprint in Central Asia is modest and has fluctuated over recent years. Kazakhstan is the single largest beneficiary of Chinese investment and contracts into the region.

6 Book Structure

This book comprises eight chapters. Chapter 2 compares and contrasts various alternative infrastructure financing initiatives that have been put forward by other global and regional powers subsequent to the announcement of the BRI such as Japan's Enhanced Partnership for Quality Infrastructure, India's sub-regional initiatives in South Asia, the United States' Indo-Pacific infrastructure strategy, and the EU's Strategy for Connecting Europe and Asia. While all these initiatives seek to reconnect Eurasia, the chapter shows that the BRI is in a class of its own by virtue of its ambition and scale.

Chapter 3 investigates the potential economic impact of the BRI by simulating a CGE model. The results suggest that reducing transport cost and lowering tariffs would both generate economic benefits but the latter appears to have a higher beneficial impact. Land-locked countries and countries with high initial tariff levels are likely to be the largest beneficiaries of the BRI. For the MSR, it is projected that countries already embedded in the global maritime shipping networks would reap higher economic benefits.

Chapter 4 presents the results of a perception survey of opinion leaders from 26 Asian countries that are stakeholders of the BRI. Although there were different views and opinions, most respondents felt that the BRI is a positive development that could facilitate regional cooperation and economic development. Most respondents also felt that the BRI has the potential to lead to a win-win situation and many rejected the Chinese debt trap diplomacy argument. Most respondents, however, agreed that both China and the stakeholding countries have to implement a number of policy reforms in order to realise the full potential of the BRI.

Chapter 5 analyses the BRI's impact on Southeast Asian countries. This is the region that takes part in both the SREB and the MSR. The chapter notes that the BRI is seen as a boon for the region in terms of providing infrastructure financing, closing development gap, enhancing digital connectivity and addressing urbanisation challenges. It however also argues that the BRI could have a negative impact on ASEAN Centrality and exacerbate maritime disputes in the South China Sea.

Chapter 6 focuses on South Asia. It finds that the BRI stands to benefit Pakistan and Nepal, a land-locked country, because of improved transport connectivity. The BRI can also partially resolve the energy crises in electricity-starved Pakistan and Bangladesh. Another benefit to South Asian BRI countries could be industrial development as China is building a number of industrial parks in the region. On the flip side, India's opposition to the BRI leads to some doubt about the BRI's long-term geopolitical sustainability in the region.

Chapter 7 examines the progress and prospects of the BRI for Central Asia. As is the case with other Asian sub-regions, Central Asia is experiencing both benefits and risks under the BRI. The BRI is transforming the land-locked region into a 'land bridge' between China and Europe. Financial development in the region is also getting an important boost from the BRI. Yet, Sinophobia, geopolitical undercurrents and debt situations need policy attention.

In Chap. 8, the final chapter of the book, we outline ten key policy recommendations for both China and the stakeholding countries to improve the BRI. Specifically, China and the stakeholding Asian countries should enhance transparency, strengthen governance, liberalise trade, uphold multilateralism, secure the buy-in of other major powers, manage public debt, prepare national infrastructure development strategy, empower and protect local communities, address transport bottlenecks, and transform transport corridor into economic corridor.

Appendix 1 Summary of Key Achievements of the BRI

Policy goal	*Progress*
Policy coordination	• The BRI has been incorporated into documents of several international organisations, such as the United Nations, G20 and Asia-Pacific Economic Cooperation • China has signed agreements with 16 countries to strengthen the construction of the DSR
Infrastructure connectivity	• A rail connection between Chongqing and Duisberg is operational and the number of train services is increasing • Construction has started on the Belgrade-Stara Pazova section of the Hungary-Serbia Railway in Serbia • The Western China-Western European International Expressway has been largely completed • Trial operations have begun on the China-Mongolia-Russia road • China has signed bilateral agreements on international road transport with Kazakhstan, Uzbekistan, and Turkey • Agreements on the China-Pakistan-Kazakhstan-Kyrgyzstan, China-Kazakhstan-Russia, and China-Kyrgyzstan-Uzbekistan roads have been signed • The Kunming-Bangkok Expressway has been completed, while the construction of the China-Laos and China-Thailand railways is underway. Work has started on the China-Laos Economic Corridor • Work on key projects, such as the road to the Gwadar Port, Peshawar-Karachi Motorway, Karakoram Highway Phase II, Lahore Orange Line Metro, and 1320 MW Coal-Fired Power Plants at Port Qasim has started • A Joint Committee of the China-Myanmar Economic Corridor has been established. China-Myanmar oil and gas pipelines have been completed • Progress is being made on the Jakarta-Bandung high-speed railway • A pre-feasibility study on a China-Nepal cross-border railway has been completed and a detailed feasibility study has been initiated • China has signed bilateral intergovernmental air transport agreements with 126 countries. Over the past five years or so, 1239 new international routes have opened • Progress has been made in the construction of China-Myanmar, China-Pakistan, China-Kyrgyzstan, and China-Russia cross-border fibre optic cables for information transmission

(*continued*)

(continued)

Policy goal	*Progress*
Unimpeded trade	• Since May 2017, China has signed more than 100 trade cooperation agreements with other BRI countries • China has signed, upgraded, or implemented free trade agreements with ASEAN, Singapore, Pakistan, Georgia, and the Eurasian Economic Union • From 2013 to 2018 the value of trade between China and other BRI countries surpassed $6 trillion, and China's direct investment in BRI countries surpassed $90 billion • China has established the China-Kazakhstan Khorgos International Border Cooperation Centre, and the China-Laos Mohan-Boten Cross-Border Economic Cooperation Zone
Financial integration	• China Exim Bank has issued a 2-billion-yuan green bond for global investors, and the NDB issued a 3-billion-yuan green bond to support the green development of the BRI • Eleven Chinese-funded banks have set up 76 institutions in 28 BRI countries, and 50 banks from 22 BRI countries have opened 7 corporate banks, 19 branches, and 34 representative offices in China. Two Chinese-funded securities firms have established joint ventures in Singapore and Laos • China has made bilateral currency swap arrangements with more than 20 BRI countries and renminbi clearing arrangements with 7 BRI countries. The Cross-Border Interbank Payment System now covers some 40 countries and regions involved in the BRI
People-to-people bond	• China and other BRI countries have jointly hosted events like arts festivals, film festivals, music festivals, cultural exhibitions, and book fairs • The Chinese Government Scholarship, the Silk Road Programme, has been established. China has signed agreements with 24 BRI countries on mutual recognition of higher education degrees • China has opened 153 Confucius Institutes and 149 Confucius Classrooms in 54 BRI countries. China offers post-graduate scholarships, and runs science and technology training courses to train some 5000 students from BRI countries • China has held joint year of tourism with many BRI countries, initiating cooperation mechanisms such as the Silk Road Tourism Promotion Union, Maritime Silk Road Tourism Promotion Alliance, and Tea Road International Tourism Alliance • Since the first BRF, China has signed 56 agreements on cooperation in the health sector with countries, international organisation, and non-governmental organisations • China has dispatched ophthalmology teams to Cambodia, Myanmar, Laos, and Sri Lanka to carry out the 'Brightness Action' program. Short-term medical teams to island countries such as Fiji, Tonga, Micronesia, and Vanuatu in the Pacific have been sent

Source: Office of the Leading Group for Promoting the Belt and Road Initiative (2019)

Notes

1. China is likely to benefit from the BRI in the following ways: (1) China has over-capacity in eight sectors—crude steel, aluminium, cement, chemicals, flat glass, ship building, and paper and paper board; these products could be used to build infrastructure in BRI countries; (2) BRI could elevate China's global status and put it at the centre of the world once again; (3) New corridors will provide strategic alternative routes to China to source its inputs; and (4) BRI could help in internationalising the Renminbi. On the other hand, BRI countries could benefit in the following ways: (1) Addressing the shortage of infrastructure finance and, thereby, promoting regional cooperation and economic development and (2) Attracting investment and technology from China.
2. However, a recent review of 40 instances of Chinese debt renegotiations across 24 countries, has found that 'actual asset seizures are a very rare occurrence. Apart from the Sri Lanka, the only other example we could find…was in Tajikistan where the government reportedly ceded 1158 square km of land to China in 2011. However, the limited information available, and the opacity of the process makes it difficult to determine whether this specific land transfer case was in exchange for Chinese debt forgiveness…or part of a historic dispute settlement between the two countries' (Kratz et al. 2019).
3. Central Asia comprises Armenia, Azerbaijan, Georgia, Kazakhstan, Kyrgyzstan, Tajikistan, Turkmenistan, Uzbekistan; East and Southeast Asia comprises Brunei, Cambodia, Indonesia, Laos, Malaysia, Myanmar, Mongolia, New Zealand, Philippines, Singapore, South Korea, Thailand, Vietnam; and South Asia comprises Afghanistan, Bangladesh, Maldives, Nepal, Pakistan, Sri Lanka.

References

ADB. 2017. *Meeting Asia's Infrastructure Needs*. Manila: Asian Development Bank.

Ang, Yuen Yuen. 2018. *China's Belt and Road Is a Campaign, Not a Conspiracy*. Bloomberg. https://www.bloomberg.com/opinion/articles/2018-09-27/china-s-belt-and-road-initiative-is-a-campaign-not-a-conspiracy. Accessed 5 February 2020.

Asia Times. 2020. China Rolls Out the Health Silk Road. *Asia Times*. https://asiatimes.com/2020/04/china-rolls-out-the-health-silk-road/. Accessed 4 April 2020.

Callahan, William A. 2016. China's "Asia Dream": The Belt Road Initiative and the New Regional Order. *Asian Journal of Comparative Politics* 1 (3): 226–243.

Chellaney, Brahma. 2018. China's Creditor Imperialism. *The Japan Times*. https://www.japantimes.co.jp/opinion/2017/12/21/commentary/world-commentary/chinas-creditor-imperialism/#.XjonuWgzYuU. Accessed 5 February 2020.

Clover, Charles, and Lucy Hornby. 2015. China's Great Game: Road to a New Empire. *FinancialTimes.* https://www.ft.com/content/6e098274-587a-11e5-a28b-50226830d644#axzz3oTDW37mz. Accessed 1 January 2020.

Deloitte. 2018. *Embracing the BRI Ecosystem in 2018.* Unspecified: Deloitte.

Ferdinand, Peter. 2016. Westward ho—The China Dream and 'One Belt, One Road': Chinese Foreign Policy Under Xi Jinping. *International Affairs* 92 (4): 941–957.

He, Alex. 2019. The Belt and Road Initiative: Motivations, Financing, Expansion and Challenges of Xi's Ever-Expanding Strategy. In *CIGI Papers Series.* Waterloo: Centre for International Governance Innovation.

Hillman, Jonathan. 2018. *China's Belt and Road Initiative: Five Years Later.* Washington, DC: Center for Strategic and International Studies.

Huang, Yiping. 2016. Understanding China's Belt & Road Initiative: Motivation, Framework and Assessment. *China Economic Review* 40: 314–321.

Kratz, Agatha, Allen Feng, and Logan Wright. 2019. New Data on the "Debt Trap" Question. Rhodium Group. https://rhg.com/research/new-data-on-the-debt-trap-question/. Accessed 5 February 2020.

Lim, Linda. 2018. *China's Belt-and-Road Initiative: Future Bonanza or Nightmare? RSIS Commentary.* Singapore: S. Rajaratnam School of International Studies.

Maddison, Angus. 2007. *Contours of the World Economy 1–2030 AD: Essays in Macro-Economic History.* New York: Oxford University Press.

Manuel, Ryan. 2019. Twists in the Belt and Road. *China Leadership Monitor* (61).

Office of the Leading Group for Promoting the Belt and Road Initiative. 2019. *The Belt and Road Initiative: Progress, Contributions and Prospects.* Beijing: Foreign Languages Press.

Oxford Economics. 2017. Global Infrastructure Outlook - 2017. Unspecified: Oxford Economics.

Pence, Mike. 2018. Remarks by Vice President Pence on the Administration's Policy Toward China. The White House. https://www.whitehouse.gov/briefings-statements/remarks-vice-president-pence-administrations-policy-toward-china/.

Rana, Pradumna B., and Wai-Mun Chia. 2017. *Jumpstarting South Asia: Revisiting Economic Reforms and Look East Policies.* New Delhi: Oxford University Press.

Rimmer, Peter. 2018. China's Belt and Road Initiative: Underlying Economic and International Relations Dimensions. *Asian-Pacific Economic Literature* 32 (2): 3–26.

Rolland, Nadège. 2017. China's "Belt and Road Initiative": Underwhelming or Game-Changer? *The Washington Quarterly* 40 (1): 127–142.

The Economist. 2020. China Wants to Put Itself Back at the Centre of the World. *The Economist*. https://www.economist.com/special-report/2020/02/06/china-wants-to-put-itself-back-at-the-centre-of-the-world. Accessed 12 February 2020.

United States-China Economic and Security Review Commission. 2018. China and the World. In *2018 Report to Congress*. Washington, DC: United States-China Economic and Security Review Commission.

Vanham, Peter. 2019. A Brief History of Globalization. *World Economic Forum*. https://www.weforum.org/agenda/2019/01/how-globalization-4-0-fits-into-the-history-of-globalization/. Accessed 7 January 2020.

Wang, Jisi. 2014. "Marching Westwards": The Rebalancing of China's Geostrategy. In *The World in 2020 According to China*, ed. Shao Binhong. Leiden: Brill.

Wei, Wei. 2014. China: Opportunity for India's Economic Take-Off. *The Economic Times*. https://economictimes.indiatimes.com/opinion/et-commentary/china-opportunity-for-indias-economic-take-off/articleshow/35612805.cms?from=mdr. Accessed 5 February 2020.

World Bank. 2019. *Belt and Road Economics: Opportunities and Risks of Transport Corridors*. Washington, DC: World Bank.

Xi, Jinping. 2013. Promote Friendship Between Our People and Work Together to Build a Bright Future. *Ministry of Foreign Affairs, China*. https://www.fmprc.gov.cn/mfa_eng/wjdt_665385/zyjh_665391/t1078088.shtml. Accessed 5 February 2020.

———. 2019. Working Together to Deliver a Brighter Future for Belt and Road Cooperation. *Ministry of Foreign Affairs, China*. https://www.fmprc.gov.cn/mfa_eng/zxxx_662805/t1658424.shtml. Accessed 5 February 2020.

Xinhua. 2017. China Focus: What to Expect from Belt and Road Forum. http://www.xinhuanet.com/english/2017-05/01/c_136248648.htm. Accessed 20 December 2019.

Yeh, Emily T., and Elizabeth Wharton. 2016. Going West and Going Out: Discourses, Migrants, and Models in Chinese Development. *Eurasian Geography and Economics* 57 (3): 286–315.

CHAPTER 2

Proliferating Major Power Infrastructure Initiatives

1 Introduction

Alongside the BRI, a proliferation of major power infrastructure initiatives is underway. Japan's Expanded Partnership for Quality Infrastructure (EPQI), various India-centred connectivity schemes in South Asia and elsewhere, the infrastructure components of Washington's 'Free and Open Indo-Pacific' vision, and the European Union Strategy on Connecting Europe and Asia are making Eurasia 'the world's great construction site' (Szczudlik 2016).

In this chapter, we provide a preliminary assessment of these initiatives highlighting their scopes and comparative policy strengths and weaknesses. The objective is to put the BRI into perspective and draw Asian countries' attention to a menu of alternative opportunities available for infrastructure finance and cooperation.

2 Infrastructure Initiatives

2.1 *Expanded Partnership for Quality Infrastructure*

In the past, Japan was the leading source of infrastructure finance in Asia. With the launch of the BRI, Japan has ramped up its infrastructure diplomacy further. In May 2015, Prime Minister Shinzo Abe announced the 'Partnership for Quality Infrastructure' which sought to co-invest approximately $110 billion with ADB in the transport sectors of ADB's developing member countries in Asia. In 2016, the initiative was upgraded to the

P. B. Rana, X. Ji, *China's Belt and Road Initiative*,
https://doi.org/10.1007/978-981-15-5171-0_2

EPQI which, among others, doubles the funding available to $200 billion and covers the entire world.

The EPQI enhances Japan's role in infrastructure finance in four ways (MOFA Undated; METI 2016). First, official development assistance (ODA) project appraisal time will be reduced from 3 years at present to 1.5 years (for high-priority projects) and 2 years for other projects. Also, Japanese financial assistance can be extended directly to sub-sovereign entities like local governments and public corporations without central government guarantee.

Second, Japan reforms and resources relevant government agencies so that they can better support a coherent foreign infrastructure strategy that prioritises financing for strategic and high-risk projects. Specifically, the EPQI allows for subsidised partnership with private sector through the Japan International Cooperation Agency (JICA) and enhanced insurance provided by the Nippon Export and Investment Insurance (NEXI) to high-risk projects. It also permits the Japan Bank for International Cooperation (JBIC) to issue loans denominated in local currencies while focusing on high-risk infrastructure projects.

Third, the EPQI deepens Japan's collaboration with multilateral development banks (MDBs). In 2016–2017, Japan created three new trust funds administered by ADB. They are the Leading Asia's Private Sector Infrastructure Fund ($16 billion) for co-financing non-sovereign infrastructure projects, the High-Level Technology Fund ($40 million) for localised technological development, and the Domestic Resource Mobilisation Trust Fund to strengthen developing country's domestic resource mobilisation capability. Outside Asia, the JBIC and NEXI, together with the European Investment Bank, are jointly underwriting infrastructure projects in the Middle East and Africa.

Finally, under the EPQI campaign, Japan is coming up with a global definition of 'high-quality infrastructure'. A quality infrastructure, in Japan's narrative, should be cost-effective, environment friendly, disaster resilient, socially inclusive, transparent, and locally empowering. Notably, Japan has coined the term 'high-quality infrastructure' to explicitly differentiate the EPQI from the BRI which is perceived to follow a quantity-driven approach at the expense of project quality. To build up international support for the definition it espouses, Japan initiated, with the World Bank, the International Conference on Sustainable Development through Quality Infrastructure in 2016 and aligned the infrastructure development guidebook of the Asia-Pacific Economic Cooperation with the EPQI principles in

2018. At the 2019 Osaka G20 Summit, Japan furthermore convinced world leaders to enshrine those principles as the grouping's 'common strategic direction and high aspiration' for future infrastructure commitments.

Since the onset of the EPQI, Japan has solidified its ground in Asia with new road, railway, and port projects (see Table 2.1). Elsewhere, Japan is investing in deep-sea ports in Africa (e.g., Mombasa container port in Kenya) and in the littoral states in the Indian Ocean (e.g., East Container Terminal at the Port of Colombo, Sri Lanka).

2.2 *India-led Connectivity Initiatives*

India is another prominent champion of Asian connectivity, spearheading a suite of infrastructure initiatives in South Asia and beyond (Fig. 2.1). Initially, India had pushed for regional infrastructure cooperation through the South Asian Association for Regional Cooperation (SAARC). But this did not succeed because of intra-SAARC Indo-Pakistani rivalry. Therefore, since the mid-1990s, India began assembling smaller 'coalitions of the willing' (Karim 2017) outside the SAARC framework. In 1997, imitating the growth triangles in Southeast Asia, the eastern members of SAARC (Bangladesh, Bhutan, India, and Nepal, known collectively as BBIN) formed the South Asian Growth Quadrangle (SAGQ). In light of their weak capacity, the SAGQ countries turned to ADB for assistance. That prompted the establishment of the South Asia Sub-regional Economic Cooperation (SASEC) programme in 2001. SASEC took in two additional members (Maldives and Sri Lanka) at a later stage. As of October 2018, SASEC countries had implemented 50 regional projects worth over $11 billion. By contrast, SAARC-led cooperation remains weak. A case in point is the SAARC Motor Vehicle Agreement (MVA) proposed by India in 2015. Again, Pakistani opposition stifled the proposal. India went instead for the BBIN-MVA which has been highly successful to date (although Bhutan has withdrawn temporarily).

India's sub-regional connectivity drive is motivated by two lines of thinking, one of which is that if India does not enhance its regional clout through new and improved connectivity initiatives, it might lose its regional prominence in the sub-continent to China. There is also a recognition that a physically connected and geo-economically stable South Asia is important for India's own growth and prosperity.

In addition to sub-regional connectivity initiatives, India is backing several inter-regional connectivity schemes (Yhome 2017). India is the

Table 2.1 Selected Japan-funded infrastructure projects under the EPQI

No	*Country*	*Project name*	*Sector*	*Loan*[a] *($ million)*	*Repayment period (years)*	*Grace period (years)*	*Interest rate (%)*	*Executing agency*
1	Bangladesh	Matarbari Ultra Super Critical Coal-Fired Power Project (V)	Energy	1304	30	10	0.9	Coal Power Generation Company, Power Grid Company, Ministry of Road Transport and Bridges (Bangladesh)
2	Cambodia	Sihanoukville Port New Container Terminal Development Project	Ports	214	40	10	0.01	Port Authority of Sihanoukville (Cambodia)
3	India	Project for the Construction of Mumbai-Ahmedabad High Speed Rail (II)	Railways	1366	50	15	0.1	National High-Speed Rail Corporation (India)
4	Indonesia	Patimban Port Development Project	Ports	1083	40	12	0.1	Ministry of Transportation (Indonesia)
5	Kyrgyzstan	International Main Roads Improvement Project	Roads	109	40	10	0.1	Ministry of Transport and Communications (Kyrgyzstan)
6	Laos	Vientiane Capital Water Supply Expansion Project	Water	94	30	10	0.7	Department of Public Works and Transport in Vientiane Capital (Laos)
7	Mongolia	New Ulaanbaatar International Airport Construction Project (II)	Airports	336	40	10	0.1	Ministry of Road and Transport (Mongolia)

8	Myanmar	Yangon-Mandalay Railway Improvement Project Phase II (I)	Railways	516	40	10	0.01	Myanmar Railways, Ministry of Transport and Communications (Myanmar)
9	Nepal	Nagdhunga Tunnel Construction Project	Roads	152	40	10	0.01	Ministry of Physical Infrastructure and Transport (Nepal)
10	Papua New Guinea	Nadzab Airport Redevelopment Project	Airports	245	40	10	0.1	National Airports Corporation (Papua New Guinea)
11	Philippines	Malolos-Tutuban Commuter Railway Project	Railways	2204	40	10	0.1	Department of Transportation and Communications (Philippines)
12	Sri Lanka	Bandaranaike International Airport Development Project (II)	Airports	414	40	10	0.1	Airport and Aviation Services (Sri Lanka) Ltd.
13	Vietnam	Ho Chi Minh City Urban Railway Construction Project	Railways	1643	40	10	0.1	Management Authority for Urban Railways, the People's Committee of Ho Chi Minh City (Vietnam)

Source: JICA database

[a]Loan amounts are converted to US dollar using market rates from Japanese yen

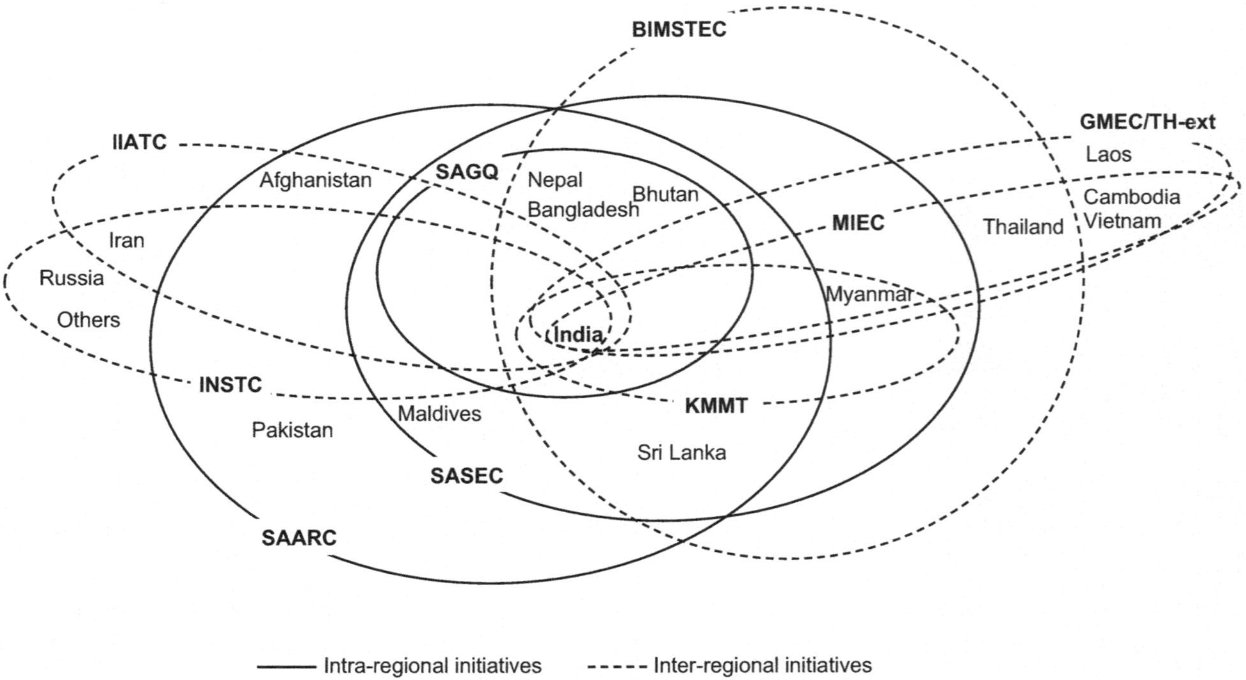

Fig. 2.1 India-led architecture for connectivity and economic cooperation in South Asia and beyond.
Source: Authors' illustration

leading proponent of the International North-South Transport Corridor (INSTC), a land and sea-based 7200 km corridor consisting of rail, road, and water routes. The corridor will give rise to the so-called Mumbai-Bandar Abbas-Baku-Astrakhan-Moscow-Saint Petersburg 'Axis of Goodwill' (Shinde 2018). The prime objectives of the INSTC are to provide a shorter alternative to the conventional Asia-Europe commercial routes (which go through the Suez Canal) and to facilitate energy trading within the group. India is also venturing north via the India-Iran-Afghanistan Transit Corridor (IIATC) into Central Asia, a region cut off from India by Pakistan. A focus of the IIATC is the southern Iranian port of Chabahar, which is situated strategically at the mouth of the Strait of Hormuz and close to the China-funded Gwadar port in Pakistan.

India's efforts to enhance connectivity with Southeast Asia rely on five initiatives: the Kaladan Multi-modal Transit Transport Corridor (KMMT), the Bay of Bengal Initiative for Multi-Sectoral Technical and Economic Cooperation (BIMSTEC), the Trilateral Highway and its extension (TH-ext), Ganga-Mekong Economic Corridor (GMEC), and the Mekong-India Economic Corridor (MIEC). The KMMT is a sea-river-land hybrid corridor which will deliver improved transport links between India's land-locked North-Eastern Region (NER) and various Indian cities and ports. The corridor begins from Kolkata using a sea route towards the Myanmar sea-port of Sittwe, which is subsequently connected to Paletwa by an inland water transport component on the Kaladan River. The corridor finally loops back to India's Aizawl in the NER through the dry port of Zorinpuri. The construction of KMMT has repeatedly missed deadlines because of the recurring violence in Myanmar's Rakhine state. The KMMT is expected to be operational by 2020. BIMSTEC, established in 1997, is an inter-regional cooperation scheme between five SAARC member states (BBIN plus Sri Lanka) and two ASEAN states (Thailand and Myanmar). The Trilateral Highway (TH) was launched in 2002 as a 1360 km 'highway of opportunity and friendship' between India's Moreh, Myanmar's Bagan and Thailand's Mae Sot. In 2012, it was decided that the TH should be extended to Laos, Cambodia, and Vietnam. The GMEC seeks to enhance cooperation on tourism, culture, education, and transport between India and five greater Mekong countries (Thailand, Myanmar, Cambodia, Laos, and Vietnam). Its focus on cultural interconnectedness and social infrastructure is a distinctive feature. As with the GMEC, the MIEC is meant to jumpstart India-Southeast Asia trade and investment linkages by connecting Ho Chi Minh City and Chennai through Phnom Penh, Bangkok, and Dawei.

2.3 *US Infrastructure Engagement in Indo-Pacific*

The United States is a significant extra-regional actor in the infrastructure sector of Asia. The idea of resurrecting the ancient Silk Road was believed to be the brainchild of the Obama administration which in 2011 put forward a vision of the 'New Silk Road' for the reconstruction of Afghanistan. International infrastructure development is now re-emerging on the agenda of policy-makers in Washington at a time when China advances a similar objective through the BRI.

Since 2017, the Trump administration has progressively fleshed out its economic vision for the Indo-Pacific region under the broad mantra of the 'Free and Open Indo-Pacific' (FOIP). Three thematic initiatives of infrastructure development under the FOIP vision are: Digital Connectivity and Cybersecurity Partnership (DCCP), Infrastructure Transaction and Assistance Network (ITAN), and Enhancing Development and Growth through Energy Initiative (Asia EDGE). Operating with a budget of $25 million, the DCCP aims to develop 'an open, secure, and reliable internet' network in the Indo-Pacific region using American digital technology. ITAN (with nearly $30 million in funding) is mandated to provide technical assistance, capacity building, and access to private professional services[1] to developing countries when it comes to scouting, assessing, negotiating, and implementing infrastructure projects. Under the ambit of the Asia EDGE, $50 million will be spent on enhancing energy security in the Indo-Pacific region by optimising regional energy policy regimes and building high-tech infrastructure like smart grids.

More recently, in October 2018, President Trump signed into law the Better Utilization of Investments Leading to Development Act (BUILD Act of 2018). This Act established the US International Development Finance Corporation (DFC) to replace the Overseas Private Investment Corporation (OPIC) as the leading institution for overseas infrastructure investment. The DFC has a larger investment portfolio ceiling of $60 billion as compared to $29 billion of OPIC, and more functions and staff resources. It officially started operation in January 2020.

The transformation of OPIC to the DFC signals Washington's intent to increase its infrastructure diplomacy overtures amid great power geo-economic competition. Adam Boehler, the chief executive of the DFC, has made it clear that the DFC is part and parcel of the Trump administration's wider Indo-Pacific strategy aiming to compete with China (Lo 2020). This is manifested in the 'Triple Aim' approach followed by the DFC. That is to focus on promoting global development, advancing US foreign policy, and generating returns for American taxpayers all at the same time. To that end, the DFC will provide integrated services that cover debt and equity financing, investment funds, loan guarantee, political risk mitigation, and technical assistance to developing countries which are looking for alternatives to China's BRI (Akhtar and Tarnoff 2018). See Table 2.2 for a list of selected active projects sponsored by OPIC/DFC since 2017 in Asia.

Apart from the DFC, the US's 2017 National Security Strategy reaffirmed the strategic importance of Millennium Challenge Corporation (MCC). A unique development assistance agency, the MCC is designed to reward countries moving towards good governance, free market and liberal democracy and punish those moving in opposite directions. Practically, it firstly identifies poor but well-governed countries and then signs compact agreements for development financing (which can last up to five years) with them. Presently, the MCC has active compact arrangements with Mongolia ($250 million for water supply), Nepal ($500 million for electric power and transport) and Sri Lanka ($480 million for transport and land reform) in Asia (Brown 2019). The so-called 'MCC Effect' of initial MCC aid setting off subsequent policy and institutional reforms in recipient countries in order for them to maintain eligibility for further MCC assistance is the core concept underpinning the operation of this institution. The latest research by Parks and Davis (2019) has found beneficial MCC Effect in 45 out of 118 recipient countries but the authors also reveal that Washington's security allies are likely to be rewarded by the MCC anyway with or without the requisite governance reform. A greater controversy is the MCC's implications on national sovereignty. In February 2020, for instance, the Sri Lankan Cabinet of Ministers decided to suspend the signing of the MCC compact after considering the recommendations of a committee set up to review the agreement. Nepal's compact agreement has also become controversial because it states that the MCC agreement 'will prevail over the domestic laws of Nepal' (Amatya 2020).

2.4 *EU Strategy on Connecting Europe and Asia*

The EU adopted an infrastructure investment strategy labelled 'Connecting Europe and Asia' (CEA) in September 2018 in preparation for the 12th Asia-Europe Meeting (ASEM) Summit. The CEA's stated objective is to improve connections between Europe and Asia by supporting transport, energy, digital and people-to-people networks. The EU's infrastructure drive to the East is motivated by three broad factors. First, Asia is an

Table 2.2 Selected active OPIC/DFC projects in Asia (2017–2019)

Year	*Region*	*Country*	*Type*	*Project*	*Commitment*
2019	South Asia	India	Finance	Vehicle finance on-lending for Indian small and medium-sized enterprises	$185 million
2019	Central Asia	Armenia	Finance	Expansion of mortgage lending portfolio in Armenia	$10 million
2019	Central Asia	Georgia	Finance	Expansion of existing port operations including a new multifunctional dry cargo terminal and warehouses on the Black Sea port of Poti	$50 million
2019	East Asia	Mongolia	Finance	Construction of a new facility for finished cashmere clothing	$3.25 million
2019	Southeast Asia	Regional	Investment funds	Navis Capital Partners focuses on control investments in middle-market companies across Southeast Asia	$200 million
2018	South Asia	India	Finance	Loan proceeds to be used to expand microfinance lending to women	$100 million
2018	South Asia	India	Finance	Construction and operation of an up to 252 MW wind farm in Tamil Nadu	$225 million
2018	South Asia	Afghanistan	Finance	Re-capitalizing an existing borrower in order to reopen apparel production operations at its factory located in Kabul	$1.85 million
2018	South Asia	Pakistan	Finance	Expansion of the borrower's microfinance lending portfolio in Pakistan	$7 million
2018	East Asia	Mongolia	Finance	Expansion of an existing institution to support Mongolian micro and small and medium-sized enterprises and to finance short-term consumer loans	$2 million

(*continued*)

Table 2.2 (continued)

Year	*Region*	*Country*	*Type*	*Project*	*Commitment*
2018	Asia	Regional	Investment funds	Healthcare-focused growth equity fund investing in Asia's healthcare space: 40 per cent South Asia/60 per cent Southeast Asia	$150 million
2017	South Asia	Sri Lanka	Finance	Expansion of borrowers' microfinance lending portfolio in Sri Lanka	$14.6 million
2017	East Asia	Mongolia	Finance	Expansion of International School of Ulaanbaatar	$20 million
2017	Central Asia	Tajikistan	Insurance	Processing local agricultural crops to sell snack products that are currently imported or unavailable in Tajikistan	$4.5 million
2017	Southeast Asia	Cambodia	Finance	Refinancing of a commercial loan used for the construction of a new elementary and secondary school campus	$20 million
2017	Southeast Asia	Myanmar	Finance	Development of an 18-story quality office building in Yangon	$19.9 million
2017	Asia	Regional	Finance	Funding water and sanitation micro-loans in India, Cambodia, Indonesia and the Philippines, mainly for women	$20 million

Source: DFC project database

increasingly important market that must be more accessible to European businesses. Second, Europe believes that it has expertise in financing economically, environmentally, and socially sustainable infrastructures that abide by international norms (dubbed the 'European way to connectivity'). Third, Brussels looks set to contest China's rising infrastructure might. To a large extent, the CEA is an EU-wide response to the BRI as China has been persistently pushing its connectivity agenda at various ASEM meetings. According to the ASEM Connectivity Inventory, seven out of 12 events organised by China between 2014 and 2018 were focused on infrastructure and connectivity (Okano-Heijmans et al. 2018).

To operationalise the CEA strategy, the EU intends firstly to extend the Trans-European Network for Transport to Asian countries on Europe's periphery. This can be seen as the EU's plan to invest in integration towards the East given China's infrastructure charm offensive towards the West. The CEA agenda also extends beyond transport infrastructure to include customs cooperation, inter-regional access to digital services, transport de-carbonisation, exchange in research and cultural activities, and protection of personal data. In addition, through the CEA, the EU aspires to lay the groundwork for an international governance system for regulating the flow of goods, people, capital and services. In this regard, the EU prepares to form partnerships with like-minded countries such as China, Japan, and ASEAN for inter-regional connectivity governance and pursue technical collaborations with international standardisation organisations (e.g., the Intergovernmental Organisation for International Carriage by Rail) to set internationally acceptable standards. As to the financing of the CEA, however, the EU has expressly mentioned that it will not establish any financial institutions to underwrite the strategy. Rather, the EU will explore co-funding opportunities with private European companies, EU member states' public financial institutions (e.g., sovereign wealth funds) and MDBs.

3 Comparative Strengths and Weaknesses of Various Initiatives

The above mentioned initiatives each displays a distinct set of policy characteristics. Below, a tentative comparative analysis is provided.

BRI First, as elaborated in Chap. 1, the scope of the BRI is open-ended, making it the broadest and most ambitious initiative of all. Once focusing on Eurasian countries that lie along the bygone silk road, the BRI now is open to all countries that are willing to embrace it. The sectoral coverage of the BRI is likewise all-encompassing, including transport, industrial parks and special economic zones, space and scientific exploration, digital economy, trade liberalisation and facilitation, natural resources and financial integration. Other initiatives are much narrower in scope. Second, the amount of political capital and economic resources China has put into the BRI dwarfs all the other competing initiatives by a significant margin.

Politically, China has written the delivery of the BRI into the constitution of the Communist Party. President Xi is even personally identified with the initiative. Financially, following a state-directed financing model, strong Chinese commercial and policy banks stand ready to finance BRI projects when called upon. In comparison, the budget set aside by Tokyo, New Delhi, Washington and Brussels for their respective infrastructure strategy is either undefined or smaller in scale. Third, large Chinese companies have the expertise of constructing all types of sophisticated infrastructure that are needed by developing BRI countries. China Communications Construction Group, China State Construction Engineering Corporation and Power Construction Corporation of China are among the largest in the world; whereas no American, Japanese, or Indian construction companies have made it to the top ten globally in terms of revenue (Ellis 2019).

The BRI also has many downsides (Kliman and Grace 2018; Kliman et al. 2019). The lack of transparency is widespread, considering the scarcity of publicly available information on the bidding process and on the exact terms of the contracts awarded. Moreover, there is an excessive concentration of BRI funding sources in a handful of Chinese banks (see Chap. 1). This is of concern partly because these Chinese banks are self-sustaining entities, meaning they often charge for-profit interest rates. For example, the AidData suggests that for the period of 2000–2014 three-quarters of Chinese foreign loans charge for-profit commercial interest rates (The Economist 2018). This makes BRI funding analogous to the World Bank's non-concessional loans (Dollar 2018). Sri Lanka's Hambantota port is an often-quoted example of costly BRI financing. China's loan for the Phase I of the project carried an interest rate of 6.3 per cent and it had to be repaid in 13 years (inclusive of one-year grace period). Sri Lanka lost a certain degree of sovereign control over the port after it failed to pay back the debt. By contrast, Japanese ODA-oriented financing features more generous lending rates and repayment terms (see Table 2.1). China's non-participation in the Organisation for Economic Co-operation and Development's Development Assistance Committee (OECD DAC) and the Paris Club has also generated additional apprehensions against the BRI. Without a rules-based protocol, China is predisposed to handling sovereign default in an ad hoc, case-by-case manner, provoking criticisms of 'debt trap diplomacy'.

EPQI Japan's EPQI is the only credible alternative to the BRI. Importantly, it is a coordinated campaign that combines infrastructure financing with standard setting. Its budget of $200 billion appears relatively small at first when compared to China's deep pocket. But that is the seed capital, serving as a catalyst to crowd-in private investment.[2] Paradoxically because of the budgetary limit, the EPQI is more demand-driven and request-based relative to the BRI which is seen by many as supply-driven. In other words, EPQI projects may better reflect local priorities rather than earmarks or directives from Tokyo. Besides, the EPQI tends to be more concessional than the BRI as noted. As such, borrowing from Japan would exert less pressure on the public finance of debtor countries.

Moreover, because Japan is a member of both the OECD DAC and the Paris Club, contractual transparency, environmental sustainability, corporate social responsibility and fewer instances of tied aid (Kawai and Takagi 2004) could constitute important sources of the EPQI's comparative advantage vis-à-vis the less internationally accountable BRI. For example, the Port Vila Urban Development project in Vanuatu, jointly developed by a JICA-led consortium, was seen as free from some of the challenges plaguing the BRI (Kliman et al. 2019). In addition, as noted in Sect. 1, the EPQI is willing to lend to countries and projects that have a higher risk of default. This enhanced risk tolerance would make the EPQI more appealing for countries that seek to pursue high-risk, high-impact development projects. A further strength of the EPQI is Japan's willingness of packaging infrastructure finance with technology transfer and training of local workforces. Consider the Mumbai-Ahmedabad bullet train project in India (Jain 2019). Japan agreed to transfer *Shinkansen* technology to India and set up an institute for training local talent to run and maintain the high-speed railway.[3] As can be seen from Table 2.1, EPQI-sponsored projects tend to be contracted to local firms and public agencies of the recipient countries that are more willing to hire local workers. In contrast, many BRI projects take the form of 'circular lending', trying to spend China-sourced funding on the use of Chinese materials, equipment, and labour (Horn et al. 2019).

The EPQI has a few shortcomings as well. First, Japan's EPQI follows stringent multilateral rules for loan provision with respect to environmental and social safeguards, therefore project preparation could be difficult and the environmental and labour clearance of proposed projects could take a long time. As observed by Yukon Huang (2015), a former World Bank Director for operations in Asia and Europe, many multilateral standards and project preparation procedures are 'frustratingly bureaucratic, costly and ill-suited to dealing with the real needs of client borrowers'. This is a problem for countries with weak state capacity and/or urgent infrastructure financing needs, and many developing countries increasingly avoid seeking MDB financing as a result (Humphrey 2016). The EPQI could fall victim to the same problems and countries may avoid the EPQI just as they stay away from MDBs. By contrast, applying for BRI funding from China is more straightforward and expeditious. Second, the politics of technology transfer, especially to countries with non-rigorous intellectual property regimes, could at times be toxic. The danger as forewarned by Japanese companies is that Japan could lose its technological edge to late adopters. One could look to the experience of Kawasaki Heavy Industry, the maker of *Shinkansen* bullet trains, in China to understand such risks. In the late 2000s, Kawasaki 'shared' its core technology with its joint venture partner Qingdao Sifang, a Chinese state-owned company, only to find itself priced out of the international market years later by Sifang which exported cheaper bullet trains by assimilating Japanese *Shinkansen* technology. Third, perhaps most importantly, the staying power of the EPQI vis-à-vis the BRI is questionable. Prime Minister Abe would step down in 2021 under the current Liberal Democratic Party rules. The imminently scheduled administration switch invites one to wonder whether the next government will support foreign infrastructure investment as Abe has done under his signature EPQI.

India-led Initiatives India is at the centre of infrastructure initiatives in South Asia. This reflects India's geographical centrality in the subcontinent. South Asia is described to be 'India-locked' because for non-Indian South Asians to access each other, they must either travel across Indian territory or meet in third countries outside South Asia (Snedden 2016). Looking beyond geography, one finds that India has been relatively open for a long time. During the two centuries of its colonial past, although they were exploited by the British, a number of Indian companies managed to establish offices in London and interacted well with the British and other European powers. They spoke fluent English and had developed good personal and diplomatic skills. After independence, such relationships continued to flourish and in turn have become India's assets. China, on the other hand, was closed economically until the late 1970s, hence the global presence of Chinese companies is relatively new. Language could be a problem for the Chinese as well. In South Asia, the extensive use of English as a link language allows India to communicate easily with its regional connectivity partners whereas BRI countries speak not only English but also a host of other languages including French, Spanish, Portuguese, Russian, and Arabic. To the extent that South Asian countries feel greater cultural and linguistic affinity with India, linguistic and cultural diversities add to the difficulty for China to maintain effective communication and trust with BRI partners. Indian initiatives also encompass human connectivity, capacity building and technical support (including through the Indian Technical and Economic Cooperation Programme). Although India is not a member of the OECD DAC or the Paris Club, transparency-related issues have not been a major talking point for India's connectivity partners.

The weaknesses of India's initiatives are also pronounced. The foremost issue is that New Delhi does not have an overarching policy brand—comparable to the BRI and the EPQI—to weave together all the existing connectivity initiatives. Nor is there any unified leadership structure to coordinate India's diverse foreign infrastructure activities. This is not the case with the BRI or EPQI. For the BRI, China's primary coordination vehicle is the Leading Small Group chaired by China's first Vice Premier Han Zheng. As for Japan, it is the Management Council for Infrastructure Strategy, tasked to improve government-wide coordination presently under the direction of Chief Cabinet Secretary Yoshihide Suga. By February 2019, the Council had held 42 meetings on a wide range of topics related to the EPQI. India's foreign infrastructure policy-making process, however, is incoherent (Samuel and George 2016) and decentralised with policy-making responsibilities dispersed across multiple departments and ministries (Katti et al. 2009). India has recently strengthened the foreign ministry's Development Partnership Administration, but its institutional deficiency remains largely unaddressed. A cabinet-level steering body might be required. India also lacks capable state agencies to translate its infrastructure aspirations into reality. For instance, it does not have a single agency responsible for international infrastructure development that acts at the government's behest. Moreover, New Delhi has limited fiscal space to increase spending on connectivity initiatives; India's public sector banks are less capitalised than their counterparts in China and Japan; and private banks in India are too risk averse to take up large-scale infrastructure projects abroad.

FOIP The infrastructure development components of the US's FOIP are the DCCP, Asia EDGE, and ITAN programmes. If fully implemented, the three programmes provide scope for promoting American values such as Internet openness and cyberspace freedom. The sectoral focus on digital economy, energy and capacity-building is also well-founded as it targets sectors where American firms are globally competitive and where US economic and geopolitical stakes are high.

The formation of the DFC as a fundamental institution to implement the FOIP's infrastructure vision could further bolster America's influence (Kliman 2019). Yet, the DFC has two main defects. First, remoulding a floundering and old-fashioned OPIC—which had not been reformed much since it was first established in 1971 (Leo and Moss 2015)—into the DFC is a difficult endeavour. Fitting new functions, products, services, and tools into OPIC's existing business mode and rooting out outdated ones can be challenging and time-consuming. It is open to discussion as to when the DFC will operate at full steam. It is still early days. But most likely by the time the DFC sorts itself out, the United States would be way behind the influence curve of its competitors and partners alike which enjoy significant first-mover advantage in investing in Asia's infrastructures. Second, the $60 billion-strong DFC is under-resourced compared with the EPQI, not to mention the BRI. The total DFC investment in the Indo-Pacific region is presently only around $4.3 billion. It is 'a drop in the ocean' against the huge need that Asia has in infrastructure build-out (Scott-Bell 2019). The DFC could punch above its weight by seeking to unlock private infrastructure investment, but analysts caution that this would be a daunting task because most infrastructure investment by US businesses is domestic and most US outbound private financing goes to the de-risked and profitable OECD economies (Barshefsky and Hadley 2019). The DFC's ability to redirect private capital flows from their preferred investment destinations in the OECD to frontier BRI markets in keeping with the government's foreign policy interests is therefore questioned.

CEA The EU's CEA occupies a special place in the Eurasian infrastructure financing landscape. For one, it is not a tool of realpolitik because the EU is arguably not a hard power. For another, it outranks other initiatives for prioritising niche cooperation areas, such as interoperability (i.e., technical compatibility) between different transport modalities, decarbonisation of international transport, and rules-based infrastructure cooperation. Brussels has already built its reputation on conformity with sustainable and transparent infrastructure development practices. In the context of the CEA, the EU links the strategy with the Sustainable Development Goals of the United Nations. The EU is widely applauded for launching the ASEM Sustainable Connectivity Portal in 2018 to track physical, economic/financial, political, people-to-people and institutional connectivity between Asian and European countries, as well as to measure social, economic/financial and environmental sustainability of connectivity relationships. None of the other major power connectivity initiatives has a comparable online tool to map out the state and sustainability of connectivity between its members. The EU's membership of OECD DAC also lends additional credibility to the CEA.

That said, the CEA has a few critical shortcomings that makes it the least concrete initiative of all. To start with, the CEA is not about taking practical measures to bridge EU-Asia connectivity gaps, but preaching the specific normative conditions on which the EU is willing to engage with Asian partners on connectivity-related matters (Gaens 2019). This apparently 'paternalistic' approach to international infrastructure cooperation (Bonnet and Martin 2018) may not go down well with Asian countries which need infrastructure financing rather than development mentorship. In addition, concerns have risen about three perceived 'lows': low political ambition, low financial commitment, and low policy specificity. First, the EU is not politically committed to carrying through the strategy. This can be discerned from the relatively vague language used in the EU communication document to unveil the strategy (Broer 2018). The CEA strategy paper contained mainly best-endeavour languages like 'should', 'could', and 'may consider'. Second, the CEA is likely to fall short on financial commitments. The EU has indicated that it may put aside an amount of up to €60 billion ($67 billion) for total external investment in its next Multiannual Financial Framework 2021–2027 (which is still being negotiated at the writing) but the exact portion to be spent on the CEA is left out of the document. Third, the substance of the CEA is not fully spelled out. The additionality of the new strategy over many pre-existing EU programmes such as the Asia Investment Facility is not fleshed out. The strategy is also consciously light on how to mobilise private investment into EU-Asian connectivity projects. Finally, unfavourable geopolitics could hold back the CEA, the implementation of which depends on the support of Russia and Turkey. The EU's foreign relations with both countries are fraught with difficulties and the EU has yet to win their support of its CEA agenda. For these reasons, the CEA should best be understood as a rhetorical response to China's BRI.

4 Conclusion

A cursory comparison across various major power infrastructure initiatives reveals that China's BRI, by virtue of its scale, scope and visibility, is in a class of its own. Japan's EPQI comes in a close second. The EPQI can both counter-balance China's infrastructure dominance and provide countries with an alternative to borrowing from China for infrastructure projects. It has the potential to deliver financially and environmentally sustainable infrastructure solutions at a lower cost to developing countries. A major concern, however, is that the EPQI may lose momentum should Abe leave office in 2021. India is in a dominant position in South Asia. Though the sub-regional and inter-regional connectivity initiatives led by India are of smaller scale and less ambitious compared to the BRI and the EPQI, they serve India's national interests well and place India at the centre of South Asian infrastructure diplomacy. A successful implementation of the BRI in South Asia would necessitate reconciliation with India and synergies with on-going initiatives.

Trailing behind the three Asian frontrunners are the United States and the EU. The former has planned to step up infrastructure engagement in the Indo-Pacific through specific programmes and by setting up a new institution of development finance at home. The DFC has been established but it will take some time for it to be fully operational. The United States is, therefore, unlikely to rival China or Japan on infrastructure diplomacy in the short to medium run. The EU's CEA is the least concrete policy proposal. It is less detailed with the scale of funding still unknown.

The relationship between these connectivity initiatives is still evolving. They can be organised either to pursue mutually beneficial connectivity goals, complementing each other and looking upon each other as development partners in shaping the economic geography of Eurasia, or to develop competing and adversarial relationships that result in duplication, race to the bottom in standards, and geopolitical rivalry. Policy-makers should ensure that cooperation prevails over competition.

Notes

1. ITAN has established a dedicated Transaction Advisory Fund for this purpose.
2. For instance, the JBIC has partnered with Toyota Tsusho in a public-private partnership to develop port and supply chain infrastructure worth approximately $643 million in Angola.
3. Separately, Japan pledged in November 2018 to train 80,000 manufacturing and digital industry specialists in five years for ASEAN countries.

References

Akhtar, Shayerah Ilias, and Curt Tarnoff. 2018. OPIC, USAID, and Proposed Development Finance Reorganization. In *CRS Report*. Washington, DC: Congressional Research Service.

Amatya, Kripendra. 2020. The MCC and Nepal's Strategic Ties with the US. *The Diplomat*. https://thediplomat.com/2020/02/the-mcc-and-nepals-strategic-ties-with-the-us/. Accessed 5 March 2020.

Barshefsky, Charlene, and Stephen J. Hadley. 2019. *The Higher Road: Forging a U.S. Strategy for the Global Infrastructure Challenge*. Washington, DC: Center for Strategic and International Studies.

Bonnet, Philippe, and Antoine Martin. 2018. An EU Strategy on Connecting Europe to Asia… the European Way?. https://asiapacificcircle.org/asia-pacific-insights-trends/an-eu-strategy-on-connecting-europe-to-asia-the-european-way/. Accessed 19 April 2019.

Broer, Bart. 2018. *The EU's Connectivity Strategy: An Answer to China's Belt and Road Initiative?* Brussels: EU-Asia Centre.

Brown, Nick M. 2019. *Millennium Challenge Corporation: Overview and Issues*. Washington, DC: Congressional Research Service.

Dollar, David. 2018. Is China's Development Finance a Challenge to the International Order? *Asian Economic Policy Review* 13: 283–298.

Ellis, Grace. 2019. Top 10 Construction Companies in the World. *Construction Productivity Blog*. https://blog.plangrid.com/2019/05/top-10-construction-companies-in-the-world-slideshare/. Accessed 14 February 2020.

Gaens, Bart. 2019. The EU-Asia Connectivity Strategy and Its Impact on Asia-Europe Relations. In *Trade and Economic Connectivity in the Age of Uncertainty*. Singapore: Konrad Adenauer Stiftung.

Horn, Sebastian, Carmen M. Reinhart, and Christoph Trebesch. 2019. China's Overseas Lending. In *NBER Working Paper No. 26050*. Cambridge, MA: National Bureau of Economic Research.

Huang, Yukon. 2015. China Has a Role to Play in Setting the 'Right' Standards. *Financial Times.* https://www.ft.com/content/b1a49850-23bb-3f1d-9400-9c96d09cbc60. Accessed 1 March 2020.

Humphrey, Chris. 2016. *Time for a New Approach to Environmental and Social Protection at Multilateral Development Banks.* London: Overseas Development Institute.

Jain, Purnendra. 2019. Japan's Foreign Aid and 'Quality' Infrastructure Projects: The Case of the Bullet Train in India. In *JICA-RI Working Paper.* Tokyo: JICA Research Institute.

Karim, Tariq A. 2017. South Asia's Efforts at Regional Reintegration: Fantasy or Feasible? In *Asia Pacific Bulletin.* Washington, DC: East-West Center.

Katti, Vijaya, Tatjana Chahoud, and Atul Kaushik. 2009. India's Development Cooperation – Opportunities and Challenges for International Development Cooperation. In *Briefing Paper.* Bonn: German Development Institute.

Kawai, Masahiro, and Shinji Takagi. 2004. Japan's Official Development Assistance: Recent Issues and Future Directions. *Journal of International Development* 16 (2): 255–280.

Kliman, Daniel. 2019. *To Compete with China, Get the New U.S. Development Finance Corporation Right.* Washington, DC: Center for a New American Security.

Kliman, Daniel, and Abigail Grace. 2018. *Power Play: Addressing China's Belt and Road Strategy.* Washington, DC: Center for a New American Security.

Kliman, Daniel, Rush Doshi, Kristine Lee, and Zack Cooper. 2019. *Grading China's Belt and Road.* Washington, DC: Center for a New American Security.

Leo, Benjamin, and Todd Moss. 2015. Bringing US Development Finance into the 21st Century: Proposal for a Self-Sustaining, Full-Service USDFC. In *Rethinking US Development Policy.* Washington, DC: Center For Global Development.

Lo, Kinling. 2020. US International Development Finance Corporation Targets Asia as Washington Seeks to Offer Alternative to Chinese Cash. *South China Morning Post.* https://www.scmp.com/news/china/diplomacy/article/3045686/us-international-development-finance-corporation-targets-asia. Accessed 10 February 2020.

METI. 2016. *G7 Ise-Shima Summit "Expanded Partnership for Quality Infrastructure".* https://www.meti.go.jp/english/press/2016/pdf/0523_01b.pdf.

MOFA. Undated. Partnership for Quality Infrastructure. https://www.mofa.go.jp/files/000117998.pdf.

Okano-Heijmans, Maaike, Anita Prakash, and Wouter Zweers. 2018. *ASEM Connectivity Inventory.* Jakarta and The Hague: ERIA and Clingendael.

Parks, Bradley C., and Caroline Davis. 2019. When do Governments Trade Domestic Reforms for External Rewards? Explaining Policy Responses to the

Millennium Challenge Corporation's Eligibility Standards. *Governance* 32 (2): 349–367.

Samuel, John, and Abraham George. 2016. *Future of Development Cooperation: Policy Priorities for an Emerging India*. Kerala and New Delhi: Institute for Sustainable Development & Governance and Oxfam India.

Scott-Bell, Thomas. 2019. The Belt and Road Is Funding Global Infrastructure Investment. What About the Rest?. *China Focus*. http://www.cnfocus.com/the-belt-and-road-is-funding-global-infrastructure-investment-what-about-the-rest/. Accessed 11 February 2020.

Shinde, Shankar. 2018. International North South Transport Corridor (INSTC). FIATA World Congress 2018, New Delhi, 26 September.

Snedden, Christopher. 2016. *Shifting Geo-politics in the Greater South Asia Region*. Honolulu: Daniel K. Inouye Asia-Pacific Center for Security Studies.

Szczudlik, Justyna. 2016. Many Belts and Many Roads: The Proliferation of Infrastructure Initiatives in Asia. In *PISM Policy Paper*. Warsaw: Polish Institute of International Affairs.

The Economist. 2018. China Has a Vastly Ambitious Plan to Connect the World. *The Economist*. https://www.economist.com/briefing/2018/07/26/china-has-a-vastly-ambitious-plan-to-connect-the-world. Accessed 16 April 2019.

Yhome, K. 2017. India's Evolving Subregional Strategy. In *Asia Pacific Bulletin, No. 403*. Washington, DC: East-West Center.

CHAPTER 3

Potential Economic Impact of BRI: A Computable General Equilibrium Analysis

1 Introduction

Infrastructure plays an indispensable role in economic development and is a necessity for increased cross-border trade. Trade liberalisation is also a well-known driver of economic growth and regional integration. Improved transport connectivity and unimpeded trade are two priority areas of cooperation under the BRI. This chapter quantifies the potential economic gains (defined as increase in national real GDP) to countries from the BRI corridors by simulating a computable general equilibrium (CGE) model. Its value-added is that it provides empirical evidence on the possible benefits of the BRI corridors to stakeholder countries and identifies the groups of countries that are more likely to benefit from the BRI than others. This quantitative evidence supplements the qualitative discussion of the benefits in Chaps. 5–7.

So far, there are only a handful of quantitative studies that assess the economic impact of the BRI. These fall into two methodological groups. One group estimates the trade effects of the BRI by utilising gravity models. An example is Herrero and Xu (2017) who use this approach to analyse the BRI's impact on Europe, concluding that European countries would benefit considerably from the Chinese initiative. Lu et al. (2018) also find a positive correlation between improved transport connectivity and bilateral trade volumes within BRI regions and beyond. Similarly, Baniya et al. (2019) estimate that the BRI could increase trade flows among BRI countries by up to 4.1 per cent.

P. B. Rana, X. Ji, *China's Belt and Road Initiative*,
https://doi.org/10.1007/978-981-15-5171-0_3

The other group of researchers use economy-wide CGE models to quantify the potential macroeconomic impact of the BRI. One such study is Villafuerte et al. (2016) which finds that improved transport networks among BRI countries could raise GDP growth in Central, West, and South Asian countries by amounts up to 0.19 per cent. Also by simulating a recursive dynamic CGE model, Zhai (2018) suggests that, if the BRI were to invest $1.4 trillion in Asian transport infrastructure, Asian BRI countries could realise an annual real GDP gain of 2.9 per cent.

A problem with existing studies is that they focus only on the reduction of transport cost through the BRI and neglect the potential gains from the BRI's trade liberalisation agenda. This chapter, therefore, uses a CGE model to capture the effects of both improving transport connectivity (i.e., reducing transport cost) and liberalising trade (i.e., eliminating tariffs) under the BRI. Our study is similar to the two recent studies by the World Bank (de Soyres et al. 2019; Maliszewska and van der Mensbrugghe 2019), a key difference being that unlike these studies we estimate the impacts of individual overland corridors and the Maritime Silk Road (MSR) and aggregate them to get the combined effect of the BRI. Another shortcoming of the World Bank studies is that they look at how the BRI might reduce the shortest transport distances between pairs of major cities in Eurasia, so they cannot attribute the estimated economic gains to any specific BRI corridor.

2 Modelling Framework and Database

Our economic assessment of the BRI is based on the Global Trade Analysis Project (GTAP) model, which is a multi-region, multi-sector, comparative-static CGE model of the world economy (Hertel 2013). The GTAP database describes the global economy in an initial state of general equilibrium where all markets clear. When a policy shock is introduced, the world economy goes into a temporary state of disequilibrium. GTAP's behavioural equations and parameters describing the assumed responses of market agents (e.g., private household, company, and government) then adjust and come up with a new set of market clearing prices and quantities so that the world economy settles into a new general equilibrium state. Comparing variables of interest in the original and the new general equilibria, one can determine the effects of the policy shock, all else being equal.

The standard GTAP model adopts a short-term macroeconomic closure in which cross-border mobility of capital is prohibited. In order to estimate the longer-term effects of the BRI, we modify the closure to create a longer-term macro-environment where capital is mobile across countries in search of the highest return. This calibration of the GTAP model closure has been used by the Australian Productivity Commission (2010), Gretton (2017) and Ji et al. (2018).

Our study uses the latest GTAP database available, Version 10 released in July 2019. The database provides data until 2014 and covers 121 countries representing 98 per cent of the global economy and 65 economic sectors (Aguiar et al. 2019). Countries and sectors in the GTAP database are bundled into aggregates to enhance computational efficiency. The regional aggregation procedure in our study takes into account country participation in various BRI corridors and the MSR. Southeast Asian and South Asian BRI countries are retained individually, while other countries are aggregated according to whether they (1) lie along BRI corridors, (2) participate in more than one corridor, or (3) belong to a conventional grouping. Countries involved in more than one corridor (e.g., Kazakhstan) are not aggregated. Countries that form a natural geographical grouping such as the Caucasus (Armenia, Azerbaijan, and Georgia) are grouped together. The detailed regional and sectoral aggregations used are in Appendix Tables 3.11 and 3.12.

In the GTAP model, the difference between the value of a commodity at exporter's and importer's borders is analytically considered as the transport cost. Bilateral international transport cost is thus imputed from the Cost, Insurance, and Freight/Free-on-Board ratio of a traded commodity. Three transport modalities are covered by the GTAP database: air, sea, and ground transport. For the purpose of this study, we assume that BRI infrastructure development reduces ground and sea transport costs for overland BRI countries and member states of the MSR, respectively. This approach of lowering *ad valorem* transport cost to provide a proxy of improvement in international transport condition is widely adopted including by Menon and Warr (2006), Stone et al. (2012) and Villafuerte et al. (2016). International organisations like UNCTAD (2017) regularly employs this method to track global changes in international transport cost.

Nevertheless, our modelling approach has a number of methodological drawbacks that deserve attention. First, it only captures the static effects of lowering transport cost, and cannot account for the dynamic economic effects such as new trading opportunities and revolutionary commercial patterns that could arise because of enhanced transport connectivity. Second, our approach does not allow for domestic transport improvement even though the BRI also builds and improves in-country transport infrastructure. Third, indirect cost-raising factors such as delivery reliability, customs checks, and border delays (Hummels and Schaur 2013) are unaccounted for in the simulations. Finally, the ground transport data as compiled by GTAP harmonises together road, railway, and pipeline; singling out a particular transport mode or a specific transport route for analysis is not possible. As such, our CGE modelling results do not correspond to the full benefit of the BRI undertaking. Despite these limitations, our results shown below are not far-off from existing CGE studies on the relationship between infrastructure improvement and economic growth including non-BRI studies such as Wignaraja et al. (2015).

3 Simulation Scenarios

We simulate the real GDP impacts of reductions in transport costs and tariff eliminations along each of the seven BRI land corridors and the MSR. We also estimate the aggregate real GDP impacts of the seven land corridors and the MSR combined.

In the case of each land corridor and the MSR, we consider three scenarios:

S1: Reduction in transport costs ranging from 5 to 50 per cent at 5 per cent intervals;
S2: Trade liberalisation (zero tariffs) along each BRI land corridor or the MSR;
S3: Combined impact of transport cost reduction plus trade liberalisation.

The S1 assumption is based on studies reviewed by Stone and Strutt (2010) which suggest that infrastructure-induced transport cost reduction (in the Greater Mekong sub-region) can be about 45 per cent at best. Furthermore, it should be noted that the assumed transport cost reductions are un-weighted across corridor and MSR countries.[1]

In the case of estimating the aggregate impact of the seven land corridors and the MSR, we further consider two scenarios: the low case (defined as 5% trade cost reduction for all countries excluding India) and high case (50% trade cost reduction and full tariff liberalisation including India's participation in the BRI) scenarios.

4 Estimation Results

4.1 *Impact of Land Corridors*

4.1.1 New Eurasian Land Bridge

Table 3.1 shows that the projected economic gain from the hypothesised transport cost reduction (Scenario S1) is the highest for Kazakhstan which is a land-locked country in Central Asia. The country's GDP elasticity (defined as percentage growth in real GDP divided by percentage reduction in transport cost reduction) is 0.0086, meaning that one per cent reduction in transport cost across all NELB countries leads to an increase in Kazakhstan's real GDP by 0.0086 per cent. European BRI countries and Russia also benefit from the NELB albeit to lesser degrees; the GDP elasticity is 0.0022 in the former and 0.0013 in the latter. China's GDP gain from transport cost improvement alone is negligible. This is in part because the sea routes have been more important than land route for China–Europe trade. That said, it should be noted that the GTAP model we use is a static model; the benefits would have been higher had we used a dynamic one.

The simulation results also show that if China, Kazakhstan, and Russia abolish all tariffs (but keep inter-state transport costs unchanged), that is

Table 3.1 NELB Corridor: Estimated real GDP impact of Scenarios S1, S2, and S3 (%)

	0	*5*	*10*	*15*	*20*	*25*	*30*	*35*	*40*	*45*	*50*
		Scenario S1									
China	–	–	–	–	–	0.01	0.01	0.01	0.01	0.01	0.01
Kazakhstan	–	0.06	0.11	0.15	0.2	0.24	0.27	0.31	0.34	0.37	0.4
Russia	–	0.01	0.02	0.02	0.03	0.03	0.04	0.05	0.05	0.05	0.06
European Belt countries	–	0.01	0.03	0.04	0.05	0.06	0.07	0.08	0.09	0.1	0.1
	Scenario S2	Scenario S3									
China	0.08	0.08	0.08	0.08	0.08	0.09	0.09	0.09	0.09	0.09	0.09
Kazakhstan	0.87	0.92	0.98	1.03	1.07	1.11	1.15	1.19	1.22	1.26	1.29
Russia	0.19	0.2	0.21	0.21	0.22	0.23	0.23	0.24	0.24	0.25	0.25
European Belt countries	–	–	0.01	0.02	0.03	0.04	0.05	0.06	0.07	0.08	0.08

Source: Authors' estimates

Scenario S2, the estimated real GDP increases to these countries are relatively higher, amounting to 0.08 per cent, 0.87 per cent, and 0.19 per cent, respectively. Comparing the data in S2 column with those in S1 and S3 columns also shows that trade liberalisation tends to generate greater economic gains than reduction in transport cost.

4.1.2 *China-Mongolia-Russia Economic Corridor*

The China-Mongolia-Russia (CMR) Economic Corridor is projected to have a minimal impact on both China and Russia from a transport perspective but could confer a significant economic boost to the land-locked Mongolia (see Table 3.2, S1 columns). The estimated GDP elasticity for Mongolia is high at 0.021. That is to say if the CMR corridor reduces transport cost by 10 per cent, Mongolia's real GDP will up by 0.21 per cent. CMR-based trade liberalisation will also benefit Mongolia (1.72%) to a greater extent than it does to China (0.06%) and Russia (0.22%) as S2 column in Table 3.2 shows. Since transport enhancement and trade liberalisation simulate economic growth through different channels, the gains from them tend to be additive and non-overlapping (Table 3.2, S3 columns).

4.1.3 *China-Central Asia-West Asia Economic Corridor*

The China-Central Asia-West Asia (CCAWA) Economic Corridor connects China with Central Asia and West Asia. Under Scenario S1 (Table 3.3), all participating countries are expected to benefit, and the top winners from the CCAWA connectivity cooperation are the Caucasus

Table 3.2 CMR Corridor: Estimated real GDP impact of Scenarios S1, S2, and S3 (%)

	0	*5*	*10*	*15*	*20*	*25*	*30*	*35*	*40*	*45*	*50*
		Scenario S1									
China	–	–	–	–	–	–	–	–	–	–	0.01
Mongolia	–	0.14	0.26	0.37	0.48	0.58	0.67	0.75	0.83	0.9	0.97
Russia	–	–	0.01	0.01	0.01	0.01	0.01	0.02	0.02	0.02	0.02
	Scenario S2	Scenario S3									
China	0.06	0.06	0.07	0.07	0.07	0.07	0.07	0.07	0.07	0.07	0.07
Mongolia	1.72	1.86	1.99	2.11	2.22	2.32	2.41	2.5	2.58	2.66	2.73
Russia	0.22	0.22	0.22	0.23	0.23	0.23	0.23	0.23	0.24	0.24	0.24

Source: Authors' estimates

Table 3.3 CCAWA Corridor: Estimated real GDP impact of Scenarios S1, S2, and S3 (%)

	0	*5*	*10*	*15*	*20*	*25*	*30*	*35*	*40*	*45*	*50*
		Scenario S1									
China	–	–	–	–	–	0.01	0.01	0.01	0.01	0.01	0.01
Kazakhstan	–	0.04	0.07	0.1	0.13	0.16	0.19	0.21	0.23	0.25	0.27
Other Central Asian BRI countries	–	0.03	0.06	0.08	0.11	0.13	0.15	0.17	0.19	0.2	0.22
Caucasus	–	0.04	0.08	0.11	0.15	0.18	0.2	0.23	0.25	0.28	0.3
Turkey	–	0.02	0.03	0.05	0.06	0.08	0.09	0.1	0.11	0.12	0.13
Iran	–	0.04	0.08	0.11	0.14	0.17	0.2	0.22	0.24	0.26	0.28
Saudi Arabia	–	0.01	0.01	0.02	0.03	0.03	0.04	0.04	0.05	0.05	0.06
Other West Asian BRI countries	–	0.02	0.04	0.05	0.06	0.08	0.09	0.1	0.11	0.12	0.13
	Scenario S2	Scenario S3									
China	0.17	0.17	0.17	0.17	0.17	0.17	0.18	0.18	0.18	0.18	0.18
Kazakhstan	0.86	0.9	0.94	0.97	1	1.03	1.06	1.09	1.11	1.13	1.15
Other Central Asian BRI countries	0.67	0.7	0.73	0.76	0.78	0.8	0.82	0.84	0.86	0.88	0.89
Caucasus	0.36	0.4	0.44	0.48	0.51	0.55	0.58	0.6	0.63	0.65	0.68
Turkey	−0.31	−0.3	−0.28	−0.27	−0.26	−0.25	−0.24	−0.23	−0.22	−0.21	−0.2
Iran	7.53	7.59	7.64	7.68	7.72	7.76	7.79	7.83	7.86	7.89	7.91
Saudi Arabia	0.21	0.22	0.22	0.23	0.24	0.24	0.25	0.25	0.26	0.26	0.26
Other West Asian BRI countries	0.33	0.34	0.36	0.38	0.39	0.4	0.42	0.43	0.44	0.45	0.46

Source: Authors' estimates

countries (Armenia, Azerbaijan, and Georgia), Iran and Kazakhstan. They register a GDP elasticity of 0.0064, 0.0061, and 0.0058, respectively. China benefits the least followed by Saudi Arabia. This is in part because Saudi Arabia has much stronger commercial ties with non-CCAWA countries such as Japan, India, South Korea, the United States, and Germany.

Under the tariff scenario S2, however, Iran emerges as the single largest winner should CCAWA countries reciprocally eliminate tariffs. Iran's real GDP could go up by 7.53 per cent. Turkey's real GDP, on the other hand, is projected to contract by 0.31 per cent due to its presumed exclusion from BRI trade liberalisation (as Turkey binds its trade policy with the EU's Common Commercial Policy). When the effects of tariff elimination and transport cost reduction are combined (S3 columns in Table 3.3), the results indicate that land transport costs pose a lesser obstacle than prohibitive tariff protections in the CCAWA countries for traders. Indeed, Iran's weighted average applied tariff rate as of 2011 (the latest available year) was over 15 per cent, making it one of the most protectionist countries in the world. Geopolitically speaking, for this positive scenario to become reality, it is essential for China to broker an early restoration of economic and diplomatic ties between two West Asian regional hegemons, Iran and Saudi Arabia.

4.1.4 China-Indochina Peninsula Economic Corridor

The China-Indochina Peninsula Economic Corridor (CICPEC) reduces the transport cost of trading between China and countries in mainland Southeast Asia. The economic relationship between China and Southeast Asia is already strong (Salidjanova et al. 2015) but the CICPEC will further integrate the participating economies. As shown in Table 3.4, the major beneficiaries of the CICPEC's infrastructure agenda are Vietnam and Laos (S1 columns). They have a GDP elasticity of 0.0151 each. Thailand and Myanmar are also projected to be big winners. In comparison, the expected economic benefits for Cambodia, China, Singapore, and Malaysia from transport cost reduction are less.

Under the tariff reduction scenario (column S2 in Table 3.4), Cambodia (2.32%) and Vietnam (1.63%) are likely to see the highest real GDP increases. Aside from China, the country that benefits the least from CICPEC tariff liberalisation is Singapore. This is not surprising as the city-state has long been a free-trade entrepôt pre-BRI. The data in the table show once again that real GDP gains from trade liberalisation are higher than from transport cost reduction.

Table 3.4 CICPEC Corridor: Estimated real GDP impact of Scenarios S1, S2, and S3 (%)

	0	*5*	*10*	*15*	*20*	*25*	*30*	*35*	*40*	*45*	*50*
		Scenario S1									
China	–	–	–	0.01	0.01	0.01	0.01	0.01	0.02	0.02	0.02
Vietnam	–	0.1	0.19	0.27	0.34	0.41	0.48	0.54	0.6	0.65	0.7
Malaysia	–	0.01	0.02	0.03	0.04	0.05	0.06	0.07	0.07	0.08	0.09
Singapore	–	0.01	0.02	0.04	0.05	0.05	0.06	0.07	0.08	0.08	0.09
Thailand	–	0.06	0.12	0.17	0.22	0.27	0.31	0.35	0.39	0.42	0.45
Laos	–	0.1	0.19	0.27	0.35	0.42	0.48	0.55	0.6	0.65	0.7
Cambodia	–	0.01	0.03	0.04	0.05	0.06	0.07	0.08	0.08	0.09	0.1
Myanmar	–	0.05	0.10	0.14	0.17	0.21	0.24	0.27	0.3	0.32	0.34
	Scenario S2	Scenario S3									
China	0.05	0.05	0.05	0.05	0.06	0.06	0.06	0.06	0.06	0.06	0.06
Vietnam	1.63	1.73	1.83	1.91	1.99	2.07	2.14	2.2	2.26	2.32	2.37
Malaysia	0.24	0.26	0.27	0.28	0.29	0.29	0.3	0.31	0.32	0.32	0.33
Singapore	0.19	0.2	0.22	0.23	0.24	0.24	0.25	0.26	0.27	0.27	0.28
Thailand	0.5	0.56	0.62	0.68	0.73	0.77	0.82	0.86	0.89	0.93	0.96
Laos	0.99	1.09	1.18	1.26	1.33	1.4	1.46	1.52	1.58	1.63	1.68
Cambodia	2.32	2.33	2.34	2.35	2.36	2.37	2.38	2.39	2.4	2.4	2.41
Myanmar	0.33	0.38	0.42	0.47	0.5	0.54	0.57	0.6	0.62	0.65	0.67

Source: Authors' estimates

4.1.5 *China-Pakistan Economic Corridor*

Table 3.5 shows the estimated economic impact of China-Pakistan Economic Corridor (CPEC). The economic benefit to China is negligible according to the simulations. This finding is consistent with the perception that to China CPEC is a foreign policy initiative for achieving a geopolitical foothold in South Asia, rather than a business proposition. Pakistan, by contrast, can expect sizeable economic benefits from CPEC. Its GDP elasticity under CPEC is 0.0032. Pakistan's gain from trade liberalisation with China is equivalent to 0.39 per cent in comparison with China's modest gain of 0.02 per cent. When connectivity improvement and trade liberalisation are considered together, CPEC would have a positive economic impact in the range of 0.39 and 0.56 per cent in Pakistan (S3 columns in Table 3.5). Again, Pakistan benefits not so much from enhancing connectivity as from liberalising trade with China.

Table 3.5 CPEC Corridor: Estimated real GDP impact of Scenarios S1, S2, and S3 (%)

	0	*5*	*10*	*15*	*20*	*25*	*30*	*35*	*40*	*45*	*50*
		Scenario S1									
China	–	–	–	–	–	–	–	–	–	–	–
Pakistan	–	0.02	0.04	0.06	0.07	0.09	0.1	0.12	0.14	0.14	0.15
	Scenario S2	Scenario S3									
China	0.02	0.02	0.02	0.02	0.02	0.02	0.02	0.02	0.02	0.02	0.02
Pakistan	0.39	0.42	0.44	0.46	0.48	0.49	0.51	0.52	0.54	0.55	0.56

Source: Authors' estimates

4.1.6 Bangladesh-China-India-Myanmar Economic Corridor

Our modelling results (Fig. 3.1) suggest that the real GDP impact of reduced transport cost (Scenario S1) along the Bangladesh-China-India-Myanmar Economic Corridor (BCIM) is the highest for Myanmar. India could see a marginal real GDP gain of 0.01 per cent provided that transport cost is brought down by around 35 per cent or more. Real GDP gains to China and Bangladesh are estimated to be near zero in the connectivity scenario. More importantly, Fig. 3.1 implies that excluding India from the BCIM corridor does not dampen the economic impact as far as only transport connectivity is concerned. With an averaged GDP elasticity of around 0.0053, Myanmar derives benefits predominately from reducing transport cost with China. Two-way merchandise trade between Myanmar and China is more than five times as much as Myanmar-India trade ($12.8 billion vs. $1.9 billion in 2017). Going ahead with the China-Myanmar Economic Corridor as an interim alternative to the BCIM appears to be a sound policy choice given India's non-committal attitude.

Results for the tariff reduction scenario (column S2 in Table 3.6) show that with India's participation, the projected gains in real GDP for Bangladesh, China, India, and Myanmar are 1.48 per cent, 0.09 per cent, 0.2 per cent and 0.13 per cent, respectively. Without India, real GDP gains for Bangladesh, China, and Myanmar are 1.23 per cent, 0.02 per cent, and 0.29 per cent, respectively. The discrepancy means that India's non-participation in BCIM trade liberalisation reduces gains for China and Bangladesh but increases economic benefits for Myanmar.

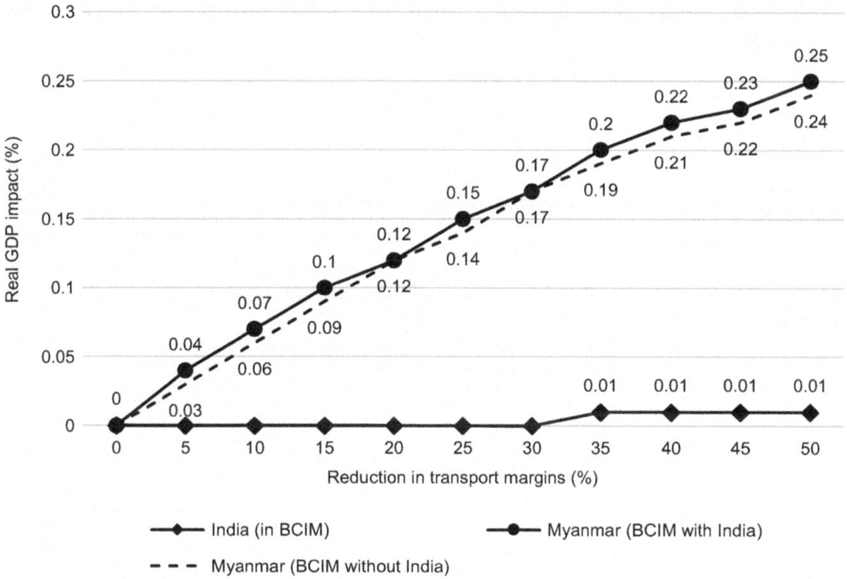

Fig. 3.1 Estimated real GDP impact of transport cost reduction for BCIM countries (S1).
Note: Projected impacts on China and Bangladesh are zero
Source: Authors' estimates

Taking into consideration both transport cost reduction and trade liberalisation (Scenario S3), the estimated impact of the BCIM corridor, with or without India, as Table 3.6 shows, is that Bangladesh, China and India benefit significantly more from removing tariffs whereas Myanmar benefits almost equally from trade liberalisation and transport cost reduction within the simulated range.

4.1.7 Trans-Himalayan Economic Corridor

The Trans-Himalayan Economic Corridor (THEC) connects China with India through Nepal. As Fig. 3.2 illustrates, reducing trans-Himalayan transport cost (Scenario S1) has a positive effect on Nepal but real GDP gains for the other two countries are relatively small (which is zero in the case of China). India starts to realise real GDP gains only if trans-Himalayan

Table 3.6 BCIM Corridor: Estimated real GDP impact of Scenarios S2 and S3 (%)

	Scenario S2	*Scenario S3*									
	0	*5*	*10*	*15*	*20*	*25*	*30*	*35*	*40*	*45*	*50*
BCIM											
Bangladesh	1.48	1.48	1.48	1.48	1.48	1.48	1.48	1.48	1.48	1.48	1.48
China	0.09	0.09	0.09	0.09	0.09	0.09	0.09	0.09	0.09	0.09	0.09
India	0.2	0.2	0.2	0.2	0.2	0.2	0.2	0.2	0.21	0.21	0.21
Myanmar	0.13	0.16	0.2	0.23	0.25	0.28	0.3	0.33	0.35	0.37	0.39
BCIM w/o India											
Bangladesh	1.23	1.23	1.23	1.23	1.23	1.23	1.23	1.23	1.23	1.23	1.23
China	0.02	0.02	0.02	0.02	0.02	0.02	0.02	0.02	0.02	0.02	0.02
Myanmar	0.29	0.32	0.35	0.38	0.41	0.43	0.45	0.48	0.5	0.51	0.53

Source: Authors' estimates

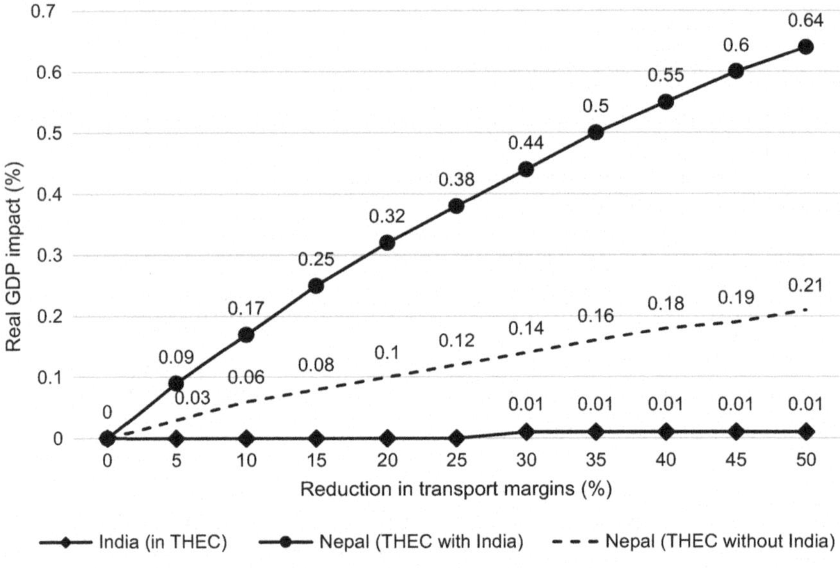

Fig. 3.2 Estimated real GDP impact of transport cost reduction for THEC countries (S1).
Note: Projected impact on China is zero
Source: Authors' estimates

Table 3.7 THEC Corridor: Estimated real GDP impact of Scenarios S2 and S3 (%)

	Scenario S2	*Scenario S3*									
	0	*5*	*10*	*15*	*20*	*25*	*30*	*35*	*40*	*45*	*50*
THEC											
China	0.07	0.07	0.07	0.07	0.07	0.07	0.07	0.07	0.07	0.07	0.07
India	0.19	0.19	0.2	0.2	0.2	0.2	0.2	0.2	0.2	0.2	0.2
Nepal	0.42	0.51	0.58	0.65	0.71	0.77	0.82	0.87	0.92	0.96	1.01
THEC w/o India											
China	–	–	–	–	–	–	–	–	–	–	–
Nepal	−1.58	−1.56	−1.53	−1.51	−1.49	−1.48	−1.46	−1.45	−1.43	−1.42	−1.41

Source: Authors' estimates

transport cost is reduced by at least 30 per cent. Also noteworthy is that, unlike the BCIM corridor, the economic impact of the THEC on Nepal is determined by India's stand on the BRI. If India is in, Nepal enjoys a reasonably high GDP elasticity of 0.0139 but the figure diminishes by two-thirds to 0.0045 if India stays out of the THEC connectivity cooperation. The same can be said with respect to the tariff liberalisation scenario (column S2 in Table 3.7). With India's participation, the Chinese, Indian, and Nepali real GDPs increase by 0.07 per cent, 0.19 per cent, and 0.42 per cent, respectively. India's non-participation, however, causes China's gain to be wiped out and turns Nepal's economic gains into losses.

4.2 *Impact of Maritime Silk Road*

Table 3.8 presents the estimated real GDP impact of various scenarios under the MSR. The results suggest that under the transport cost reduction scenario (Scenario S1), Sri Lanka, Malaysia, Singapore, and Kenya would benefit the most. These are the countries which are already well integrated with the existing global maritime trade networks. Vietnam benefits less in comparison. However, under the tariff reduction scenario (S2), Vietnam is one of the largest beneficiaries with a projected real GDP gain of 1.57 per cent, next only to Sri Lanka (1.85%) and Kenya (1.79%). These three countries are also projected to do well in Scenario S3.

Table 3.8 MSR: Estimated real GDP impact of Scenarios S1, S2, and S3 (%)

	0	*5*	*10*	*15*	*20*	*25*	*30*	*35*	*40*	*45*	*50*
		Scenario S1									
China	–	0.01	0.01	0.02	0.03	0.03	0.04	0.04	0.05	0.05	0.06
Vietnam	–	0.4	0.07	0.11	0.14	0.16	0.19	0.21	0.24	0.26	0.28
Malaysia	–	0.1	0.19	0.27	0.34	0.41	0.48	0.54	0.6	0.65	0.7
Singapore	–	0.06	0.12	0.18	0.22	0.27	0.31	0.35	0.39	0.42	0.45
Indonesia	–	0.02	0.04	0.06	0.08	0.10	0.11	0.13	0.14	0.15	0.17
Myanmar	–	0.03	0.05	0.08	0.1	0.12	0.14	0.15	0.17	0.18	0.2
Sri Lanka	–	0.1	0.2	0.29	0.37	0.44	0.51	0.58	0.64	0.7	0.75
Pakistan	–	0.02	0.04	0.05	0.07	0.08	0.09	0.1	0.11	0.12	0.14
Kenya	–	0.06	0.12	0.17	0.21	0.26	0.3	0.34	0.37	0.41	0.44
Italy and Greece	–	0.01	0.02	0.02	0.03	0.03	0.04	0.05	0.06	0.07	0.07
	Scenario S2	Scenario S3									
China	0.07	0.08	0.09	0.09	0.1	0.11	0.11	0.12	0.12	0.13	0.13
Vietnam	1.57	1.61	1.65	1.68	1.71	1.74	1.76	1.79	1.81	1.83	1.85
Malaysia	0.3	0.4	0.49	0.58	0.65	0.72	0.79	0.85	0.91	0.96	1.01
Singapore	0.33	0.4	0.46	0.51	0.56	0.61	0.65	0.69	0.72	0.76	0.79
Indonesia	0.11	0.13	0.16	0.18	0.19	0.21	0.23	0.24	0.26	0.27	0.28
Myanmar	0.29	0.32	0.34	0.36	0.39	0.41	0.42	0.44	0.46	0.47	0.49
Sri Lanka	1.85	1.98	2.09	2.2	2.29	2.38	2.47	2.55	2.62	2.69	2.76
Pakistan	0.55	0.58	0.59	0.61	0.63	0.65	0.66	0.67	0.69	0.7	0.71
Kenya	1.79	1.85	1.91	1.97	2.02	2.07	2.12	2.16	2.2	2.24	2.28
Italy and Greece	−0.01	0	0.01	0.02	0.03	0.03	0.04	0.04	0.05	0.06	0.06

Source: Authors' estimates

4.3 Cumulative Impact of BRI's Overland and Maritime Corridors

We now turn to the combined impacts of all BRI corridors and the MSR under the low case and high case scenarios (Table 3.9). Recall that India is included in the high case scenario as it might eventually opt in some time in the future when it sees economic benefits materialise in presently participating countries.

Table 3.9 shows that Vietnam and Malaysia are expected to be the major beneficiaries in the low case scenario. Their relatively higher real GDP gains can be explained by the fact that they are dual-track economies that participate in both the Belt (i.e., CICPEC) and the Road. The BRI also yields considerable economic benefits to land-locked and sea-locked nations like Mongolia, Sri Lanka, and Laos. In contrast, the BRI generates only modest

Table 3.9 Estimated real GDP impacts of the BRI in the 'low case' and 'high case' scenarios

	Real GDP impact (%)	
Country	*Low case scenario*[a]	*High case scenario*[b]
Bangladesh	–	1.35
Cambodia	–	1.97
Caucasus countries	0.04	0.66
China	0.01	0.5
European Belt countries	0.01	0.04
European Road countries	0.01	−0.02
India	−0.01	0.04
Indonesia	0.02	0.22
Iran	0.03	7.63
Kazakhstan	0.07	1.29
Kenya	0.05	2.11
Laos	0.1	1.57
Malaysia	0.11	0.96
Mongolia	0.12	2.58
Myanmar	0.08	0.72
Nepal	0.02	0.79
Other Central Asian BRI countries	0.03	0.77
Other West Asian BRI countries	0.02	0.32
Pakistan	0.04	0.64
Russia	0.01	0.22
Saudi Arabia	0.01	0.2
Singapore	0.07	0.73
Sri Lanka	0.1	2.46
Thailand	0.05	0.55
Turkey	0.01	−0.41
Vietnam	0.13	2.34

Source: Authors' estimates

[a]5 per cent reduction in transport cost (India excluded)

[b]50 per cent reduction in transport cost plus full trade liberalisation (India included)

gains for Turkey, Saudi Arabia, Russia, and European stakeholder countries. A general trend to note from the low case scenario in Table 3.9 is that as a country's distance from China increases, its gain under the BRI's transport cost reduction component becomes less. The distribution of real GDP gains in the high case scenario presents a slightly different picture. Iran is likely to gain the most with a real GDP increase of 7.63 per cent, nearly three times that of Mongolia (2.58%), which is the second highest. Sri Lanka, Vietnam, Kenya, Cambodia, Laos, and Bangladesh can also expect real GDP gains exceeding 1 per cent. Nepal gains 0.79 per cent.

From a global perspective, our CGE modelling estimates that the global GDP could increase by 0.004 per cent (or $3 billion) in the low case scenario and by 0.12 per cent (or $90.9 billion) in the high case scenario, respectively. Our estimates are higher than those of Villafuerte et al. (2016) who have forecasted negative global impacts, but lower than Maliszewska and van der Mensbrugghe (2019) who suggest that global real income (roughly equivalent to real GDP) could increase by 0.7 per cent in 2030. This discrepancy could be because Villafuerte et al. (2016) do not incorporate tariff elimination like we do. They also use the default short-term macro closure of the standard GTAP model, meaning that their results reflect the immediate and short-run effects of the BRI's connectivity agenda. Maliszewska and van der Mensbrugghe (2019) project higher global gains because the authors use a more advanced dynamic CGE model and factor in additional considerations not accounted for by this study such as savings in trading time and improvement in domestic transport conditions.

5 Conclusion

In this chapter, we have estimated the economic impacts of transport cost reduction and trade liberalisation along the BRI land corridors and the MSR using a modified comparative-static CGE model. The following conclusions can be drawn from the simulation results.

First, although both reduction in transport cost and trade liberalisation will generate economic benefits to countries along the BRI corridors and the MSR, the latter policy action will likely bring larger GDP benefits than the former. The policy implication is that China should push BRI countries to liberalise trade through tariff reductions while implementing hard infrastructure projects. In recent years, a formidable international movement has been launched by China and others to establish a dense global network of free trade agreements which are in part intended to be complementary with the BRI (see Table 3.10).

Table 3.10 Major free trade initiatives between China and BRI countries

FTA status	*Agreement*	*BRI countries involved*	*Non-BRI member(s)*
Signed and in effect	China-Eurasian Economic Union FTA	Armenia, Belarus, China, Kazakhstan, Kyrgyzstan, Russia	None
	ASEAN-China FTA	Brunei, Cambodia, China, Indonesia, Laos, Malaysia, Myanmar, Philippines, Singapore, Thailand, Vietnam	None
	China-Georgia FTA	China, Georgia	None
	China-Switzerland FTA	China, Switzerland	None
	China-Pakistan FTA	China, Pakistan	None
	China-Peru FTA	China, Peru	None
	China-Costa Rica FTA	China, Costa Rica	None
	China-Chile FFTA	China, Chile	None
	China-New Zealand FTA	China, New Zealand	None
	China-Korea FTA	China, South Korea	None
Signed but not yet in effect	China-Maldives FTA	China, Maldives	None
Under negotiation	Regional Comprehensive Economic Partnership	Brunei, Cambodia, China, Indonesia, Laos, Malaysia, Myanmar, New Zealand, Philippines, Singapore, South Korea, Thailand, Vietnam	Australia, (India), Japan
	China-Gulf Cooperation Council FTA	Bahrain, China, Kuwait, Oman, Qatar, Saudi Arabia, United Arab Emirates	None
	China-Southern African Customs Union FTA	Botswana, China, Lesotho, Namibia, South Africa	Eswatini
	China-Japan-Korea FTA	China, South Korea	Japan
	China-Sri Lanka FTA	China, Sri Lanka	None
	China-Israel FTA	China, Israel	None
	China-Panama FTA	China, Panama	None
	China-Moldova FTA	China, Moldova	None

(*continued*)

Table 3.10 (continued)

FTA status	*Agreement*	*BRI countries involved*	*Non-BRI member(s)*
Proposed/ under consultation	Shanghai Cooperation Organization FTA	China, Kazakhstan, Kyrgyzstan, Pakistan, Russia, Tajikistan, Uzbekistan	India
	China-Mongolia FTA	China, Mongolia	None
	China-Nepal FTA	China, Nepal	None
	Bangladesh-China FTA	Bangladesh, China	None
	China-MERCOSUR FTA	China, Uruguay	Argentina, Brazil, Paraguay
	China-Papua New Guinea FTA	China, Papua New Guinea	None
	China-Fiji FTA	China, Fiji	None

Source: ADB Asia Regional Integration Center

Second, the results suggest that land-locked countries like Mongolia, Kazakhstan, and Nepal are likely to benefit the most from the BRI. Countries with relatively high tariffs like Iran will benefit more from the trade liberalising policies than transport cost reduction. In relation to the MSR, it is the countries that are already well-embedded in the global maritime shipping networks (e.g., Malaysia and Singapore) that are expected to experience higher real GDP gains from reductions in maritime transport cost.

Third, the impact of India's stance on the BRI has implications that are corridor-specific. In the case of the BCIM corridor, India's participation (or absence) does not substantially alter the economic gains to other partners. In the case of the THEC, however, the inclusion of India could be a precondition for Nepal to secure significant economic benefits.

Technical Appendix

Table 3.11 Regional aggregation

No.	*Aggregated region*	*BRI corridor(s)*	*Code*	*GTAP economy(s) in the region*
1	China	All	China	China
2	Rest of Asia	–	R_A	Philippines; Brunei; Japan; South Korea; Taiwan; Hong Kong; Rest of East Asia; Rest of South Asia
3	Vietnam	CIP; MSR	Vietnam	Vietnam
4	Malaysia	CIP; MSR	Malaysia	Malaysia
5	Singapore	CIP; MSR	Singapore	Singapore
6	Thailand	CIP	Thailand	Thailand
7	Laos	CIP	Laos	Laos
8	Cambodia	CIP	Cambodia	Cambodia
9	Indonesia	MSR	Indonesia	Indonesia
10	Myanmar	CIP; BCIM; MSR	Myanmar	Rest of Southeast Asia
11	India	BCIM	India	India
12	Bangladesh	BCIM	Bangladesh	Bangladesh
13	Pakistan	CPEC; MSR	Pakistan	Pakistan
14	Nepal	THEC	Nepal	Nepal
15	Sri Lanka	MSR	Sri Lanka	Sri Lanka
16	Russia	CMR; NELB	Russia	Russia
17	Mongolia	CMR	Mongolia	Mongolia
18	Kazakhstan	CCAWA; NELB	Kazakhstan	Kazakhstan
19	Other Central Asia BRI Countries	CCAWA	O_CA	Kyrgyzstan; Tajikistan; Rest of Former Soviet Union (Uzbekistan)
20	Caucasus	CCAWA	Caucasus	Armenia; Azerbaijan; Georgia
21	Iran	CCAWA	Iran	Iran
22	Turkey	CCAWA	Turkey	Turkey
23	Saudi Arabia	CCAWA	SArabia	Saudi Arabia
24	Other Western Asia BRI Countries	CCAWA	O_WA	Kuwait; United Arab Emirates; Qatar; Oman; Bahrain

(*continued*)

Table 3.11 (continued)

No.	*Aggregated region*	*BRI corridor(s)*	*Code*	*GTAP economy(s) in the region*
25	Rest of Western Asia	–	R_WA	Israel; Jordan; Rest of Western Asia
26	Oceania	–	Oceania	Australia; New Zealand; Rest of Oceania
27	European BRI Countries	NELB	EBRI	Belarus; Poland, Germany; Netherlands
28	European MSR Countries	MSR	EMSR	Italy; Greece
29	Rest of Europe	–	R_ER	Austria; Belgium; Cyprus; Czech Republic; Denmark; Estonia; Finland; France; Hungary; Ireland; Latvia; Lithuania; Luxembourg; Malta; Portugal; Slovakia; Slovenia; Spain Sweden; United Kingdom; Switzerland; Norway; Rest of European FTA; Albania; Bulgaria; Croatia; Romania; Ukraine; Rest of Eastern Europe; Rest of Europe
30	North America	–	NRA	Canada; United States; Mexico; Rest of North America
31	Central and Latin America	–	CLA	Argentina; Bolivia; Brazil; Chile; Colombia; Ecuador; Paraguay; Peru; Uruguay; Venezuela; Rest of South America; Costa Rica; Guatemala; Honduras; Nicaragua; Panama; El Salvador; Rest of Central America; Dominican Republic; Jamaica; Puerto Rico; Trinidad and Tobago; Rest of Caribbean
32	Kenya	MSR	Kenya	Kenya
33	Rest of Africa	–	R_AF	Egypt; Morocco; Rest of North Africa; Benin; Burkina Faso; Cameroon; Cote d'Ivoire; Ghana; Guinea; Nigeria; Senegal; Togo; Rest of Western Africa; Rest of Central Africa; South Central Africa; Ethiopia; Madagascar; Malawi; Mauritius; Mozambique; Rwanda; Tanzania; Uganda; Zambia; Zimbabwe; Sudan; Tunisia; Rest of Eastern Africa; Botswana; Namibia; South Africa; Rest of South African Customs
34	Rest of World	–	ROW	Rest of the World

Note: Afghanistan, Djibouti, Yemen, Iraq, and Lebanon have all signed BRI MOUs but are excluded from the present analysis due to GTAP data unavailability. The MSR refers to the East-West MSR; South Pacific and Trans-Pacific MSRs are not considered

Table 3.12 Sectoral aggregation

No.	*Aggregated sector*	*Code*	*Sub-sectors and products*
1	Grains and Crops	GrainsCrops	Paddy rice; Wheat; Cereal grains; Vegetables, fruit, nuts; Oil seeds; Sugar cane, sugar beet; Plant-based fibres; Other crops; Processed rice
2	Livestock and Meat Products	MeatLstk	Cattle, sheep, goats, horses; Animal products; Raw milk; Wool, silk-worm cocoons; Meat: cattle, sheep, goats, horse; Meat products
3	Mining and Extraction	Extration	Forestry; Fishing; Coal; Oil; Gas; Other extraction
4	Processed Food	ProcFood	Vegetable oils and fats; Dairy products; Sugar; Food products; Beverages and tobacco products
5	Textiles and Clothing	TextWapp	Textiles; Wearing apparel
6	Light Manufacturing	LightMnfc	Leather products; Wood products; Paper products, publishing; Motor vehicles and parts; Transport equipment; Manufactures
7	Heavy Manufacturing	HeavyMnfc	Petroleum, coal products; Chemical products; Basic pharmaceutical products; Rubber and plastic products; Mineral products; Ferrous metals; Metals; Metal products; Computer, electronic and optical products; Electrical equipment; Machinery and equipment
8	Land Transport	LandTpt	Transport
9	Sea Transport	SeaTpt	Sea transport
10	Other	OthServices	Electricity; Gas manufacture, distribution; Water; Construction; Trade; Accommodation and food; Air transport; Warehousing and support activities; Communication; Financial services; Insurance; Real estate; Business services; Recreation; Public administration and defence; Education; Human health and social work; Dwellings

Note

1. When simulating the impact of trade liberalisation, tariffs between European countries and their Asian partners remain unchanged. This is because this cluster of countries are bound by the EU's Common Commercial Policy which prevents them from unilaterally liberalising trade policy vis-à-vis third countries outside the bloc. In the same vein, this assumption is applicable for Turkey which is in a Customs Union with the EU.

References

Aguiar, Angel, Maksym Chepeliev, Erwin L. Corong, Robert McDougall, and Dominique van der Mensbrugghe. 2019. The GTAP Data Base: Version 10. *Journal of Global Economic Analysis* 4 (1): 1–27.

Baniya, Suprabha, Nadia Patrizia Rocha Gaffurri, and Michele Ruta. 2019. Trade Effects of the New Silk Road: A Gravity Analysis. In *World Bank Policy Research Working Paper No. 8694.* Washington, DC: World Bank.

de Soyres, François, Alen Mulabdic, and Michele Ruta. 2019. Common Transport Infrastructure: A Quantitative Model and Estimates from the Belt and Road Initiative. In *Policy Research Working Paper 8801.* Washington, DC: World Bank.

Gretton, Paul. 2017. Bilateral and Regional Trade Agreements: Detangling the Noodle/Spaghetti Bowl. In *EABER Working Paper 130.* Canberra: East Asian Bureau of Economic Research.

Herrero, Alicia Garcia, and Jianwei Xu. 2017. China's Belt and Road Initiative: Can Europe Expect Trade Gains? *China & World Economy* 25 (6): 84–99.

Hertel, Thomas. 2013. Global Applied General Equilibrium Analysis Using the Global Trade Analysis Project Framework. In *Handbook of Computable General Equilibrium Modeling*, ed. Peter B. Dixon and Dale W. Jorgenson. Amsterdam: North Holland.

Hummels, David L., and Georg Schaur. 2013. Time as a Trade Barrier. *American Economic Review* 103 (7): 2935–2959.

Ji, Xianbai, Pradumna B. Rana, Wai-Mun Chia, and Changtai Li. 2018. Post-TPP Trade Policy Options for ASEAN and its Dialogue Partners: "Preference Ordering" Using CGE Analysis. *East Asian Economic Review* 22 (2): 177–215.

Lu, Hui, Charlene Rohr, Marco Hafner, and Anna Knack. 2018. *China Belt and Road Initiative.* Santa Monica and Cambridge: RAND Corporation.

Maliszewska, Maryla, and Dominique van der Mensbrugghe. 2019. The Belt and Road Initiative: Economic, Poverty and Environmental Impacts. In *Policy Research Working Paper 8814.* Washington, DC: World Bank.

Menon, Jayant, and Peter Warr. 2006. Does Road Improvement Reduce Poverty? A General Equilibrium Analysis for Lao PRD. *Third LAEBA Annual Meeting*, Seoul, 16 November.

Productivity Commission. 2010. *A CGE Analysis of Some Economic Effects of Trade Agreements.* Melbourne: Productivity Commission.

Salidjanova, Nargiza, Iacob Koch-Weser, and Jason Klanderman. 2015. *China's Economic Ties with ASEAN: A Country-by-Country Analysis.* Washington, DC: U.S.-China Economic and Security Review Commission.

Stone, Susan, and Anna Strutt. 2010. Transport Infrastructure and Trade Facilitation in the Greater Mekong Subregion. In *Trade Facilitation and Regional Cooperation in Asia*, ed. Douglas H. Brooks and Susan F. Stone. Cheltenham and Northampton: Edward Elgar.

Stone, Susan, Anna Strutt, and Thomas Hertel. 2012. Socio-economic Impact of Regional Transport Infrastructure in the Greater Mekong Subregion. In *Infrastructure for Asian Connectivity*, ed. Biswa Nath Bhattacharyay, Masahiro Kawai, and Rajat M. Nag. Cheltenham and Northampton: Edward Elgar.

UNCTAD. 2017. *Review of Maritime Transport 2017*. Geneva: United Nations Conference on Trade and Development.

Villafuerte, James, Erwin Corong, and Juzhong Zhuang. 2016. Trade and Growth Impact of One Belt, One Road on Asia and the World. *19th Annual Conference on Global Economic Analysis*, Washington DC.

Wignaraja, Ganeshan, Peter Morgan, Michael G. Plummer, and Fan Zhai. 2015. Economic Implications of Deeper South Asian–Southeast Asian Integration: A CGE Approach. *Asian Economic Papers* 14 (3): 63–81.

Zhai, Fan. 2018. China's Belt and Road Initiative: A Preliminary Quantitative Assessment. *Journal of Asian Economics* 55 (C): 84–92.

CHAPTER 4

The Perception Survey of Asian Opinion Leaders

1 Introduction

This chapter presents the results of a perception survey that we conducted for assessing the views of Asian opinion leaders on the BRI. Specifically, we want to capture their perceptions on:

1. Why China was interested in launching the BRI;
2. Components of the BRI that would be of interest to the recipient countries;
3. Perceived benefits and costs of the BRI; and
4. Policy actions that they would like to recommend to both China and home governments in order to enhance the effectiveness of the BRI.

A number of survey studies of the BRI have been conducted in the past, but their scopes are relatively narrow. These include the Economist Corporate Network survey (ECN 2017) which reached out to 77 business leaders and two annual surveys conducted by the International Financial Forum in 2017 and 2018 (IFF 2018, 2019) which surveyed central bankers from 25 BRI countries mainly from Europe. None of these surveys, however, focused on deriving policy implications.

The scope of our survey is broader as it captures the perceptions of a much wider range of opinion leaders and experts from Asian BRI countries. Our survey also offers perception-based policy recommendations on

P. B. Rana, X. Ji, *China's Belt and Road Initiative*,
https://doi.org/10.1007/978-981-15-5171-0_4

how to improve the BRI for the mutual benefit of both China and Asian BRI participating countries. At the Second Belt and Road Forum in 2019 President Xi had acknowledged various constructive criticisms and pledged to reform the BRI. Fine tuning and quality control were to be done with emphasis on 'high quality' infrastructure projects. Green and clean cooperation was also pledged. In this context, in anticipation of a revival of the Physical BRI post-COVID-19, China should give considerations to the various reform proposals that have been advocated by Asian opinion leaders. To our knowledge, this policy-relevant survey is the first of its kind.

2 Survey Methodology

For the purpose of this survey, we focused on 'opinion leaders' (defined as government officials and international civil servants, academics, business leaders, media, and civil society and non-governmental organisation [NGO] representatives) from Asian countries that have signed a memorandum of understanding or joint communique with China in supportive of the BRI. Other Asian countries (e.g., India and Japan) were excluded from our survey because we only want to capture the views of the BRI stakeholders. Our sample, therefore, comprised 26 countries from three Asian sub-regions: East and Southeast Asia (13 countries), South Asia (6 countries) and Central Asia (7 countries).

We developed a questionnaire comprising 12 questions that were divided into four parts. The first part aimed to sketch out the respondents' profile by asking about their institutional affiliation and country of citizenship. The second part explored the multifaceted motivations behind China's launch of the BRI. Part III consisted of seven questions about the perceived benefits and costs of the BRI. And in part four, respondents were asked what policy recommendations they would offer to Chinese and home country policy-makers to enhance the prospect of a win-win BRI. Under each question and at the end of the survey, respondents were at liberty to provide additional comments and feedback.

We performed a test run of the survey among several doctoral students and researchers from our institution. Following the attainment of the research ethics clearance from the university's institutional review board,[1] we put up the survey online between 20 June and 19 July 2019. Using a sampling method known as the purposive sampling technique, we sent out email invitations along with informed consent forms to 16,069 identified opinion leaders from 26 Asian BRI countries.[2]

At the end of the four weeks we received a total of 1230 responses (627 responses from East and Southeast Asia, 393 responses from South Asia, and 74 responses from Central Asia, see Table 4.1), corresponding to 7.7 per cent of the sample. This response rate was reasonable for an online perception survey and in fact higher than our earlier survey on East Asia-South Asia connectivity (Rana and Chia 2017). The response rate could possibly have been higher had we engaged a professional survey firm followed by offline interviews or translated the questionnaire in English into different local languages. The budget for the study, however, restricted us from such a sophisticated approach.

The highest survey responses were from Pakistan (11.2%), Singapore (10.0%), Bangladesh (9.2%), the Philippines (8.2%), followed by Malaysia (7.6%), Nepal (7.1%), Thailand (5.9%), Indonesia (4.6%), Sri Lanka (3.5%), South Korea (2.6%), New Zealand (2.5%), Cambodia (2.4%), Vietnam (2.4%), Myanmar (2.0%), and Georgia (1.9%). The responses collected from Kazakhstan, Kyrgyzstan, Laos, Mongolia, Armenia, Afghanistan, Brunei, Uzbekistan, Azerbaijan, Maldives, and Tajikistan were fewer than 20 each. Internet penetration, English literacy rate and the size of the intellectual community are also proportionally lower in these countries.

In terms of affiliation, the academic and think-tank community made up the largest respondent group at 56 per cent.[3] More than one-fifth of the respondents (22.5%) were from various central government agencies and departments (e.g., monetary authorities, and ministries of finance, national planning, economy, trade, industry, foreign affairs, infrastructure, and transport) and regional and international organisations (e.g., United Nations, ADB, APEC, and ASEAN secretariat). The business and consultancy cluster (7.9%), civil society and NGO (6.1%), and media (5.7%) made up the bulk of the remaining 21.5 per cent of the respondents. A small percentage (1.8%) was from 'Other', primarily consisting of retired government officials and experts who have multiple affiliations.

Table 4.1 Survey respondents' profile

		Government	*Business*	*Academia*	*NGO*	*Media*	*Other*	*Total*
East and Southeast Asia	Brunei	2	2	4	1	0	0	9
	Cambodia	0	1	15	14	0	0	30
	Indonesia	12	2	35	6	2	0	57
	Korea	2	0	30	0	0	0	32
	Laos	9	0	3	0	0	0	12
	Malaysia	29	3	47	6	8	1	94
	Mongolia	0	1	10	0	1	0	12
	Myanmar	11	0	10	4	0	0	25
	New Zealand	2	4	25	0	0	0	31
	Philippines	45	3	27	10	15	1	101
	Singapore	18	15	74	1	15	0	123
	Thailand	17	3	50	0	1	1	72
	Vietnam	5	0	24	0	0	0	29
	Subtotal	152	34	354	42	42	3	627
South Asia	Afghanistan	2	0	7	0	0	0	9
	Bangladesh	35	11	51	7	2	7	113
	Maldives	1	0	1	0	1	0	3
	Nepal	8	28	30	11	5	5	87
	Pakistan	32	11	85	4	2	4	138
	Sri Lanka	22	2	15	3	1	0	43
	Subtotal	100	52	189	25	11	16	393
Central Asia	Armenia	2	0	6	1	1	0	10
	Azerbaijan	1	0	1	0	1	0	3
	Georgia	0	0	21	1	0	1	23
	Kazakhstan	3	0	12	1	1	0	17
	Kyrgyzstan	1	0	12	0	2	0	15
	Tajikistan	0	0	1	0	0	0	1
	Uzbekistan	2	0	3	0	0	0	5
	Subtotal	9	0	56	3	5	1	74
Others		16	11	90	5	12	2	136
Grand total		277	97	689	75	70	22	1230

Note: Respondents identified themselves as citizens of 'other' countries were mainly expatriates based in Asian institutions

Source: Authors' compilation of survey data

3 Survey Results

3.1 *China's Motives*

Understanding China's motives in launching the BRI in the first place is essential to developing an appropriate characterisation of the initiative. The survey provided 11 options (see Fig. 4.1) for respondents to identify the top five motives which they think China attaches to the BRI. Four options received more than half of the responses—the BRI helps China 'promote regional integration, infrastructure connectivity and economic development' (58.8%); 'assert influence on international economic governance' (53.8%); 'construct and control key supply chains and energy

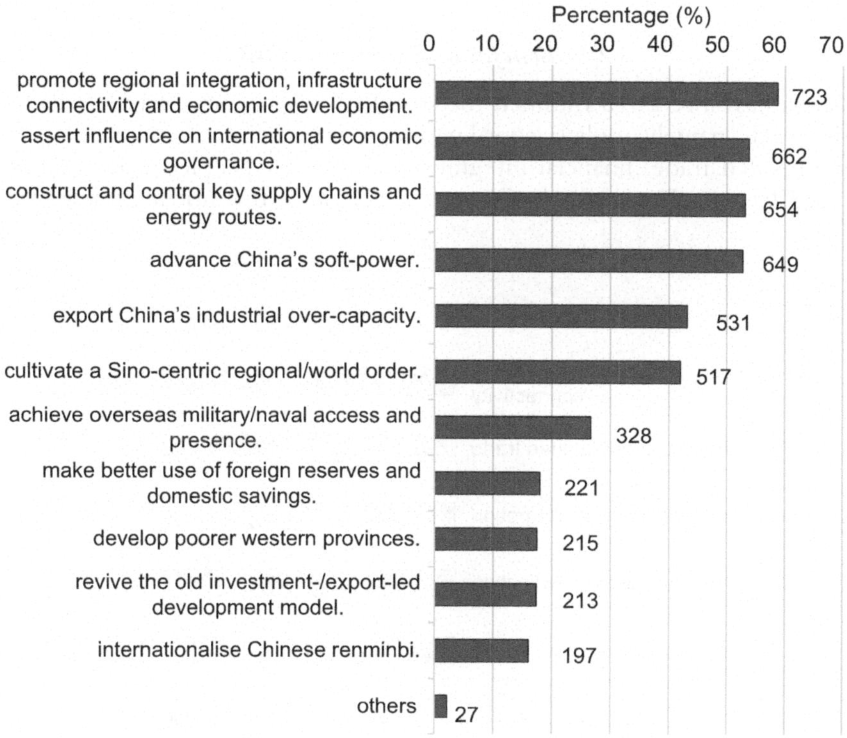

Fig. 4.1 China's motives behind the BRI. The BRI helps China... (Answered: 1230; Skipped: 0).
Source: Authors

routes' (53.2%); and 'advance China's soft-power' (52.8%). To lesser degrees, the respondents also believed that Beijing aims to leverage the BRI to 'export China's industrial over-capacity' (43.2%); 'cultivate a Sino-centric regional/world order' (42.0%); and 'achieve overseas military/naval access and presence' (26.7%). In comparison, less important in the views of the respondents were domestic factors (e.g., developing impoverished inland provinces and reviving the old investment-led development model) and financial considerations (e.g., internationalising the Chinese currency renminbi and making better use of domestic savings and foreign reserves). In other words, the respondents largely saw the BRI as an outward-looking geopolitical and geo-economic undertaking rather than something that China pursues for solely domestic economic and financial reasons.[4]

3.2 *Benefits and Costs of the BRI*

China has since 2015 outlined the so-called 'Five Connectivity' goals of the BRI, namely, policy coordination, connectivity of infrastructure, unimpeded trade, financial integration, and closer people-to-people ties (see Chap. 1). The survey findings (Fig. 4.2) show that not all dimensions

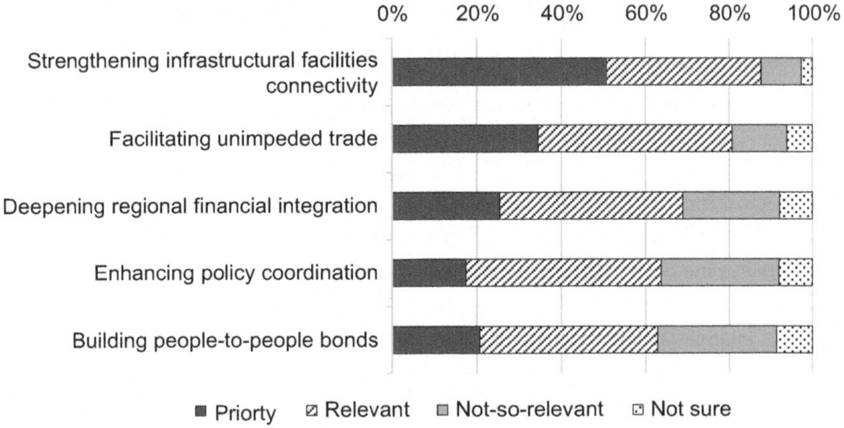

Fig. 4.2 Relevance of BRI's five stated connectivity goals to your country (Answered: 1205; Skipped: 25).
Source: Authors

of the BRI's connectivity vision were viewed as equally important in Asian partner countries.

The respondents overwhelmingly felt that strengthening infrastructure connectivity is the most relevant component of the BRI (87.7% rated as priority plus relevant). This finding echoes the ADB's assessment that infrastructure in developing Asian countries remains inadequate and needs $1.7 trillion per year in new investment to sustain growth while responding to climate change (ADB 2017). Trade facilitation was rated as the second most important component of the BRI. Over four-fifths (80.7%) of all surveyed respondents rated the BRI's trade facilitation and liberalisation agenda as either priority or relevant. By contrast, 'enhancing policy coordination', 'deepening financial integration', and 'building people-to-people bonds' ranked relatively lower in terms of relevance from the perspective of Asian BRI participating countries.

As to which specific types of infrastructure the BRI should focus on, Fig. 4.3 illustrates that most of the respondents deemed transport infrastructure either as a priority (59.3%) or a relevant (27.2%) sector for their country. The respondents also believed that the BRI should focus its operation and funding on energy-related (e.g., power plants) and industrial infrastructure (e.g., industrial estates and special economic zones). In

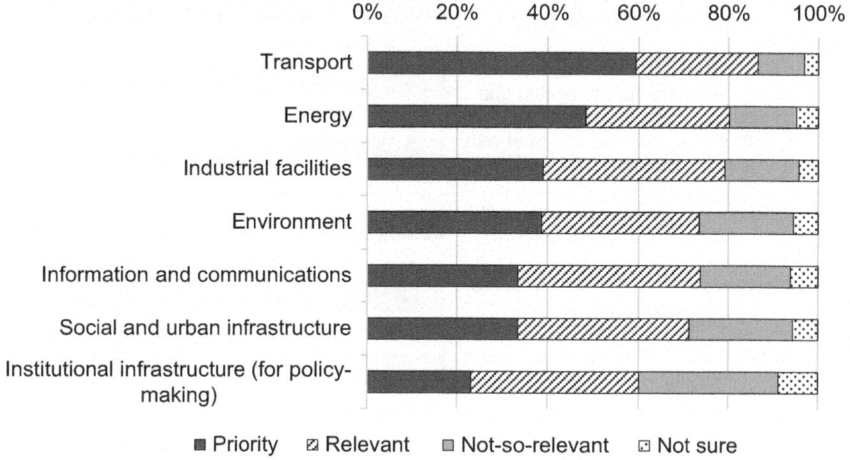

Fig. 4.3 Which infrastructure sectors should the BRI focus on in your country? (Answered: 1173; Skipped: 57).
Source: Authors

particular, Pakistani (99.2%) and Bangladeshi (95.5%) respondents almost unanimously perceived energy infrastructure as priority or relevant. This could attribute to the World Bank statistics that there are on average 75 and 65 power outages a month in Pakistan and Bangladesh, respectively.[5] Energy shortages in these two countries have severely disrupted supply chains and hindered productivity growth. Environmental, digital, and social infrastructures trailed by a bit but not so much. Despite its theoretical importance, institutional infrastructure was given a low relevance rating by the respondents. This means the BRI's role in enhancing BRI partner countries' governance standards and policy-making capacity is not yet openly recognised by local opinion leaders.

When it comes to the key benefits that their countries could obtain from the BRI (Fig. 4.4), a decisive majority (76.4%) of the respondents felt that the initiative holds significant potential to 'expand trade, investment and tourism with China and other BRI countries'. In addition, around two-thirds (66.8%) of the respondents felt that the BRI could

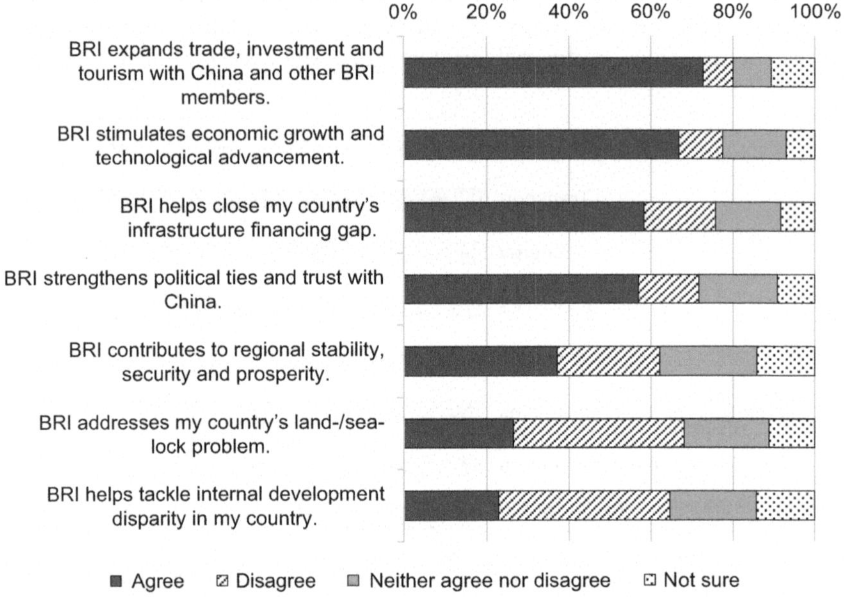

Fig. 4.4 Likely benefits for BRI countries (Answered: 1152; Skipped 78). Source: Authors

stimulate economic growth and help their countries move up the value chain. In light of the massive infrastructure financing gap in Asia, 58.3 per cent of the respondents were of view that the BRI could bring in much-needed funding to 'close my country's infrastructure financing gap'. A similar share (56.9%) of the respondents felt that the 'BRI strengthens my country's political ties and trust with China'.[6]

On the other hand, only 37.1 per cent of the respondents felt that the BRI would contribute to regional security and international stability. Meanwhile, the surveyed respondents did not envisage a meaningful amelioration of internal development imbalances in their home countries just because of the implementation of the BRI (22.8%). Even fewer respondents expected the BRI to address their countries' sea- or land-lockedness problem (26.4%).[7]

One of the most common and controversial criticisms against the BRI is that China deliberately engages in predatory lending practices, known as debt trap diplomacy (DTD), in order to buy influence or seek dominance in sovereign BRI debtor countries. More than 42 per cent of the respondents, however, rejected such an alarmist narrative (Fig. 4.5) although it is important to bear in mind that 30.6 per cent felt otherwise. Still more than a quarter (27.3%) of the respondents had not made up their minds on this issue.[8]

A number of reasons were offered by the respondents in their comments below the question on why they disagreed with the DTD hypothesis. First, some respondents argued that domestic factors which were in the purview of host government (e.g., corrupted administration, reckless borrowing propensity, pre-existing macroeconomic vulnerability and inherent governance deficiency) should be responsible rather than Chinese

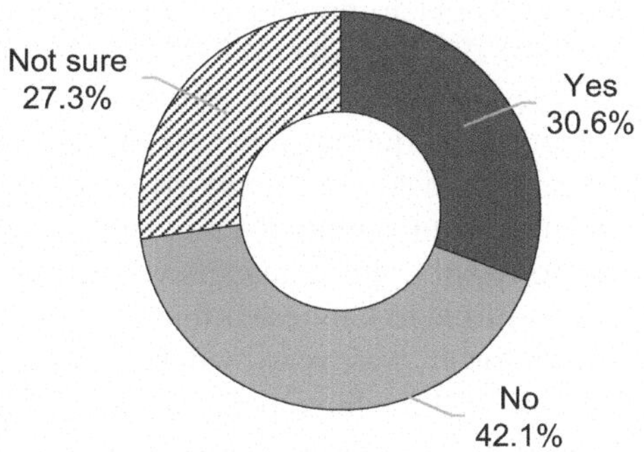

Fig. 4.5 Do you think China is deliberately engaging in 'debt-trap diplomacy' in your country in order to buy influence or seek dominance? (Answered: 1152; Skipped: 78). Source: Authors

BRI financing when a country runs into a difficult debt situation. For instance, a Pakistani official remarked that 'I do not think [that] China is deliberately engaging in debt trap diplomacy but public sector corruption and poor governance at our end may lead to this result in Pakistan'. Second, some respondents argued that the perceived DTD was not the outgrowth of a coordinated Chinese strategy but the unintended consequence of inappropriate project implementation. According to a Malaysian trade official, one possibility is that 'newly internationalising' private Chinese companies strike unfairly lopsided contracts that 'maximise the returns of their investment' at the expense of local interest, or it could be the by-product of state-to-state 'bargaining that occurs only on elite policy levels without proper consultation of other stakeholders'. Along similar lines, a Singaporean journalist opined that the DTD theory 'is not so much a cautionary tale of borrowing from China, but of what happens when weak governance is married with the unforgiving demands of international financial markets' (Tan 2019). Some opinion leaders went as far as describing the DTD as the manufactured fear by biased western countries. Lashing out at the West, a Nepali diplomat-turned-scholar contended that the DTD 'is propaganda of some [W]estern countries which are seeking to dissuade the countries which have already signed up or are preparing to sign up MOU on BRI with China'.

Despite some disagreements to the DTD rhetoric, a not-insignificant proportion (30.6%) of the respondents did believe that China knowingly drowns their countries in unsustainably high levels of debt with the malicious aim of securing undue political or foreign policy gains. The strongest reservation in relation to the DTD came from Vietnam (65.4%), followed by the Philippines (60.6%) and Sri Lanka (48.7%). Respondents from the civil society (Yes: 45.8%; No: 26.4%) were most predisposed to agreeing with the DTD argument, whereas respondents with business (Yes: 25.0%; No: 50.0%) and media (Yes: 25.4%; No: 47.6%) backgrounds were significantly less inclined to buy into the DTD thesis.

In the next question, we asked the respondents what they perceived to be the (up to five) most worrisome costs, risks, and challenges to their countries from the involvement in the BRI (Fig. 4.6). The greatest concern to Asian opinion leaders was the prospect that their countries could be susceptible to Chinese influence (48.8%). Such fear of being drawn into China's orbit was very widely shared among respondents from New Zealand (69.0%), Singapore (64.3%), and Cambodia (60.7%). The second most significant uneasiness with the BRI was the influx of Chinese migrant

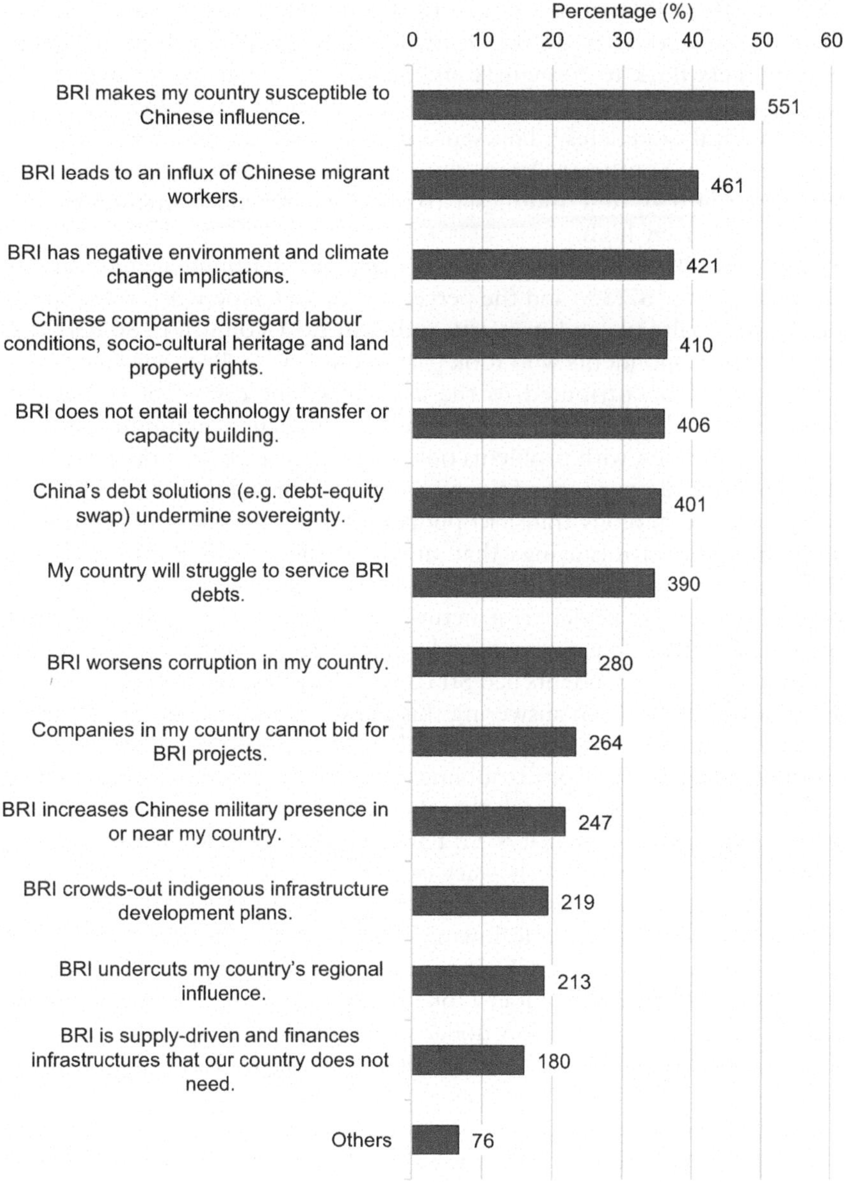

Fig. 4.6 Likely costs associated with the BRI (Answered: 1129; Skipped: 101). Source: Authors

workers (40.8%). For various reasons, Chinese companies prefer importing Chinese workers to do the construction work. When those construction workers flock to foreign lands, they could create social and ethnic tensions and are seen as taking up jobs that could have otherwise been filled by local candidates.[9] This sense of local disengagement was particularly acute in Southeast Asian countries like the Philippines (66.7%), Vietnam (64.0%), and Indonesia (62.3%) where youth unemployment rates are relatively high.

The fear that BRI projects entail negative environment and climate change impacts (37.3%) and the perceived risk of Chinese firms disregarding labour, cultural, and property rights in host countries (36.3%) also worried the respondents who took part in our survey. Both senses of foreboding could be attributed to the alleged 'Chinese way' of rushing to make quick deals (without adequate due diligence and community engagement) and dealing with problems only when they arise down the road. At the same time, 36 per cent of the respondents worried that the BRI might not present technology transfer opportunities or up-skilling programmes. Two inter-related misgivings that surround the debt implication of the BRI ranked in the sixth and seventh places. 35.5 per cent of the respondents felt that possible debt restructuring solutions in the event of a default on Chinese BRI loans could undermine their countries' sovereignty. Presumably the respondents had Sri Lanka's Hambantota port debt-equity swap case in mind when answering this question. Indeed, 44.7 per cent of the Sri Lankan respondents suspected that the BRI's potential sovereignty-eroding effect is a deeply troubling risk. More generally, over a third (34.5%) of the respondents felt that their countries could struggle to make payments to Chinese financiers. Sri Lankan (63.2%) and Malaysian (59.1%) respondents were particularly wary of this risk given the twists and turns associated with their countries' experiences with the BRI. In both countries, a new administration following election victory moved to renegotiate contractual terms with China or scale back BRI projects. Malaysia cut the cost of the East Coast Rail Link (ECRL) project by a third and cancelled two other multi-billion-dollar mega-projects. Respondents on the whole were noticeably less bothered by other risks we had listed for them to choose.[10]

On balance, 41.6 per cent of the respondents, adding up all the likely economic and political benefits and subtracting potential fallouts, believed that the BRI represents a net opportunity for their countries (Fig. 4.7).[11] The strongest endorsements of the BRI came from Georgia (69.6%),

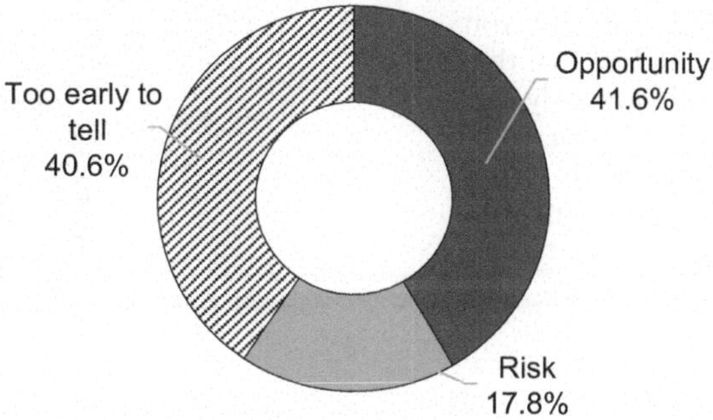

Fig. 4.7 In your opinion, on balance for your country, the BRI represents a net... (Answered: 1128; Skipped: 102). Source: Authors

Bangladesh (64.5%), Pakistan (59.7%), and Nepal (58.8%) whereas the opinion leaders from the Philippines (opportunity: 21.2%; risk: 47.5%) were among the least receptive to the proposition that the BRI is an economic and development opportunity to be embraced. South Korean (62.1%), Burmese (60.0%), and Vietnamese (60.0%) opinion leaders tended to take a more neutral and nuanced stance, saying that it was too early to ascertain if the BRI presents an opportunity or a risk for their respective countries. Breaking down the affiliations shows that respondents from the business community (opportunity: 50.6%) and government agencies and international institutions (opportunity: 46.4%) were more bullish than others on the BRI, while approximately 40 per cent of the surveyed academics, think tankers and civil society stakeholders were on the fence. Also, more than half of the Central Asian respondents (61.4%) were positively inclined towards the BRI. Somewhat fewer but still the majority in South Asia (58.8%) concurred. Such optimism did not carry through to East and Southeast Asia though. There, opinion leaders were less upbeat about the BRI. 44.8 per cent of the respondents harboured the view that it was still too soon to make a definitive judgement on whether their countries stood to win or lose out from the BRI.

Looking forward, 35.8 per cent of the respondents felt that they are confident that the BRI would ultimately result in win-win situations benefiting both China itself and partner countries; and only 21.2 per cent suggested otherwise (Fig. 4.8). 43 per cent of the respondents, however, remained undecided. At the country-level, the most positive views on the BRI's long-term economic and development promise were found in such South Asian nations as Nepal (Yes: 57.5%), Bangladesh (Yes: 57.0%), and Pakistan (Yes: 51.2%), while a lack of faith in the eventuality of the BRI

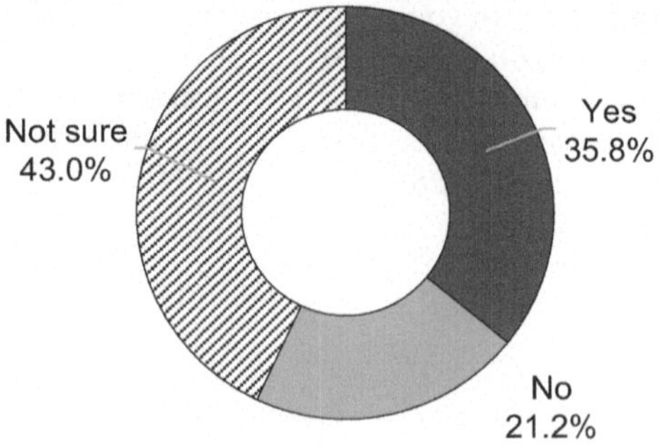

Fig. 4.8 Are you confident that the BRI will ultimately lead to win-win situations? (Answered: 1128; Skipped: 102). Source: Authors

being a win-win initiative was most pronounced in New Zealand (No: 48.3%), Vietnam (No: 44%), and the Philippines (No: 40.4%).

3.3 Policies to Improve the BRI

The BRI is a work-in-progress and clearly needs to be improved. To obtain additional insights into what policy measures should be adopted to ensure the success of the BRI, the respondents were presented with a list of policy recommendations that we think could be helpful and asked which ones they would endorse based on their local perspectives. Each respondent was allowed to choose a maximum of five options.

Figure 4.9 summarises the respondents' views on policies that should be implemented by the Chinese government in the next phase of BRI implementation. The six policy recommendations that topped the list were:

- China should enhance transparency[12] (61.7%)
- China should offer employment, capacity-building and technology transfer opportunities (56.3%)
- China should be attentive to national sensitivities and adapt the BRI to each partner's specific needs (49.5%)
- China should allow local contractors to bid for BRI projects and treat foreign companies fairly (43.7%)
- China should refrain from supporting corrupt governments and political parties (38.4%)
- China should move towards a rules-based system of infrastructure financing (35.4%)

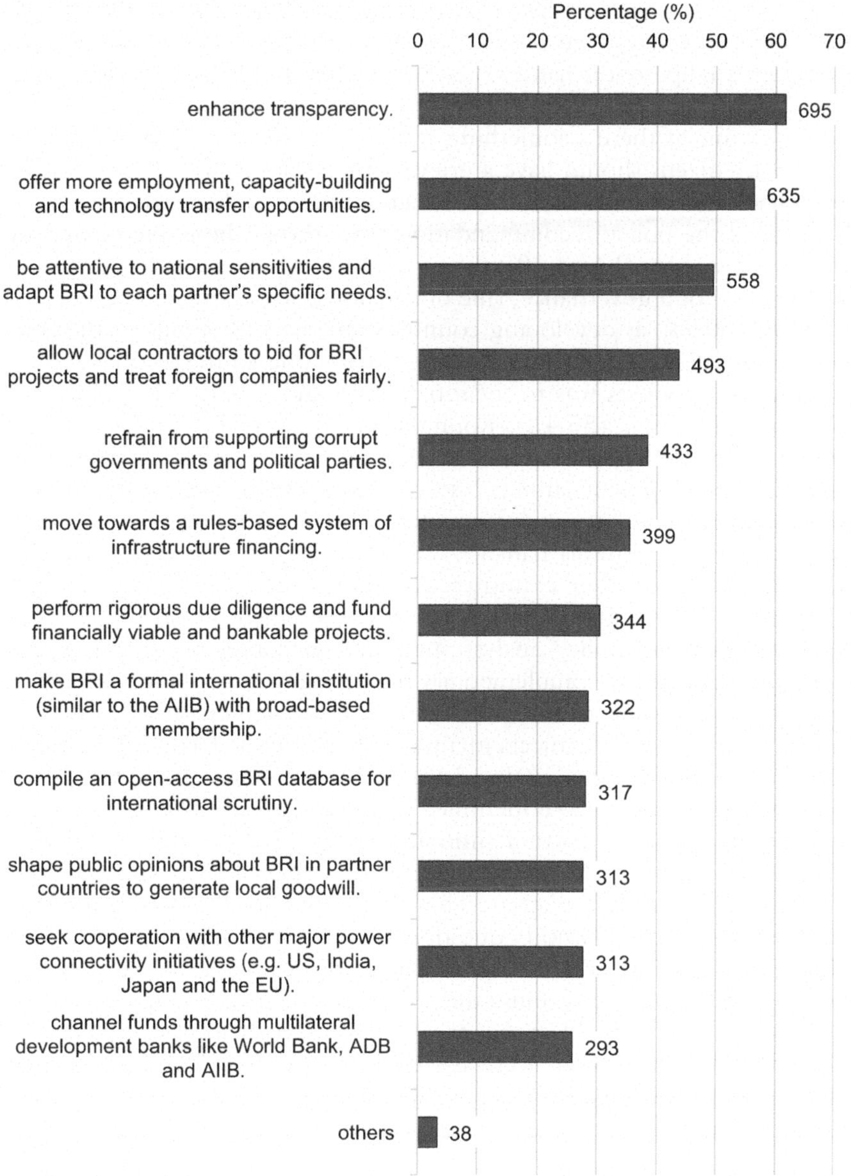

Fig. 4.9 Policy recommendations for China. China should... (Answered: 1127; Skipped: 103).
Source: Authors

Other policy options listed in the questionnaire also seemed to be appropriate as they were selected by over 200 opinion leaders each. In addition, a Filipino journalist noted that China should institute appropriate dispute resolution and grievance mechanisms to address local concerns, saying 'if there's something wrong with these projects, countries and their citizens should have a grievance mechanism where they can air out their concerns. In short, the BRI should have a safeguards policy'.

Among the policy recommendations that should be implemented by the host countries (Fig. 4.10), the most important one was to put a high priority on good governance, rule of law, anti-corruption, and democracy at home (60.2%) as developing countries interact with China in the context of the BRI.[13] The recommendation that gathered the second-highest number of responses was to 'negotiate hard and smartly with China for best possible terms' (55.4%). Rounding up the top three recommendations was the policy advice for BRI countries to 'prepare a national infrastructure development strategy' so that they could engage China in a more organised and purposive manner (52.0%). Notably, nearly eight in ten respondents from Sri Lanka (78.9%) and Nepal (77.5%) felt that this was important for their countries. A regional (as opposed to national) infrastructure strategy for infrastructure development could be useful as well. A Malaysian policy analyst suggested in comments that regional countries should 'use complementary regional governance mechanisms to improve BRI prospects where available, e.g., matching BRI projects to priority infrastructure projects identified in ASEAN's upcoming [priority infrastructure] database.' Being level with the public about the BRI's potential pros and cons was identified by 47 per cent of the respondents as being useful. Perhaps worth mentioning is that the respondents tended to think it was primarily the host governments' responsibility to inform their citizens on BRI-related matters. This is because only 27.8 per cent of the respondents in the previous question encouraged China to proactively shape public opinions in BRI recipient countries to make the initiative more embraceable. Performing due diligence and investing in only financially viable and bankable projects and insisting that local companies be allowed to bid for projects were also chosen by 44.5 and 41.2 per cent of the respondents respectively as pivotal to the success of the BRI. The rest of the proposed suggestions were seen as comparatively less important.

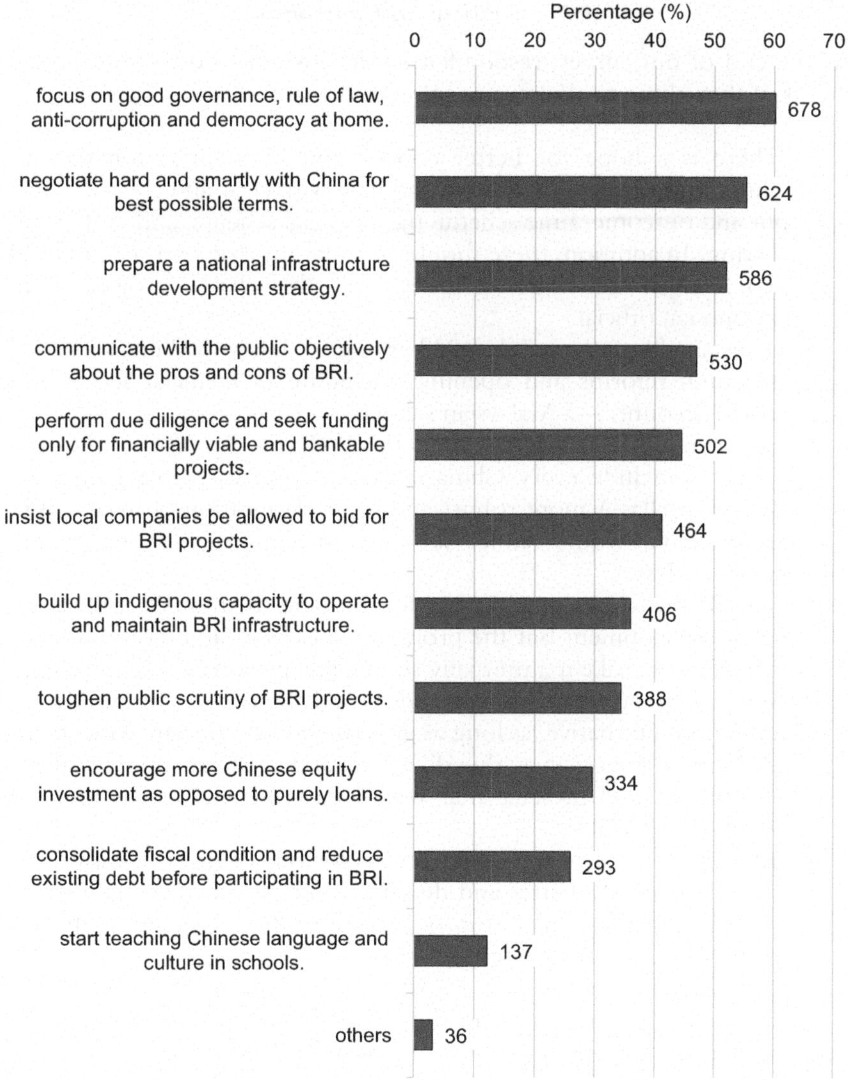

Fig. 4.10 Policy recommendations for BRI countries. My country should... (Answered: 1127; Skipped: 103).
Source: Authors

3.4 Additional Comments

At the end of our survey, respondents were invited to offer some comments, if they chose to. Below are some of them:

- 'There is a hope for better cooperation between Indonesia and China. But, there should be a road map with clear and concrete output and outcome, time scheduling, financial scheme, and cost-profit sharing. In addition, there should be more involvement of [...] local people on the management of the BRI projects.'—an Indonesian official
- 'A sustainable and credible BRI has to go along with China's internal structural reforms and opening, including in financial sector and capital account.'—a Malaysian scholar
- 'Some misunderstandings about the BRI arise because of the tendency to include every China-associated overseas project into the BRI umbrella. A more robust and strict clarification of what a BRI project entail would reduce such misconceptions.'—a Singaporean policy analyst
- 'The BRI offers an opportunity for Asia and the non-West for alternative development but the programme lacks local interest and participation to make it a mutually sustainable project.'—a Thai scholar
- 'When US plays hardball on trade, the BRI does not seem like an unfriendly alternative, as long as governments participate with stronger internal governance, due diligence, and a proper strategy on the investments and projects that would most benefit the nation.'—a Malaysian official
- 'BRI can be one of the major means for our country to move forward to achieve a better and developed life, at the same time it can be the important tool for our country to negotiate with our neighbours.'—a Bangladeshi official
- 'New Zealand's enthusiasm for BRI will be determined by the extent to which it is consistent with the country's core goal of maintaining an independent foreign policy.'—a New Zealand scholar
- '[China] has to communicate in local languages of the relevant countries to make awareness about the projects to local people.'—a Sri Lankan diplomat
- 'BRI needs to reach out to the private sector stakeholders properly informing the government, motivate them, engage them, and part-

ner in realising objective[s] in a professional manner that helps for shared prosperity.'—a Nepali consultant

- 'Most suspicions about the BRI stems [sic] from a lack of transparency in China's political system. Hence, countries can't be quite sure how much BRI is a tool for promoting economic development and political influence.'—a Singaporean official
- 'It is an ambitious, exciting and challenging endeavour. It is a very long-term initiative and therefore expectations about the results and benefits have to be managed well. Some mechanisms have to be developed to ensure long-term success despite change of governments in the participating countries.'—a Singaporean scholar
- 'Walk the ground more to sense the effects of whatever projects are planned to be in touch with people['s] sentiments. It's too top-down at this stage.'—a Singaporean businessperson
- 'The government has to do a better job in getting the visions, aspirations, benefits as well as costs associated with the BRI across. The awareness of the initiative in my country is very low for now.'—an Armenian scholar
- 'Implementation of BRI is certainly fraught with difficulties and challenges. Additional risks are laid in the complex reality of current geopolitical confrontation. That is why China needs to reach consensus with key actors on a number of issues.'—an Azerbaijani official
- 'There is great hope that BRI will bring Central Asia the same prosperity as the Silk Way in the past.'—a Kazakh scholar

4 Conclusion

Our survey results present a fairly positive, yet mixed, assessment of China's BRI from the perspectives of Asian opinion leaders and stakeholders. Over half of the respondents believed that China pursues the BRI with an eye to promoting regional integration and connectivity, asserting influence on global economic governance, constructing key supply chains and energy routes, and advancing Chinese overall soft power.

Among the BRI's five connectivity objectives, the respondents generally felt that achieving infrastructure connectivity and unimpeded trade are more relevant to their countries than financial integration, policy coordination, and people-to-people relations. On infrastructure types, the respondents were of the opinion that energy, transport, and industrial infrastructure should be the ones which the BRI needs to focus in Asia.

A majority of the respondents felt that the BRI provides a platform for BRI countries to attract trade, investment, and tourists from China and elsewhere. They also expected the BRI to stimulate economic growth and technological advancement while closing infrastructure financing gaps. Better political relations with China due to the BRI was also highlighted by close to three-fifths of the respondents as a key benefit. On the other hand, respondents expressed concerns over potential downsides like China's influence expansion, influx of Chinese migrant workers, BRI projects' environmental implications, lack of technology transfer opportunities, and risks related to debt overhang.

On balance, the respondents had fairly positive views of the BRI. The opinion leaders who categorised the BRI as a 'net opportunity' significantly outnumbered those who saw the BRI as a 'net risk'. Similarly, the respondents were more confident than not that the BRI would lead to win-win outcomes eventually. More than two-fifths of the respondents also rejected the notion of Chinese 'debt trap diplomacy'. These findings, however, must be interpreted with caution as for each of the three questions a large chunk of the respondents were undecided.

In terms of policy actions that should be taken to ensure a successful BRI, enhancing transparency, offering more capacity building and local employment, adapting the BRI to specific needs of foreign partners, and allowing non-Chinese contractors to bid for projects topped the list of recommendations for Beijing to maximise developmental impact and inclusiveness of the BRI. As for their home governments, the respondents felt that they should focus on good governance, negotiate with China for best possible terms, make sure that the BRI fits in a national infrastructure development strategy, perform due diligence, and communicate with the general public about the pros and cons of the BRI if they were to make the most of the BRI.

Notes

1. The IRB reference number is IRB-2019-04-006.
2. The sample was developed by augmenting the email banks used in Rana, Chia, and Jinjarak (2012), Rana and Chia (2017) and Ji et al. (2016) with publicly available email addresses and mailing lists of interest.
3. For readability, the figures in this chapter are rounded to one decimal point.

4. Additional driving factors suggested by respondents (i.e., 'others' in Figure 4.1) include 'stav[ing] off environmental pollution in China', overtaking the United States as the world's preeminent power, rebalancing trade relations from the United States to Asian next-door neighbours, resuscitating the 'good old days' of Chinese tributary system, achieving 'digital dominance', setting global technical standards, and 'building new visions for domestic politics to legitimise [Chinese Communist Party's] rule at the new stage of development'.
5. https://www.enterprisesurveys.org/data/exploretopics/infrastructure
6. In this regard, the highest degrees of scepticism of the BRI being an economic instrument to bolster political ties came from South Korea and New Zealand (33.3% each).
7. This is mainly due to the fact that most respondents were from countries that are not sea-/land-locked. Examining specifically responses collected from Asian land-locked developing countries (LLDCs), the survey finds that close to 75 per cent of the respondents agreed that the BRI could address their countries' geographical isolation problem. Asian LLDCs' economic structures traditionally reply on resource-intensive extractive industries to propel growth (Bolesta 2019); thus, the BRI if done right is uniquely well positioned to help with their economic transformation and diversification efforts.
8. This is in part due to a lack of concrete evidence. A Filipino respondent from the Department of Trade and Industry explained: 'This issue [DTD] has been proliferating in the media discussion for some time but I have not seen any document to support it'.
9. A Malaysian journalist observed, 'Frankly having been to BRI nations like Cambodia, my personal observation is the jobs are given to Chinese companies and Chinese workers.'
10. In the comments, a few respondents mentioned additional sensitivities about Chinese companies growing genetically modified crops in foreign countries and the BRI putting their countries' relationship with other great powers, mostly the United States and India, under strain.
11. This finding must be interpreted with caution as 40.6 per cent noted that it was too early to tell.
12. For example, China should enhance transparency in relation to procurement practice, contract-awarding mechanism and financing terms and conditions (see Chap. 8 for more discussion).
13. One exception is Georgia where only around a third (34.8%) of the respondents held this view.

References

ADB. 2017. *Meeting Asia's Infrastructure Needs.* Manila: Asian Development Bank.

Bolesta, Andrzej. 2019. *Asia's Landlocked: Tackling Development Challenges Through Structural Transformation and Trade.* United Nations Economic and Social Commission for Asia and the Pacific. https://www.unescap.org/blog/asia-s-landlocked. Accessed 8 July 2019

ECN. 2017. *Up and Running? Opportunity and Risk Along China's Belt and Road Initiative.* Singapore: Economist Corporate Network.

IFF. 2018. A Route to Economic Growth – The Belt and Road Initiative 2018 Survey. In *The IFF China Report 2018.* Beijing: International Finance Forum.

———. 2019. The Belt and Road Initiative 2019 Survey – A New Driver for Globalisation? In *The IFF China Report 2019.* Beijing: International Finance Forum.

Ji, Xianbai, Pradumna B. Rana, Wai-Mun Chia, and Changtai Li. 2016. Economic and Strategic Dimensions of Mega-FTAs: A Perception Survey of Asian Opinion Leaders. In *RSIS Working Paper.* Singapore: S. Rajaratnam School of International Studies.

Rana, Pradumna B., and Wai-Mun Chia. 2017. *Jumpstarting South Asia: Revisiting Economic Reforms and Look East Policies.* New Delhi: Oxford University Press.

Rana, Pradumna B., Wai-Mun Chia, and Yothin Jinjarak. 2012. Monetary Integration in ASEAN+3: A Perception Survey of Opinion Leaders. *Journal of Asian Economics* 23 (1): 1–21.

Tan, Hui Yee. 2019. Chinese Debt Trap? Host Countries Bear Responsibility Too. *Straits Times.* https://www.straitstimes.com/opinion/chinese-debt-trap-host-countries-bear-responsibility-too.

CHAPTER 5

BRI and Southeast Asia

1 Introduction

Southeast Asia is the focal point for the implementation of the BRI as it links the land-based Belt and the ocean-going Road (Liu and Lim 2019). All ten members of the Association of Southeast Asian Nations (ASEAN) have signed a BRI memorandum of understanding with China. Several joint statements of China-ASEAN Summit have taken note of the synergies between the Master Plan on ASEAN Connectivity 2025 (MPAC 2025) and the BRI, not least because of ASEAN's vast infrastructure financing needs.

The G20's Global Infrastructure Outlook estimates that between 2016 and 2040 Southeast Asian countries together need to invest about $4.2 trillion for infrastructure development, of which based on current trends only $3.6 trillion is forthcoming. Hence they face a financing gap of about $600 billion. The gap is negligible in the case of Singapore, and the largest in Myanmar ($112 billion), Vietnam ($102 billion), and Thailand ($100 billion). With the exception of Indonesia, financing gap is the largest in the transport sector followed by the water sector (Table 5.1). In the past, Chinese investment went mainly to the energy sector but, as the next sections show, in more recent years the share of the transport sector has been increasing.

The large financing gap suggests that Southeast Asian countries could potentially benefit from the BRI. But they should be aware of the dual nature of China's north-south charm offensive, as it could be a vehicle for

P. B. Rana, X. Ji, *China's Belt and Road Initiative*,
https://doi.org/10.1007/978-981-15-5171-0_5

Table 5.1 Cumulative infrastructure financing gaps in Southeast Asia, 2016–2040 ($ billion)

Country	*Investment needed*	*Current investment trends*	*Total investment gap*	*Investment gap*			
				Energy	*Telecom*	*Transport*	*Water*
Cambodia	87	59	28	7	7	14	0
Indonesia	1.7 (trillion)	1.6 (trillion)	70	0	3	2	65
Malaysia	460	383	77	0	0	77	0
Myanmar	224	111	112	1	9	75	28
Philippines	498	429	69	0	0	36	33
Singapore	94	94	0	0	0	0	0
Thailand	494	394	100	0	5	96	0
Vietnam	605	503	102	9	0	70	23

Source: Global Infrastructure Outlook

both economic development as well as geopolitical dominance. This is indeed the case in Southeast Asia, where apart from admiration and hope, the BRI is also viewed with scepticism and suspicion (LSE IDEAS and CIMB ASEAN Research Institute 2018). Various intertwining factors lie behind the mixed feelings including the ways in which BRI infrastructure projects are carried out, and the likelihood of BRI installing China as a dominant power challenging the much cherished ASEAN Centrality.

Against the above background, this chapter assesses the major benefits and risks of the BRI in Southeast Asia. It also highlights the key BRI projects in the countries of the region.

2 BRI Projects in Southeast Asia

The China-Indochina Peninsula Economic Corridor (CICPEC) is the BRI corridor that has direct relevance to Southeast Asia. Analysts hope that the CICPEC will 'take regional economic integration [between China and Southeast Asia] to a whole new level' (Luft 2016). A key component of the CICPEC is the China-Laos Economic Corridor (CLEC) which comprises a high-speed railway (HSR) linking Kunming of China and Vientiane of Laos. This HSR is expected to be operational in 2021; by September 2019, 80 per cent of the construction work had been completed (Xinhua 2019b). It will boost bilateral border trade between the two countries especially at the Mohan-Boten cross-border economic cooperation zone which is being expanded under the BRI.

The extension of the HSR south to Bangkok via the Nong Khai gateway of Thailand gives rise to the China-Laos-Thailand (CLT) HSR, another key BRI project pushed by Beijing. The CLT HSR will transform Laos from a land-locked nation to a land-bridge between China and Thailand. Divided into two phases, the construction of the first phase (from Bangkok to Nakhon Ratchasima) has been completed with Thailand bearing the entire construction cost of $4 billion. The second phase (from Nakhon Ratchasima to Nong Khai) costing $6.4 billion will be jointly financed by China and Thailand (Charoenpoin 2019). The CLT HSR is set to start services in 2023 (Charoenpoin 2019). Sensing the emerging economic opportunities presented by the CLT HSR, Thailand has charted out an Eastern Economic Corridor (EEC) spanning Chonburi, Rayong, and Chachoengsao provinces (Phuangketkeow 2020). Presently, more than 100 Chinese companies have established factories in the Thai-Chinese industrial zone in Rayong. The ports in Sattaship, Laem Chabang, and Map Ta Phut, which are being modernised or expanded under the BRI, are also key nodes that make up the Maritime Silk Road (MSR).

Malaysia is also in the midst of implementing several MSR-related projects, including the Kuala Linggi port expansion, the Penang port refurbishment, and the Kuantan port expansion projects. The Malaysia-China Kuantan Industrial Park is being developed as the sister park of the China-Malaysia Qinzhou Industrial Park in Guangxi, China following a distinctive 'Two Countries, Twin Parks' model. Another major BRI project in Malaysia is the Melaka Gateway project, launched in 2014. The Gateway encompasses a mix of port facilities, specialised industrial parks, and tourism attractions (Hutchinson 2019). As concieved by Putrajaya, it would be a logistical alternative and competitor to Singapore. There are, however, doubts over the project's commercial viability and geopolitical repercussions (Hutchinson 2019). The East Coast Rail Link (ECRL) is yet another key BRI transport project (Lim 2018). With China Communications Construction as the lead contractor, the 640 km ECRL will connect Port Klang on the Strait of Malacca with Kota Bharu in northeast Malaysia. The project was nearly derailed because of cost overrun and corruption allegations (see Sect. 4.3).

Similarly, the Kyaukpyu port in Myanmar's Rakhine state is in the spotlight. In 2016, China and Myanmar had agreed to a $7.2 billion port development contract. The deal stalled soon afterwards partly due to negative public opinion in Myanmar questioning the local benefits from China-sponsored infrastructure projects. The Kyaukpyu port project was revived in August 2018 after China agreed to drastically scale down the project to $1.3 billion. As of this writing, the political will to push ahead the Kyaukpyu project is high because China has provided strong diplomatic backing to Myanmar against international criticisms about Naypyidaw's role in the Rohingya crisis. Two other on-going BRI projects in Myanmar are a border economic cooperation zone along the Kunlong-Chinshwehaw border area and the New Yangon City project (see Sect. 3.3). One completed project is the oil and gas pipelines from Kyaukpyu to Kunming. The crude oil pipeline was put into operation in 2017 while the natural gas pipelines came onstream earlier in 2013. As of July 2019, China had imported more than 19 million tonnes of crude oil and more than 20 billion cubic meters of natural gas through the China-Myanmar oil and gas pipelines (Xinhua 2019a).

Sihanoukville city is the poster child of Sino-Cambodian BRI cooperation. Once a tranquil coastal town, the establishment of the Sihanoukville Special Economic Zone (SSEZ) has transformed the city into a focus of national attention and a centre of economic activities. One Cambodian observer notes that the 'SSEZ alone has helped generate income by directly employing over 20,000 Cambodian workers and promoting the social and economic inclusion of mostly low-skilled and female workers from Sihanoukville and other surrounding provinces. Over 100 factories currently in operation within the zone hire these Cambodian workers to produce garment, textiles, bags, leather products, hardware, machinery, wooden products, and other light manufacturing products for exports' (Kha 2019). The SSEZ is being connected to Phnom Penh via a four-lane expressway which is under construction. This will be Cambodia's first expressway and is funded by a $2 billion investment from China.

With Singapore, China has pursued connectivity cooperation through the China-Singapore (Chongqing) Demonstration Initiative on Strategic Connectivity (CCI). Financial services, aviation industry, transportation and logistics, and information and communications technology are priority cooperation areas under the CCI. The two sides are also developing a CCI New International Land-Sea Trade Corridor to advance physical and commercial connectivity. Since the 2015 inception of the CCI, the two countries have signed more than 160 projects worth over $26 billion (MOFCOM 2019).

Sino-Vietnamese connectivity cooperation builds on the pre-existing 'Two Corridors, One Belt' (TCOB) initiative. In 2003, China had proposed to build the 'Kunming-Laojie-Hanoi-Hai Phong-Quang Ninh' and 'Nanning-Liangshan-Hanoi-Hai Phong-Quang Ninh' economic corridors and the Beibu Bay Economic Belt (Hiep 2018). But this plan did not go ahead as planned for a number of reasons, including maritime disputes and a lack of mutual trust between the two countries. The TCOB is likely to get a new lease of life as the 2019 Belt and Road Forum (BRF) mentioned it in the leaders' joint communique. A prototype project that emerged in November 2019 was the proposed $4.3 billion refurbishment of a colonial-era railway from Hai Phong through Hanoi to Lao Cai on the border with China (Wu 2020). Prior to that, China had provided a $419 million loan to Vietnam to finance the Cat Linh-Ha Dong metro line in Hanoi.

In 2007, Brunei announced the 'Wawasan Brunei 2035' initiative (Brunei Vision 2035), the major focus of which is to diversify the monolithic Bruneian economy away from oil and gas which would be depleted. The country is seeking Chinese support under the BRI to achieve this vision. In 2014, Brunei and China signed an agreement to establish the Brunei-Guangxi Economic Corridor (BGEC). Under the BGEC, Guangxi and Brunei have invested in the capacity expansion of the Muara port (Kasim 2016). The two countries have also stepped up cooperation in agriculture, food production, and tourism. In particular, Brunei hopes to benefit from China's growing halal food market, and the cooperation between its halal-certified bio-pharmaceutical products and traditional Chinese medicines is accorded high priority within the BGEC framework (Julay 2018).

In Indonesia, the construction of the 142 km HSR between Jakarta and the textile hub of Bandung, financed by a $4.5 billion loan from China Development Bank, has started after long delays in land acquisition. There are proposals to extend the HSR to Surabaya in East Java. At the 2019 BRF, new contracts were signed to fund projects in four Indonesian 'Regional Comprehensive Economic Corridors', namely North Sumatra, North Kalimantan, North Sulawesi, and Bali (Deha 2019). An early-harvest project is the expansion of the Kuala Tanjung port in North Sumatra to handle multiple mother vessels and direct cargo flows from and to China's major ports.

In the Philippines, President Rodrigo Duterte's 'Build, Build, Build' (BBB) campaign of investing around 9 trillion pesos ($177 billion) on new infrastructure projects shares common goals with the BRI. China has pledged $24 billion for the BBB. As with other ASEAN countries, railway projects feature heavily on the agenda. China is funding and potentially building a rail line from Subic to the New Clark City (which are 85 km apart) in support of Manila's plan to create a logistics hub in the Central

Luzon Corridor. The Filipino authorities also hope that this railway, which connects the Subic port and Clark City (where a new international airport is being constructed) will reduce congestion in the Manila port and freight traffic through Metro Manila. The Philippines purchased Chinese-made trains for the first time in 2019 as well. These trains will be deployed on the rail line from Manila to Bicol.

In addition to projects in individual Southeast Asian countries, at a regional level the BRI could play an important role in contributing to ASEAN's desire for greater trans-ASEAN railway connectivity. From the 1990s, ASEAN has seen Singapore-Kunming Rail Link (SKRL) as a game-changing project that could transform and knit together regional economies (ADB and ADBI 2009). The SKRL has three main routes. The first is an Eastern Route running from Kunming through Vietnam and Cambodia to connect with Bangkok. The second is the Central Route that traverses Laos. The third is the Western Route, which will start from Kunming and end in Yangon through the Dali-Ruili railway. All the three routes will eventually link to Singapore via Kuala Lumpur. This ambitious plan had stalled for nearly two decades, but are now being reinitiated through the BRI (Ganjanakhundee 2018). It is no coincidence that the BRI's China-Laos-Thailand HSR takes the Central Route as its path. China is also reportedly funding a $600 million rail link from Phnom Penh to Ho Chi Minh City (Miu et al. 2017), which is an indentified gap in the Eastern Route (ASEAN Secretariat 2016). With BRI support, ASEAN now has a better chance of developing a seamless community and a single production base.

3 Benefits for Southeast Asia

3.1 Bridging the Development Gap

By strengthening transport connectivity in continental Southeast Asia, the BRI helps ASEAN to lessen a long-standing intra-ASEAN economic divide. That is, the development gap between six original ASEAN members (Brunei, Indonesia, Malaysia, the Philippines, Singapore, and Thailand, known collectively as ASEAN-6) and four newer mainland members, Cambodia, Laos, Myanmar, and Vietnam (CLMV). In 1999, the GDP per capita of Singapore, the region's wealthiest nation, was close to 80 times that of Laos, the region's least developed country. In 2018, the income differential between the richest (Singapore) and the poorest

(Myanmar) country was still approximately 50 times. Despite some convergence, inter-state inequality remains at a high level and this could hinder regional cohesion and economic integration. It is against this background that ASEAN enshrined 'Equitable Economic Development' as the third pillar of the ASEAN Economic Community (AEC) Blueprint 2015 and reiterated the importance of equitable growth in the AEC Blueprint 2025.

So far, ASEAN's approach to addressing the development gap has focused on the policy front. From the late 1980s, the CLMV countries reduced tariffs and liberalised investment regimes, engaged in regional trade facilitation measures, and benefited from generous development assistance programmes of multilateral institutions such as ADB's Greater Mekong Sub-region scheme (Menon 2013). But besides policy support, there is no institutionalised ASEAN-led investment scheme dedicated to CLMV infrastructure development that goes beyond the modest Initiative for ASEAN Integration (IAI) (Cuyvers 2019). Between 2002 and 2015, ASEAN invested only $103 million through IAI in CLMV countries. This has only scratched the surface. The situation could change for the better under the BRI. Through investments and project financing in transport, industrial parks and border economic zones, the BRI is complementing the 'software' enhancing steps taken by ASEAN to create the conducive 'hardware' condition for more balanced economic growth in ASEAN. It goes without saying that improved transport connectivity will facilitate the offshoring of manufacturing activities from China to the CLMV countries to generate jobs and income.

The BRI's value to ASEAN is by no means confined to infrastructure development alone. The CLMV countries lag behind the more advanced ASEAN-6 countries across a host of human and social development indicators. Expenditure in health and education in the CLMV countries needs to be increased greatly. The BRI could help in this regard. For example, China is taking the lead in global health cooperation to develop the so-called Health Silk Road involving the CLMV countries. For example, China-Mekong cooperation on the prevention and control of AIDS, malaria, dengue, flu, and tuberculosis has also been initiated and intensified under the BRI. Additionally, China has dispatched ophthalmology teams to Cambodia, Myanmar, and Laos to carry out the 'Brightness Action' programme; nearly 800 cataract patients in the three countries have had their eyesight restored (Lyu 2018).

In short, until the proposed EU-inspired multilateral ASEAN Cohesion Fund (ACF) (ADBI 2014) comes on-stream, the BRI is functioning as the de facto ACF, harnessing Chinese funds and expertise to implement projects that contribute to the long-term equalisation in development levels between the 'old' and 'new' ASEAN members.

3.2 Digital Transformation

Despite the aforementioned development gap, Southeast Asia as a whole is a rapidly growing economic zone. ASEAN's real GDP growth rate averaged 5.3 per cent from 2000 till 2018 (ASEAN 2019). Eager for higher growth momentum, ASEAN has made digital economy a new policy priority given that some 125,000 new users come onto the Internet every day. As consumers, producers, and traders increase their participation in e-commerce, it is estimated that the value of ASEAN's regional digital economy may reach somewhere between $980 billion and $1.33 trillion by 2025, up from $200 billion in 2018 (Straits Times 2018). Agreements like e-ASEAN Framework Agreement, ASEAN Digital Integration Framework, ASEAN Framework on Digital Data Governance, ASEAN Framework on International Mobile Roaming, and Policy Guideline on Digitalisation of ASEAN Micro Enterprises have been laid out, revealing ASEAN's aspiration of becoming a digital powerhouse amid the unfolding Fourth Industrial Revolution.

China through its Digital Silk Road initiative can help ASEAN realise its digital ambitions. In the first half of 2019, Chinese investment in ASEAN's digital economy reached a whopping $2.5 billion, which exceeded the total amount for 2017. Thanks to the policy support of the BRI, the presence of China's internet conglomerates 'BATJ' (Baidu, Alibaba, Tencent and JD.com) in ASEAN is on a sharp upward trend. In 2018, Baidu launched the 'Apollo Southeast Asia' Autonomous Driving Programme in Singapore, as part of the company's broader plan to commercialise Baidu driver-less transport technologies in Southeast Asia. This was followed by the provision of 'Baidu Cloud' computing services in 2019 to cater for the needs of Singapore's booming financial services and gaming industries.

Alibaba has also scaled up its data services in Southeast Asia. Given the strong demand by Indonesian enterprises for big data, analytic solutions, database services, and data storage and security, Alibaba unveiled two data centres in Indonesia in the span of less than a year between 2018 and

2019. Alibaba's investment in ASEAN's online shopping sector is even more remarkable. It has acquired a controlling stake in Lazada, a pan-regional e-commerce platform with a major presence in six ASEAN countries. It is cooperating with Nanyang Technological University, Singapore to train local e-commerce talents. Alibaba is also venturing into e-payment by leading a string of cooperative e-wallet ventures (Mulia 2019) in Indonesia (Emtek), Malaysia (Touch'n Go), the Philippines (GCash), Singapore (helloPay), Thailand (TrueMoney), and Vietnam (eMonkey). Furthermore, Alibaba has announced a new plan to raise $1 billion in additional investment in fintech start-ups and digital payment systems in Southeast Asia and India.

Tencent, meanwhile, has focused on unleashing the potential of Southeast Asia's video, music, and gaming industries (Tan 2019). With only one major pre-BRI investment in Southeast Asia, Tencent has steadily firmed up its footprint in the region during the BRI period. In 2016, it took over Sanook, a Thai entertainment company, and partnered with Sea, an online gaming company in Singapore, to publish its game titles across Southeast Asia. In 2017, Tencent invested $19 million in a joint media venture with Thailand's Ookbee. A year later, Tencent injected capital into Voyager Innovations, a fintech company in the Philippines. Tencent is also making inroads into Southeast Asia's burgeoning ride-hailing industry. It invested in Indonesia's GoJek for three consecutive years from 2017 to 2019 (Tan 2019).

JD.com's role in ASEAN's digitalisation drive is to benefit ordinary Southeast Asian shoppers. Interestingly, JD.com itself was a traditional retailer forced to go online during the 2003 SARS outbreak in China (Moh 2018). JD.com has since then invested heavily in the supply chain ecosystem, bringing its unique digitisation experience, logistics expertise, and business-to-consumer model to Southeast Asia. It has set up JD.id and built a series of warehouses in Indonesia. Separately, JD.com has invested in Thailand's online fashion brand Pomelo and Vietnam's local e-commerce site Tiki.vn. Over time, the competition between Alibaba, JD.com and other international e-commerce players such as Amazon will benefit customers in Southeast Asian countries.

3.3 Smart Urbanisation

In tandem with rapid economic growth, Southeast Asian countries are experiencing rapid urbanisation (World Bank 2015). An estimated 49 per cent of the region's population live in cities now as compared to 37 per cent merely two decades ago. Urbanisation is particularly pronounced in Laos, Vietnam, Thailand, and Indonesia. In several other countries, urban sprawl is taking place in a handful of mega and middleweight urban centres, making them over-crowded and less liveable. Cities have played an instrumental role in the region's economic ascendency but the astonishingly fast pace with which rural residents flock to urban areas also led to many sustainability challenges in relation to environment, air, and climate. Rapid and uncontrolled urbanisation also puts a severe strain on infrastructure and social fabric by creating concerns for congestion, education, health, housing, and cultural heritage.

In response, ASEAN countries are adopting, among others, information and communications technology (ICT) to tackle urbanisation-related challenges. A concept gaining traction in the region is 'smart city' (Albino et al. 2015), which combines innovative urban planning principles with modern ICT. In 2018, ASEAN launched the ASEAN Smart Cities Network (ASCN) alongside the ASEAN Sustainable Urbanisation Strategy. The ASCN involves 26 pilot cities as the test-ground for large-scale smart city development. An approach known as 'Smart City Twinning' (SCT) to pair up each designated ASEAN smart city with an external city partner for mutual learning is being explored. China is a natural partner of choice, for it is a global leader in smart city technologies and has been applying them to more than 500 Chinese cities. In October 2013, Singapore had a head-start by entering into a SCT agreement with Suzhou for synchronised development of smart cities.

Currently there are four flagship BRI-related smart city projects in Southeast Asia, first of which is the 88 km^2 New Yangon City (NYC). Yangon is the most densely populated city in Myanmar. Its urban sustainability has been under stress because of aging infrastructure, surging tourism, raging youth unemployment and explosive inflows of rural migrants. Naypyidaw therefore decided to seek the BRI's support to expand Yangon south-westward towards its periphery. The NYC, modelled after comparable Chinese cities (Suzhou, Chengdu, and Shanghai) and Ho Chi Minh City, will provide homes and jobs to over one million people by 2050 (NYDC 2019). Another notable project is the New Manila Bay-City of Pearl (NMB) project. Manila, the capital of the Philippines, faces many urbanisation challenges similar to those confronting Yangon. The NMB, due to be completed by 2030 on reclaimed land surrounding Manila, will be a self-sustaining smart community run and monitored by artificial intelligence (Espejo 2017). Malaysia's capital Kuala Lumpur is also set to be a smart city. There, Alibaba is reproducing its ET City Brain initiative, tested out originally in Hangzhou, China. The appeal of the so-called Malaysia City Brain initiative is that it employs artificial intelligence in conjunction with cloud computing and 5G networks to generate real-time traffic predictions to alleviate traffic congestion in Kuala Lumpur (Saieed 2019). In Thailand, China, and Japan are cooperating to build a smart city in Chonburi. This project is claimed to be an exemplary case of Sino-Japanese cooperation on third-country infrastructure projects. The plan is to revive an old industrial park through 'smart manufacturing' and 'smart energy' technologies.

4 Risks Posed by BRI

Despite the clear potential for the BRI to deliver socio-economic value, there are a number of risks that have to be considered.

4.1 Emerging Chinese Hegemony

ASEAN preserves its geopolitical autonomy by fostering a stable balance of power among major regional and extra-regional powers. Specifically, ASEAN as a bloc considers China as the preponderant trading partner, the United States as the paramount guarantor of security, Japan as a prominent source of inward direct investment and India as a promising market to be tapped. ASEAN thereby tries to keep all major powers engaged in Southeast Asia so that they can counter-balance each other. The equidistant diplomacy arising from such a strategy appeared to have paid off in the past decade. Southeast Asia moved from the periphery to the centre of China's foreign policy; the Obama administration courted ASEAN by signing on to the Treaty of Amity and Cooperation in Southeast Asia before being admitted to the East Asia Summit (EAS); Japan increased its financial contribution to ASEAN community-building; and India also espoused an Act East Policy (AEP) that bestowed upon ASEAN a privileged partnership position. As such, ASEAN presided over a desirable power balance. This favourable greater power equilibrium bolstered ASEAN's positioning as the linchpin of regional cooperation on trade, security, and diplomacy. A slate of ASEAN-centred arrangements such as the ASEAN+1 free trade agreements (FTA), ASEAN+6 Regional

Comprehensive Economic Partnership (RCEP) and ASEAN Regional Forum proliferated.

In recent years, however, this regional order favoured by ASEAN has been unravelling. Upon taking office, President Donald Trump masterminded America's geopolitical retrenchment and economic disentanglement from the Asia-Pacific. He jettisoned the Trans-Pacific Partnership involving four ASEAN member states (Ji and Rana 2019) and skipped all the EAS's that he could have attended. Key ambassadorial posts to ASEAN and Singapore remain vacant. While the Trump administration has outlined a Free and Open Indo-Pacific vision, the United States' staying power is being increasingly questioned by regional countries. A growing number of Southeast Asian opinion leaders have lamented the deterioration of US engagement with ASEAN during the Trump presidency (ISEAS-Yusof Ishak Institute 2019, 2020). India is taking a backseat in Southeast Asia as well. To ASEAN's dismay, India refuses to endorse the RCEP agreement, upending six years of negotiations. India also holds the ASEAN-India FTA responsible for India's current account deficits vis-a-vis Southeast Asia. Within India itself, the implementation of the AEP is falling flat, further diminishing India's economic clout in Southeast Asia. By contrast, China is solidifying its economic footprint in Southeast Asia through the BRI. Despite Japan's efforts to maintain the status quo, the BRI gives Beijing an edge to map out an alternative order with China at the centre.

This tectonic shift in the prevailing regional order from multipolarity to a unipolar one creates challenges for ASEAN to grapple with and adapt to. By virtue of geographical and economic proximity, ASEAN has always been in China's orbit. But as other major powers, which would have served as counter-balancing forces, lose ground in the face of the BRI, the danger is that China may attempt to carve out Southeast Asia as its exclusive sphere of influence and use the BRI as a source of geopolitical leverage at a time when the US-China-ASEAN security triangle and geopolitical equilibrium with stabilising effects are being upended. The rise of the BRI in Southeast Asia also carries the potential of overshadowing ASEAN-style regionalism, resulting in Sino-centric rather than ASEAN-centric regionalism. Southeast Asia's notions of 'ASEAN Centrality' and 'ASEAN Way' would give way to Xi's articulations of the 'Silk Road Spirit' and 'Asian Community of Common Destiny' as the normative underpinning of Asian integration. China's preferred bilateral approach to executing infrastructure projects has raised concerns over the BRI's negative impact on

ASEAN unity. Consequently, ASEAN's capability of balancing the (inherently imbalanced) bilateral relations of individual member countries with China would be compromised. Indeed, from the perspective of individual countries, the BRI could deepen their asymmetric economic dependence on China. The fear is that, by the time they become wholly dependent on Chinese trade, funds, technologies, and economic dynamism to propel economic growth, maintaining economic security and foreign policy autonomy would be all but impossible. ASEAN countries would have to pursue a pro-China policy, refrain from calling out Beijing's misbehaviours and cede ground on core national interests such as the South China Sea (SCS; see below) lest Beijing resorts to economic retribution (e.g., withholding BRI financing) to penalise disloyalty.

On the whole, the thorny dilemma facing Southeast Asia is that, while individual BRI projects have strong economic merits, an amalgamation of these BRI projects portends China's potential hegemony in regional affairs. Reconciling China's growing geo-economic ambition and the ASEAN Centrality, while cooperating on the BRI is the overriding issue to be addressed by both sides.

4.2 Growing Maritime Tensions

The MSR passes through the SCS which is disputed by China and Vietnam, Malaysia, Brunei, and the Philippines. Territorial dispute is a long-standing source of contention plaguing China-ASEAN political relations but there is a risk that the MSR may escalate SCS tensions. Three broad observations should be considered.

First, since the announcement of the MSR in 2013, China has been actively asserting its territorial and economic rights in the SCS. Chinese naval and coast guard vessels have begun patrolling the SCS on a near-constant basis, so have fishing fleets and scientific vessels dispatched for conducting seismic surveys. In fact, the Chinese Defence White Paper 2019 has openly reaffirmed China's resolve to 'build infrastructure and deploy necessary defensive capabilities on the islands and reefs in the South China Sea'. To the extent that sovereignty implies exclusiveness, China also puts in efforts to stop other countries laying claims to hydrocarbons and natural gas reserves in the SCS. As documented by Kuok (2019), China pressurised Vietnam to scrap two oil drilling projects and sent the survey ship Haiyang Dizhi 8 to Vietnam's coastal waters for oil and gas exploration. A more dramatic stand-off unfolded between China and the Philippines. Manila initiated a case against China's SCS territorial claims at an arbitral tribunal constituted under the United Nations Convention on the Law of the Sea in January 2013. The tribunal ruled in favour of the Philippines in July 2016, but China disregarded the ruling completely. While tensions have dissipated due to President Duterte's China-leaning foreign policy, there is no denying that China has taken advantage of Duterte's conciliatory approach to encroach on Filipino interests in the SCS.

Second, regional contestants' responses to China's assertiveness are also potentially destabilising. Although the idea of an SCS naval race is overblown, Vietnam and the Philippines have both pursued active military build-ups. Between 2008 and 2018, Vietnam's military expenditure grew by 94 per cent whereas for the Philippines the figure went up by 45 per cent. The focus of spending unsurprisingly is navy. Vietnam People's Navy is being equipped with new submarines (e.g., Kilo-class diesel-electric submarines acquired from Russia under a $2.6 billion deal). A Landing Tank Ship was put into service in December 2019 to serve amphibious operation needs. The Philippine navy plans to acquire 25–30 warships and attack vessels within the next 5–10 years (Nepomuceno 2019). At the same time, the two countries have jumped on a bandwagon with other external powers to balance China's looming naval pre-eminence. For instance, as part of Abe's 'coast guard diplomacy', Japan is donating old patrol vessels to the Philippines and Vietnam and extending concessionary financing to the two countries for building new ones (Arase 2019).

Third, major external naval powers with interests in the SCS have become increasingly hands-on to counter what they see as China's bullying tactics and interference in the SCS freedom of navigation (FON). In 2019 alone, the US navy conducted seven FON operations (the highest number since Beijing announced the MSR), sending war ships to sail near disputed SCS maritime features (e.g., islands and rocks) claimed by Beijing. Navies of Japan, Australia, Britain, and France have also joined Washington's FON efforts to ramp up international pressure on China. Moreover, these FON exercises are being backed up by joint naval drills with links to the Indo-Pacific geo-strategic mantra. In January 2019, the United States and Britain staged their first joint naval drill in the SCS. In a fresh show of naval strength and geopolitical solidarity, the United States, Japanese, Indian, and Philippine navies held a joint naval exercise in the SCS four months later.

In short, the MSR has greatly raised the economic and geopolitical stakes of the SCS. With the heightened territorialisation and securitisation of the SCS, it remains to be seen whether the MSR would transform the SCS into a bond of friendship (as Xi proclaimed in 2013) or an arena of greater power geo-strategic competition. The near collision between the USS Decatur and the Chinese Luyang destroyer during the former's September 2018 FON mission around the Spratly Islands laid bare the unabated tensions surrounding the SCS. Against the backdrop of worsening Sino-American relations, the likelihood of such conflicts, larger-scale confrontations or other 'unsafe and unprofessional' encounters at sea could be increased to the detriment of regional stability.

4.3 Governance Risks: Corruption and Debt Distress

Transparency deficit is a defining criticism against the BRI. The willingness of China to handle huge financial deals opaquely is said to breed corruption (Hillman 2019), which corrodes good governance and allows unviable infrastructure projects to be selected. Malaysia for example was embroiled in a corruption case related to the BRI.

At the heart of the scandal was the 1Malaysia Development Berhad (1MDB), a public investment fund created in 2009 by former Malaysian Prime Minister Najib Razak. Shortly after its establishment, the company became heavily indebted and mis-managed. In 2015, the 1MDB was placed under public scrutiny for its suspicious money transactions, doubtful investment decisions, and leaked evidence pointing to illicit activities such as money laundering, fraud, and embezzlement (CNA 2018). In 2016, the Najib administration proposed three multi-billion mega-projects under the banner of the BRI, namely the East Coast Rail Link (ECRL), Multi-Product Pipeline (MPP) and Trans-Sabah Gas Pipeline (TSGP), and awarded contracts to Chinese state-owned companies at inflated prices so that the surplus funds could be used to bail out the 1MDB (Povera 2019). The scandal contributed to social backlash, political upheaval and the eventual toppling of Najib in the 2018 Malaysian general election. Mahathir Mohamad who succeeded Najib Razak terminated the MPP and TSGP projects and renegotiated with China on the ECRL, citing concerns over Malaysia's ability to repay the Chinese loans and the murky ways in which the original contract was structured. It was not until China agreed to cut the cost of the rail project from 66.7 billion ringgits ($16.4 billion) to 44 billion ringgits ($10.8 billion) that the ECRL got back on track in April 2019.

Another example of governance risk posed by the BRI concerns the debt conditions in Laos for which China is the largest bilateral creditor country. During the first five years of the BRI implementation in Laos, the share of nominal public and publicly guaranteed debt (PPGD) as a percentage of GDP actually decreased slightly from 59.5 per cent in 2013 (IMF 2015) to 57.2 per cent in 2018 (IMF 2019). In the past, Laos used to source financial inflows from both China and Thailand to meet its development finance needs. But as it moves ahead with various BRI projects, the growth in external debt owed to China has significantly outpaced exposure to Thailand and other official creditors. This has entrenched Laos' financial dependence on China. Therefore as the IMF (2019) has cautioned, the challenge for Laos is 'putting debt on a sustainable path while meeting development needs'. As the next two chapters demonstrate, the same can be said of South and Central Asian developing countries that are participating in the BRI.

5 Conclusion

This chapter has assessed the impact of the BRI on Southeast Asian countries. Together with the MPAC 2025, the BRI has been a stepping stone to shore up regional connectivity and reduce the persistent development gap between the ASEAN-6 countries and the CLMV. The BRI has also resulted in increased tech investments from China to Southeast Asia. Moreover, in the era of rapid urbanisation, the BRI is supporting a number of smart city projects to help Southeast Asia address the challenges of sustainable urbanisation.

However, the BRI comes with geopolitical, security and governance risks for the countries in the region. Geopolitically, the BRI is a game-changer with a potential to disturb the regional balance of power to China's advantage. ASEAN Centrality could be called into question in the shadow of the Chinese BRI largess. China's emerging regional role could complicate the SCS issue. Governance risks like corruption and debt distress could also increase as the BRI advances in Southeast Asia.

References

ADB, and ADBI. 2009. *Infrastructure for a Seamless Asia*. Tokyo: Asian Development Bank Institute.

ADBI. 2014. *ASEAN 2030: Toward a Borderless Economic Community*. Tokyo: Asian Development Bank Institute.

Albino, Vito, Umberto Berardi, and Rosa Maria Dangelico. 2015. Smart Cities: Definitions, Dimensions, Performance, and Initiatives. *Journal of Urban Technology* 22 (1): 3–21.

Arase, David. 2019. *Japan's Strategic Balancing Act in Southeast Asia*. Singapore: ISEAS-Yusof Ishak Institute.

ASEAN. 2019. *ASEAN Key Figures 2019*. Jakarta: ASEAN Secretariat.

ASEAN Secretariat. 2016. *Master Plan on ASEAN Connectivity 2025*. Jakarta: ASEAN Secretariat.

Charoenpoin, Anucha. 2019. Thailand Turns to China for High-Speed Rail Boost. *Bangkok Post*. https://www.bangkokpost.com/business/1776144/thailand-turns-to-china-for-high-speed-rail-boost. Accessed 28 January 2020.

CNA. 2018. *1MDB Scandal: A Timeline*. https://www.channelnewsasia.com/news/asia/1mdb-scandal-a-timeline-10254406. Accessed 1 March 2020

Cuyvers, Ludo. 2019. The 'ASEAN Way' and ASEAN's Development Gap with Cambodia, Laos, Myanmar and Vietnam: A Critical View. *Asia Pacific Business Review* 25 (5): 683–704.

Deha, Daniel. 2019. Indonesia, China Signs 23 Investment and Trade Agreements. *The Insider Stories*. https://theinsiderstories.com/indonesia-china-signs-23-investment-and-trade-agreements/. Accessed 29 January 2020.

Espejo, April. 2017. City of Pearl: China Builds Massive Belt and Road Metropolis in the Philippines. *CGTN*. https://news.cgtn.com/news/3455444e35557a6333566d54/share_p.html. Accessed 28 January 2020.

Ganjanakhundee, Supalak. 2018. Completion of High-Speed Southeast Asian Rail Link Is Still Far Down the Track. *The Nation*. https://www.nationthailand.com/ann/30336801. Accessed 31 January 2020.

Hiep, Le Hong. 2018. *The Belt and Road Initiative in Vietnam: Challenges and Prospects*. Singapore: ISEAS–Yusof Ishak Institute.

Hillman, Jonathan. 2019. 1MDB Probe Shines Uncomfortable Light on China's Belt and Road. *Nikkei Asian Review*. https://asia.nikkei.com/Opinion/1MDB-probe-shines-uncomfortable-light-on-China-s-Belt-and-Road. Accessed 22 January 2020

Hutchinson, Francis E. 2019. The Melaka Gateway Project: High Expectations but Lost Momentum? In *ISEAS Perspective* Singapore: ISEAS-Yusof Ishak Institute.

IMF. 2015. *Lao People's Democratic Republic*. Washington, DC: International Monetary Fund.

———. 2019. *Lao People's Democratic Republic*. Washington, DC: International Monetary Fund.

ISEAS-Yusof Ishak Institute. 2019. *The State of Southeast Asia: 2019 Survey Report*. Singapore: ISEAS-Yusof Ishak Institute.

———. 2020. *The State of Southeast Asia: 2020 Survey Report*. Singapore: ISEAS-Yusof Ishak Institute.

Ji, Xianbai, and Rana, Pradumna B. 2019. A Deal that Does Not Die: The United States and the Rise, Fall and Future of the (CP)TPP. *Pacific Focus* 34 (2): 230–255.

Julay, Abdul Hai. 2018. An overview of "Brunei-China Relations Towards Enhancing Objective Well-Being and Sustainability: A Case Study on Brunei-Guangxi Economic Corridor". *The 3rd China-ASEAN Ethnic Cultural Forum*, Guangxi, China, 12 April.

Kasim, Leo. 2016. Brunei-Guangxi Economic Corridor supports Vision 2035. *The Jakarta Post*. https://www.thejakartapost.com/seasia/2016/04/22/brunei-guangxi-economic-corridor-supports-vision-2035.html. Accessed 28 January 2020.

Kha, Sok. 2019. The Belt and Road in Cambodia: Successes and Challenges. *The Diplomat*. https://thediplomat.com/2019/04/the-belt-and-road-in-cambodia-successes-and-challenges/. Accessed 29 January 2020.

Kuok, Lynn. 2019. *How China's Actions in the South China Sea Undermine the Rule of law*. Washington, DC: Brookings Institution.

Lim, Guanie. 2018. Resolving the Malacca Dilemma: Malaysia's Role in the Belt and Road Initiative. In *Securing the Belt and Road Initiative: Risk Assessment, Private Security and Special Insurances Along the New Wave of Chinese Outbound Investments*. Singapore: Springer Singapore.

Liu, Hong, and Guanie Lim. 2019. The Political Economy of a Rising China in Southeast Asia: Malaysia's Response to the Belt and Road Initiative. *Journal of Contemporary China* 28 (116): 216–231.

LSE IDEAS, and CIMB ASEAN Research Institute. 2018. *China's Belt and Road Initiative (BRI) and Southeast Asia*. Kuala Lumpur: CIMB Southeast Asia Research Sdn Bhd.

Luft, Gal. 2016. *It Takes a Road*. Washington, DC: Institute for the Analysis of Global Security.

Lyu, Jian. 2018. Increase Cooperation 'Will Benefit Lancang-Mekong Inhabitants'. *The Nation*. https://www.nationthailand.com/opinion/30337771. Accessed 31 January 2020.

Menon, Jayant. 2013. Narrowing the Development Divide in ASEAN: The Role of Policy. *Asian-Pacific Economic Literature* 27 (2): 25–51.

Miu, Rachel, Tjen-San Chong, and Chris Leung. 2017. *One Belt, One Road: Moving Faster Than Expected*. Singapore: DBS Group Research.

MOFCOM. 2019. *First Meeting of Joint Working Committee of China-Singapore (Chongqing) Demonstration Initiative on Strategic Connectivity Held in Beijing*. Ministry of Commerce of the People's Republic of China. http://english.mofcom.gov.cn/article/newsrelease/significantnews/201908/20190802888888.shtml. Accessed 28 January 2020.

Moh, Robin. 2018. How JD Is Making Its Mark in Southeast Asia. *KrASIA*. https://kr-asia.com/how-jd-is-making-its-mark-in-southeast-asia. Accessed 28 January 2020.

Mulia, Edison. 2019. Ant Financial Expands Network in Southeast Asia with eMonkey. *EqualOcean*. https://equalocean.com/financial/20191222-ant-financial-expands-network-in-southeast-asia-with-emonkey. Accessed 22 January 2020.

Nepomuceno, Priam. 2019. PH Navy to Get 25–30 More Warships: Empedrad. *Philippine News Agency*. https://www.pna.gov.ph/articles/1070666.

NYDC. 2019. *New Yangon City: Final Master Plan Report*. Yangon: New Yangon Development Company.

Phuangketkeow, Sihasak. 2020. *Thailand's Eastern Economic Corridor: A Bold Strategic Move*. Singapore: ISEAS-Yusof Ishak Institute.

Povera, Adib. 2019. ECRL Needs a Review, Says Anwar. *New Straits Times*. https://www.nst.com.my/news/nation/2019/09/524290/ecrl-needs-review-says-anwar. Accessed 1 March 2020.

Saieed, Zunaira. 2019. Kuala Lumpur Set to Become Smart City Next Year. *The Star*. https://www.thestar.com.my/business/business-news/2019/04/25/kuala-lumpur-set-to-become-smart-city-next-year. Accessed 28 January 2020.

Straits Times. 2018. Asean GDP Could Soar by US$1 Trillion as SMEs Go Digital. https://www.straitstimes.com/business/companies-markets/asean-gdp-could-soar-by-us1-trillion-as-smes-go-digital. Accessed 22 January 2020.

Tan, Zhixin. 2019. A Key to Decode Tencent's Southeast Asian Investment Landscape. *KrASIA*. https://kr-asia.com/a-key-to-decode-tencents-southeast-asian-investment-landscape. Accessed 22 January 2020.

World Bank. 2015. *East Asia's Changing Urban Landscape*. Washington, DC: World Bank.

Wu, Shang-Su. 2020. Belt and Rail: New Vietnam-China Train Aims to Put Relations on Track. *The Interpreter*. https://www.lowyinstitute.org/the-interpreter/belt-and-rail-new-vietnam-china-train-aims-put-relations-track. Accessed 31 January 2020.

Xinhua. 2019a. *China-Myanmar Oil Pipeline Carries 5 mln Tonnes Crude in H1*. http://www.xinhuanet.com/english/2019-07/21/c_138245542.htm. Accessed 20 February 2020.

———. 2019b. Nearly 80 pct of China-Laos Railway Construction Completed. *Xinhua News Agency*. http://www.xinhuanet.com/english/2019-09/22/c_138412982.htm. Accessed 28 January 2020.

CHAPTER 6

BRI and South Asia

1 Introduction

Six South Asian countries have signed a BRI MOU with China. They are Afghanistan, Bangladesh, Maldives, Nepal, Pakistan, and Sri Lanka. The BRI is important to South Asian countries for two reasons. First, South Asia ranks the lowest among all Asian sub-regions in terms of logistics performance (ADB and ADBI 2009), and its need of infrastructure provision and financing is large. Figure 6.1 shows large infrastructure finance gaps in Bangladesh, Nepal, and Pakistan. Sri Lanka is in a relatively better position.

Second, in order to further enhance their economic growth prospect, South Asian countries need to deepen economic integration in the areas of infrastructure, trade, energy, and tourism (May 2019). The BRI contributes in this regard. This chapter reviews the BRI corridors in South Asia. It also outlines the major benefits and risks of BRI projects in South Asia.

2 BRI Corridors in South Asia

South Asia hosts two BRI economic corridors, namely, the China-Pakistan Economic Corridor (CPEC) and the Bangladesh-China-India-Myanmar Economic Corridor (BCIM). A third overland corridor that has been also mentioned is the Trans-Himalayan Economic Corridor (THEC) which stretches from the south-western region of China to the Indo-Gangetic Plains of India through Nepal.

P. B. Rana, X. Ji, *China's Belt and Road Initiative*,
https://doi.org/10.1007/978-981-15-5171-0_6

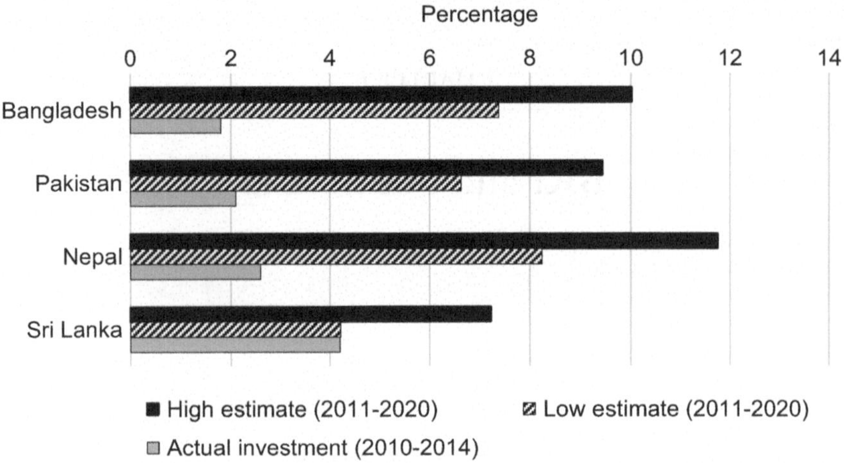

Fig. 6.1 Infrastructure needs and investment levels as percentage of GDP. Note: Data not available for Afghanistan and Maldives
Source: Andrés et al. (2014) and ADB (2017)

Labelled as the flagship project of the BRI (Khan et al. 2017), the 3000-km-long CPEC was proposed by Chinese premier Li Keqiang in May 2013 and finalised by President Xi Jinping in April 2015 during their respective visits to Pakistan.[1] The vision of CPEC is to connect China's inland Xinjiang autonomous region with Pakistan's coastal areas on the Arabian Sea through a multi-modal network of railways, highways and fibre optic cables. CPEC also covers a number of other cooperative areas including urban and social development, public sector capacity building and industrial parks and special economic zones. The construction of CPEC is to extend from 2013 to 2030 at an estimated cost of $62 billion (Siddiqui 2017). Short-term projects are to be completed by 2020, medium-term projects by 2025 and long-term projects by 2030. Beijing has a vested geo-economic interest in CPEC, which is to reduce energy and trade dependence on the strategic choke point of the Strait of Malacca (Grare 2018).

The BCIM corridor predates the BRI (Das and Thomas 2018). It grew out of the 1999 'Kunming Initiative' which focused on the so-called K2K connectivity of enhancing trade and investment ties between China's Kunming and India's Kolkata through Myanmar's Mandalay and the

Bangladeshi capital city of Dhaka. This corridor, however, has not made much progress hitherto because of India's reluctance to open its borders to China on national security and trade balance grounds (Uberoi 2016).

From late 2017, China has instead focused on the China-Myanmar Economic Corridor (CMEC) as an interim project to work around India's opposition (Aneja 2019). China's hope is that eventually India may come on board to complete the development of the envisioned BCIM corridor. The CMEC is an inverted Y-shaped corridor, running from Kunming to Mandalay before branching out to the Kyaukpyu deep-sea port on the one hand and to Yangon through Naypyidaw on the other.

As with the BCIM corridor, the development of the THEC is being held back by the Sino-Indian geopolitical discord. Hence, a bilateral Nepal-China Trans-Himalayan Multi-dimensional Connectivity Network (THMCN) has been conceived to replace the tri-partite THEC in medium term. Central to the THMCN is the extension of China's Sichuan-Tibet railway to Nepal, linking the Chinese cities of Chengdu, Ya'an, Lhasa, and Shigatse with the Nepali capital city of Kathmandu. Other important THMCN projects include Rasuwagadhi-Kathmandu road upgrade, Kimathanka-Hile road construction, Dipayal to south border with China connectivity project, Tokha-Bidur road and Galchhi-Rasuwagadhi-Kerung 400 KV transmission line (Giri 2019).

3 Benefits for South Asia

3.1 Strengthening Transport Connectivity

In the years leading up to the announcement of the BRI, the overall quality of Pakistan's railway infrastructure, as measured by the Global Competitiveness Index (GCI) published by the World Economic Forum, was deteriorating continuously due to a lack of new investment and maintenance capabilities (Fig. 6.2). The GCI railway quality index declined from 3.07 in 2010 to barely 2.51 in 2013, in comparison with the best possible score of 7. It bottomed out in 2014 and has since been on an upward trend reaching 3.33 in 2017. Considering that Pakistan has not taken up any major non-China-funded railway projects in recent years, the observed improvement in the railway quality index can largely be associated with the development of CPEC.

More specifically, the BRI is contributing to Pakistan's railway connectivity in three ways. First, the BRI has placed the impoverished region of

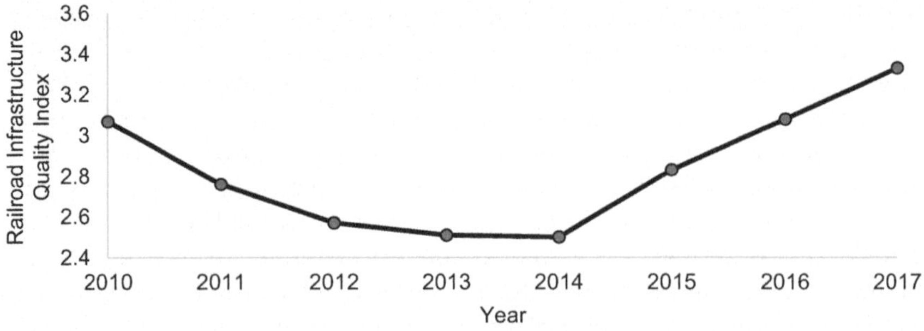

Fig. 6.2 Trend in Pakistan's Railway Infrastructure Quality Index (2010–2017). Source: World Economic Forum

Balochistan on a railway route, and thus the economic map of Pakistan. For a mix of historical, geological, demographic and political reasons, Pakistan's rail networks are concentrated in the Indus River plain and in the Punjab and Sindh provinces bordering India. The mountainous south-western province of Balochistan has long been dis-connected with the national railroad networks despite its rich mineral deposits. Islamabad had attempted to redress the problem by constructing three railway lines: the Gwadar-Panjgur-Quetta link, the Quetta-Peshawar link and the Gwadar-Panjgur-Dalbandin segment (World Bank 2008). However, none of these projects was constructed in the end. This dreadful situation will change under CPEC. The official CPEC railway map shows that a new railway will be built between Balochistan's provincial capital of Quetta and Kotla Jam of Punjab; Gwadar will be connected to Quetta and Jacobadad of Sindh; and new cargo tracks will be laid between Gwadar and Karachi, Pakistan's southern commercial hub.

Second, CPEC will improve connectivity between Khyber Pakhtunkhwa, Punjab, and the Sindh provinces. A 1600 km railway between Karachi and Peshawar via major urban centres including Hyderabad, Sukkur, Lahore, and Islamabad will be built in part by upgrading the existing rail systems. This proposed railway will improve considerably north-south connectivity in Pakistan, serving as the major transport artery to support an ever more integrated national economy. A substantial portion (85%) of the project's cost of $8.2 billion is being financed through concessional loans from China. Third, CPEC will increase Pakistan's cross-border rail connectivity with China. While in the past no major railways existed in the northern highlands of Pakistan, now a new railway is planned between China's Kashgar and the Pakistani dry port of Havelian. This railway is alternatively known as Karakoram Railway as it runs almost parallel to the Karakoram Highway between China and Pakistan.

In addition to railway projects, China and Pakistan have drawn up a master plan for highway development. Aside from the cross-border Karakoram Highway, which is under reconstruction and expansion, presently there is only one major highway within Pakistan which connects Peshawar, Lahore, and Faisalabad. After the completion of the BRI, Pakistan will have a dense network of six major highways, with three running north-south (Kashgar-Khunjerab-Gilgit-Islamabad-Dera Ismail Khan-Quetta-Basima-Gwadar; Darya Khan-Shahdādkot; and Lahore-Multan-Sukkur-Hyderabad-Karachi) and three east-west alignments (Peshawar-Faisalabad-Lahore; Besima-Sukkur; and Gwadar-Karachi). More than 40 cities, towns, and villages along the highway corridors will benefit from road connectivity and the facilitated trade.

Another country that stands to benefit greatly from the BRI's connectivity agenda is Nepal (Contessi 2019). The Himalayan republic is surrounded by India on three sides and by China in the north. Nepal depends almost exclusively on India for international trade. As Nepal is strategically located at the cross-roads of China, South Asia, and Central Asia, the planned Trans-Himalayan Economic Corridor has the potential to convert the land-locked country into a land-linked nation (Rana and Karmacharya 2016). This idea is, however, not possible at the present time because of India's unwillingness to support the BRI (see Sect. 4.2 for further discussion). China and Nepal have to be content in the meantime with the bilateral THMCN.

The main trading route between Tatopani village of Nepal and Zhangmu county of China was destroyed in the 2015 Nepal earthquake and the other Rasuwagadhi-Gyirong route has not been able to pick up the slack. As such, a lion's share of Sino-Nepali trade is routed through the Indian seaports of Kolkata and Visakhapatnam, leading to high trading costs and border delays. The THMCN will improve direct connectivity between Nepal and China (see previous section for a list of projects under the THMCN) and help Nepal diversify its international trade. In 2016, Nepal signed an Agreement on Trade and Transit with China. Under this Agreement, Nepal has access to four Chinese sea-ports (Tianjin, Shenzhen, Lianyungang, Zhanjiang) and three dry ports (Lhanzin, Lhasa, Shigatse) for carrying out trade with third countries.

Bangladesh is also leveraging its participation in the BRI to enhance transport connectivity. Construction of a 3.5 km four-lane tunnel under the Karnaphuli River commenced in December 2017 and is likely to be completed by 2022. The Shanghai-inspired tunnel will connect Chittagong and the Shah Amanat Airport on the western bank of the Karnaphuli River to the industrial zones on the eastern side of the river (Dhaka Tribune 2019), following the Chinese model of 'One City, Two Towns' that links east-Shanghai with west-Shanghai across the Huangpu River through bridges and tunnels. The cost of the Karnaphuli Tunnel is around $1.6 billion, including $570 million in loans from China's Exim bank (GCR 2019). Exim bank is concurrently funding the Padma Rail Link Project with a loan of $2.67 billion. Upon completion, this railway will connect nine major Bangladeshi cities and cut the travelling time between Dhaka and Kolkata by almost five hours (Xinhua 2018).

3.2 *Generating Electricity*

Electricity is the lifeline of modern economy, powering up irrigation, industrialisation, urbanisation, and digitalisation. In South Asia, however, 255 million people in the region lived off the grid in 2016 and manufacturing companies suffered from chronic load shedding that has an average duration of 5.3 hours per day (Zhang 2019). A World Bank study estimates that electricity shortage costs the region four to seven per cent of GDP (Zhang 2019). ADB had proposed to develop a regional power exchange project (Wijayatunga et al. 2015) so that the region could better allocate cross-border supply and demand of electricity. But volatile geopolitics had forced each country to pursue an autarchic national electricity policy which has put the region on the brink of an electricity crunch.

Among South Asian BRI countries, Pakistan has been most hampered by systematic electricity crisis. Street riots over electricity shortages and prolonged blackouts have been frequently staged in recent years, hobbling the economy, destabilising the society, and deterring foreign investment. As of fiscal 2016, Pakistan's total installed electricity generation capacity stood at 26 GW; the authorities are targeting to more than double the capacity to 62 GW by fiscal 2024 (NEPRA 2017) in order to meet the soaring household, commercial, and industrial demand. This entails yearly capacity addition of around 4.5 GW. This target is challenging for Pakistan to achieve on its own in view of the fact that self-initiated capacity upscaling and retrofitting efforts in Pakistan have been minimal. Between 2000 and 2012, Pakistan's installed generation capacity per capita did not increase at all while developing Asia as a whole saw 7.4 per cent annual growth (ADB 2017).

Against this background, CPEC can be instrumental in Pakistan's efforts to mitigate its electricity crisis. Indeed, Pakistan's crumbling electricity sector has attracted a large portion of Chinese financing subsequent to the announcement of the BRI. CPEC's seven early-harvest energy projects had already added 3.2 GW electricity to the Pakistani grid besides creating more than 30,000 local jobs by 2018 (PCI 2019). Six other energy projects are under construction. When all planned energy projects are completed, CPEC is projected to increase Pakistan's electricity generation capacity by over 11 GW. In terms of location, CPEC hydropower stations are located in the northern regions of Azad Kashmir and Khyber Pakhtunkhwa, whereas coal-fired stations and windfarms are mainly being built in the south around Hyderabad and Karachi, respectively.

Some have criticised CPEC energy projects out of environmental concerns. However, it should be pointed out that only eight CPEC electricity projects use coal as the primary input and at least half of the new coal-fired plants have adopted the supercritical electricity generation technology which is an advanced coal combustion method with reduced carbon footprint (MIT 2007). Furthermore, increasing coal-based generation capacity to a reasonable extent is in line with Pakistan's policy of rebalancing national energy mix away from imported gas and oil. Coal currently contributes to merely 3 per cent of electricity generation in Pakistan, far below the global average of 40 per cent (Ahmed 2019). By fiscal 2024, when all coal-based stations come online, coal would account for only one-fifth of the overall energy mix in the country (NEPRA 2017). Another added benefit of coal-based electricity generation is that it can enhance Pakistan's energy security since a significant proportion of the coal to be fed into the BRI electricity stations will be sourced domestically.

Bangladesh, which is another electricity-strapped country in South Asia, will also benefit from the BRI. Unlike Pakistan, Bangladesh has been successful in increasing its electricity generation capacity from 4.9 GW in 2009 to 15 GW in 2017. However, the persistent gap between electricity demand and supply continues to widen as the country urbanises and the economy grows steadily (Zhang 2019). About a quarter of Bangladeshis still lack direct access to electricity (Zhang 2019); and for those who are connected, blackouts and load shedding are a fact of life.

Under the BRI, China is financing the construction of the Payra coal-fired ultra-supercritical electricity station with a total capacity of 1320 MW and the Chittagong coal-fired electricity station with a capacity of 1224 MW. Bangladesh is also cooperating with India and Japan to enhance its coal-based electricity supply capacity. Like Pakistan, Bangladesh is embracing the use of coal to diversify its energy mix. As of June 2018, more than three-fifths of Bangladesh's electricity had come from domestically produced natural gas which has reached peak production (Yatsui 2019). There is, therefore, a pragmatic case for Bangladesh to switch to coal as a low-cost alternative.

Nepal is also in need of new power generation capacity. In 2018, the Nepali government set an ambitious target of installing 3 GW generation capacity in three years, 5 GW in five years, and 15 GW in a decade's time (MOEWRI 2018). The planned capacity addition is to meet the rising internal demand for electricity and to expand electricity trading with nearby countries. Though no major BRI-related energy projects have been launched yet, Kathmandu has proposed three projects for Beijing's consideration: Galchhi-Rasuwagadhi-Kerung-Shigatse trans-Himalayan 400 KV transmission line, Tamor hydroelectricity project (762 MW) and Phukot Karnali Hydro Electric Project (426 MW). Notably, the Galchhi-Rasuwagadhi-Kerung-Shigatse transmission line, which is under the final stage of feasibility study at the time of this writing, is designed to supply electricity to the potential cross-border railway project between China and Nepal.

3.3 Promoting Industrial Development

A third major benefit of the BRI is that it will promote industrial development in South Asia by developing special economic zones (SEZs)/industrial parks/industrial zones (Fig. 6.3). An SEZ has special tax, administrative, trade, and infrastructure arrangements that are unavailable outside the enclave to attract investment and promote merchandise exports. SEZ also plays a crucial role in industrialisation, creating jobs and catalysing wider structural reforms (Farole and Akinci 2011).

Pakistan is developing a total of nine SEZs under the BRI. Each SEZ targets a specific industry and services sector based on local resource

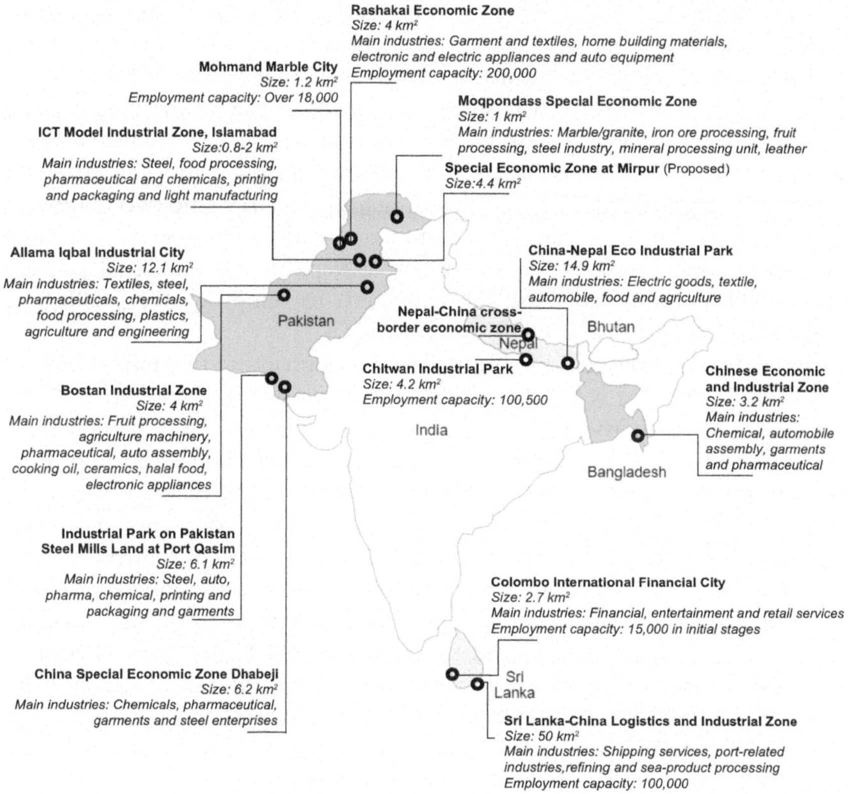

Fig. 6.3 China-funded SEZs in South Asian BRI countries.
Note: National boundaries and locations on the map are indicative only
Source: Authors' illustrations

endowment and skill availability. The SEZ which is the most advanced in terms of development is the Rashakai Special Economic Zone (RSEZ) in Nowshera. The rationale for building the RSEZ is to complement the Khyber Pakhtunkhwa Economic Zone (KPEZ) established in 1984. The KPEZ specialises in light industries like tobacco, cigarettes, maize, vegetable ghee, and cement (MDTF 2016), while the RSEZ focuses on labour-intensive sectors such as garments, home building materials, home appliance manufacturing, and financial services. Because of its location near the Pak-Afghan border, it is hoped that the RSEZ will grow into a regional industrial hub that links up nearby cities of Kashgar, Kabul, and Gwadar.

In Nepal, three major industrial zones are being developed under the BRI. In 2016, an MOU was signed to establish the China-Nepal Eco-Industrial Park in Damak. Land acquisition for an area of 15 km^2 has been completed thus far. A year later, China and Nepal signed another MOU to construct a cross-border SEZ in Rasuwagadhi. In 2019, the two countries signed a third MOU to develop an industrial park in Chitwan with a view to transforming the rural area in Central Nepal to an industrial powerhouse. This industrial park is expected to employ over 100,000 Nepali workers (Shrestha 2019).

In Sri Lanka, there are two industrial zones promoted by China as part of the BRI. The first is the Sri Lanka-China Logistics and Industrial Zone (SLCLIZ) next to the Hambantota port. The project was launched in November 2017. But because of the pushbacks and protests by members of the local community who resented the handover of Hambantota port to China (see below), it was only in June 2018 that the Sri Lankan cabinet gave the final approval for the SLCLIZ. The SLCLIZ was reduced in size (from 60 km^2 to below 50 km^2) and the focus was expanded to cover social infrastructure like hospitals and schools. At an estimated cost of $5 billion, the SLCLIZ is expected to create some 100,000 jobs (People's Daily 2017). Second, China is also supporting the Colombo International Financial City (CIFC) project, which is to be completed in 2041. The vision of the CIFC is to build 'the most liveable city in South Asia' and create a financial hub akin to Dubai and Singapore.

In Bangladesh, China is supporting the Chinese Economic and Industrial Zone (CEIZ) located in Chittagong. Unlike Bangladesh's pre-existing SEZs and export-processing zones where garment producers predominate, the CEIZ will cover chemical, automobile assembly and pharmaceutical industries. The CEIZ targets about 400 factories and hopes to attract $2 billion from Chinese multinational corporations within a three-year period (Ranjan 2019). The development of the CEIZ is expected to cost over $220 million but as of yet no Chinese fund had been provided for the project.

4 Risks Posed by BRI

4.1 Debt Distress

To assess the BRI's debt implications on South Asian and other stakeholder countries, we follow the methodology used by Hurley et al. (2018) with the Center for Global Development. We first consider the trend in a country's overall nominal public and publicly guaranteed debt (PPGD)-to-GDP ratio to identify the BRI countries that are at higher risk of sovereign debt distress.[2] The authors suggest that countries with PPGD-to-GDP ratios beyond the 50–60 per cent threshold could be vulnerable to debt distress. As a second step, we examine the composition of debt to see if China is the primary contributor to the rising debt ratios of the identified high-risk countries.

Figure 6.4 shows the trends in the PPGD-to-GDP ratios in six BRI countries of South Asia. The data show that public indebtedness does not

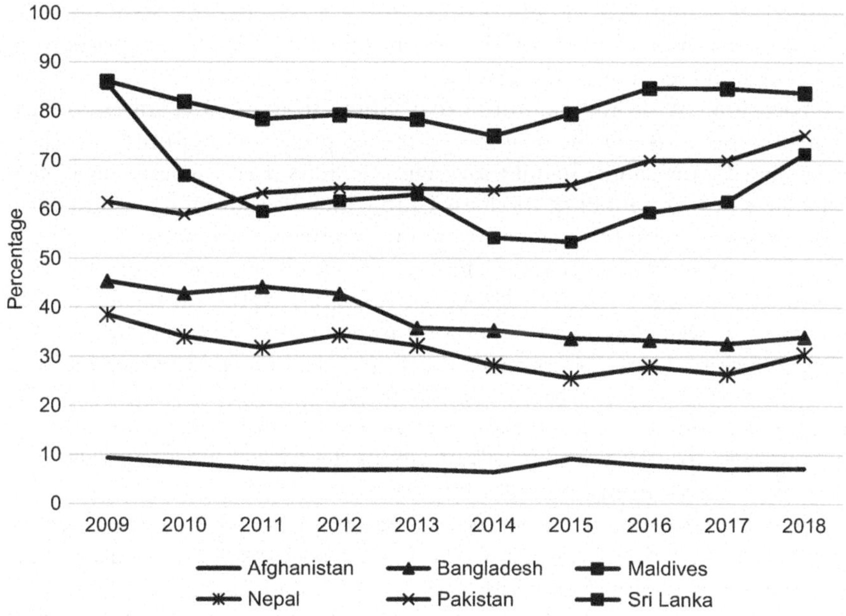

Fig. 6.4 PPGD-to-GDP ratios for six South Asian BRI countries. Source: IMF country debt sustainability reports

appear to be much of a problem in Afghanistan, Nepal, and Bangladesh where the PPGD-to-GDP ratios, although increasing slightly in 2018 compared to 2017 in the latter two countries, are still relatively low (below 40%). The same cannot be said, however, in the cases of Sri Lanka, Pakistan, and Maldives where the PPGD-to-GDP ratios have been increasing and high in recent years.

Looking deeper at the composition of external debt of these three high-risk countries, it appears that China (or the BRI) is not the primary driver of the rising debt ratios. Sri Lanka owes much more to Japan, the country's single largest creditor, than it does to China (only 3%) even though Colombo has increased its borrowings from China under the auspices of the BRI (Fig. 6.5a). According to Weerakoon and Jayasuriya (2019), Sri Lanka's foreign debt increase is due mainly to unrestrained cheap borrowing on the global capital market to finance the country's fiscal and current account deficits. Similarly, in Pakistan most of the debt is due to borrowing from multilateral development institutions and Islamic creditors rather than China (only 6%; Fig. 6.5b). Maldives has been a country at a 'high risk of debt distress' for at least a decade, with or without the BRI, as successive IMF Debt Sustainability Analysis reports have documented (see, e.g., IMF 2017).

Therefore, it should be noted that China-sourced BRI infrastructure financing per se is not the problem. The true problem lies in the uncertain ways that China might handle sovereign defaults if and when they occur. Since it is not a member of the Paris Club which has adopted a multilateral framework for debt restructuring and management, China uses a bilateral, case-by-case modality to settle debt problems. There are fears that this could lead to 'asset seizure'. However, the latest Rhodium Group report (Kratz et al. 2019) which reviewed 40 instances of China's external debt renegotiations across 24 countries has found that actual 'asset seizure' is a very rare occurrence. Most debt renegotiations involved balanced and mutually acceptable outcomes between China as the lender and borrowers, ranging from extensions of repayment deadlines to explicit refinancing, or partial or even total debt forgivenesses.

One case resembling 'asset seizure' has been Sri Lanka's Hambantota port. Constructed at $1.5 billion, the port project started in January 2008 with China providing four-fifths of the cost via high-interest (6–7%) commercial loans. However, despite the high expectations of the Sri Lankan authorities, the Hambantota port failed to attract enough ships to dock at its berths. Cash flow from low traffic volume eventually fell short of covering

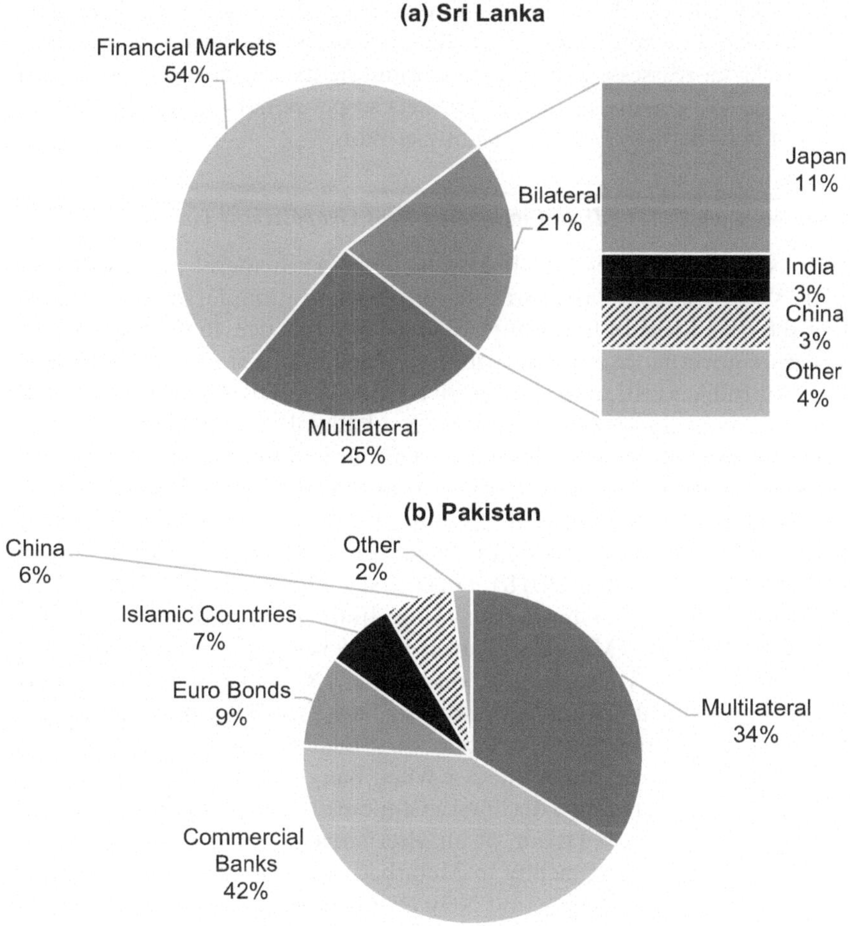

Fig. 6.5 Ownership of outstanding debt for Sri Lanka and Pakistan in 2017. Source: Central Bank of Sri Lanka and State Bank of Pakistan

debt repayment and operational expenditure. To avoid default, Sri Lanka and China settled on a debt-for-equity swap arrangement, handing over the management of the port to China Merchants Ports Holdings, a Chinese state-owned company, on a 99-year lease in 2017. While this reduced some $1.4 billion in debt for Sri Lanka, the deal has been referred to by BRI sceptics as a proof of China's ill-intentioned 'debt trap diplomacy'. The cautionary tale of Hambantota has reverberated beyond the island state. Several neighbouring countries like Bangladesh, Nepal, Myanmar, Maldives, and Malaysia reassessed their fiscal commitments and financial obligations under the BRI shortly, resulting in project suspensions or renegotiations, for fears of debt hardship and sovereignty erosion.

4.2 *Indian Opposition and Geopolitical Game*

India is South Asia's regional hegemon, but it is vehemently opposed to the BRI. There are several reasons behind India's position. First, India believes that the BRI does not follow international best practices in relation to infrastructure governance and transparency (Ministry of External Affairs 2017). Second, India is critical of the perceived 'unilateral' nature of the BRI with foreign secretary (now minister) S. Jaishankar describing it as a Chinese national initiative developed without consultations with the world or with countries that are interested in or affected by it (cited in Gokhale 2017). Third, India claims that China disregards its territorial integrity, particularly with respect to CPEC, which runs through the disputed territory of Kashmir (Baruah 2018). Finally, New Delhi sees the BRI as a geopolitical strategy of China containing India from different directions through CPEC, BCIM, and Sri Lankan port developments (Hendrix 2016).

As such, India's firm opposition to the BRI and the resulting Sino-Indian geopolitical jostling in South Asia have placed regional countries at the crosshairs of the power struggle. In some cases, the rivalry has led to project cancellations as was the case when Bangladesh, under the pressure of India, in February 2016 declined a Chinese offer to build the Chittagong and Sonadia ports in favour of an alternative proposal from Japan for building a similar port facility in Matarbari. In other cases, however, the tug-of-war between Beijing and New Delhi has led to competitive 'regime flip', forcing countries to alternate between pro-China and pro-India governments. Examples are the experiences of Sri Lanka and Maldives.

During 2005 to 2015, Sri Lanka was ruled by Mahinda Rajapaksa, a pro-China president. China assisted in Sri Lanka's post-war reconstruction and shielded the Mahinda Rajapaksa administration from international censure for human rights violations and war crimes (Hull 2011). In return, Mahinda Rajapaksa granted China extraordinary economic and security access to his country (Custer et al. 2019). A list of China-backed infrastructure projects like Hambantota port, Mattala Rajapaksa International Airport and 'Lotus Tower' project in Colombo came on board. This

China-leaning stance unnerved New Delhi, so India played on the wave of public antagonism towards opaque Chinese government-backed investments in Sri Lanka to install a pro-India coalition government led by Maithripala Sirisena in the 2015 election. Early into his presidency, Sirisena suspended all Chinese projects and ordered a full probe into all the contracts awarded to China during the reign of Mahinda Rajapaksa (Singh 2018), though he later resumed most of them. The Sirisena administration also rejected a Chinese submarine's request to dock at the Colombo port in 2017, signalling a dramatic security policy shift as a similar port call had been authorised in 2014. Despite the change in administration, China continued its elite-to-elite diplomacy to court the politically dominant Rajapaksa family. In November 2019, Gotabaya Rajapaksa, a younger brother of Mahinda Rajapaksa, won the presidential election. President Gotabaya Rajapaksa has reoriented Sri Lanka's foreign and economic policy once again towards China and appointed China-friendly Mahinda Rajapaksa as Prime Minister.

The experience of Maldives bears some similarity to that of Sri Lanka. Like Mahinda Rajapaksa, the former Maldivian President Abdulla Yameen, who was in power from 2013 to 2018, had pursued a pro-China foreign policy. During his presidency, there was a boom of Chinese capital inflow to the tune of $1.4 billion to the Maldives' transport (e.g., China-Maldives Friendship Bridge and Velana International Airport) and real estate sectors (Bhandari and Jindal 2018). A free trade deal between the two countries was also signed in December 2017 in Beijing. In the 2018 election, New Delhi once again backed then opposition leader Ibrahim Mohamed Solih who eventually won on an anti-China platform (Dutta 2018). Since Solih's coming to power, Maldives' relations with China have deteriorated. Not only did he lobby hard for debt renegotiation, but Solih also threatened to renege on the free trade pact. Solih's foreign policy was to draw the country closer to India, so much so that the *Financial Times* (2018) described the election results as a 'diplomatic win' for India. Indian Prime Minister Narendra Modi visited Maldives for Solih's inauguration in November 2018 and received Solih in New Delhi on his first presidential visit abroad in December. During his visit to India, Solih accepted a $1.4 billion bailout package from India to meet Chinese loan repayment requirements. In June 2019 as part of Modi's state visit to Maldives, the two countries inked six more MOUs and technical agreements to accelerate all-round cooperation in areas as wide as hydrography, health, passenger and cargo services by sea and customs procedures.

If Sino-Indian geopolitical rivalry and competition drag on, which is seen as the most plausible scenario by analysts like Small (2018), there will be more instances of project termination and 'regime flip' in South Asia. Policy autonomy and geopolitical manoeuvring space of regional BRI-participating countries—who have to walk a tightrope trying to balance their ties between China and India—will be constrained. Geopolitically motivated government changes entail political instability and volatile business environments, putting a brake on the economic development of the region. To rise above the zero-sum mentality, India needs to understand that there is scope for realising mutual gains under the BRI even as it stands firm on its strategic interests (Basrur 2019). China, for its part, needs to moderate its infrastructure diplomacy and economic engagement with regional countries to avoid antagonising New Delhi. After all, without India's buy-in, the BRI is geopolitically risky and divisive in South Asia.

4.3 Fuelling Corruption

Given the sheer volume of expenditure involved and the low level of transactional transparency, infrastructure projects are generally vulnerable to corruption, rent-seeking and state capture throughout the project cycle: planning, bidding, procurement, construction, operation, and maintenance. Indeed, according to the OECD (2014) Foreign Bribery Report, nearly sixty per cent of foreign bribery cases occurred within four infrastructure categories: extractive (19%), transport (15%), construction (15%), and information and communications (9%).

BRI projects in South Asia are especially corruption-prone because these countries are known for being a hotbed of endemic corruption and entrenched kleptocracy (Table 6.1). Corruption is particularly rampant in Afghanistan, Bangladesh, Nepal, and Pakistan and the ranking and score of Maldives had dropped three years in a row. The problem is compounded by Beijing's unwillingness to punish Chinese companies that are carrying out BRI projects in support of the government's foreign strategy. Evidence of BRI-fuelled corruption scandals has been publicly uncovered across the sub-region in the past few years.

In January 2018, Bangladesh blacklisted China Harbour Engineering Company (CHEC), a Chinese state-backed construction company, on corruption charges. The CHEC was accused of trying to pay off a top Bangladeshi official from the road transport ministry with around 5

Table 6.1 Corruption perception indices for South Asian BRI countries

	2016		*2017*		*2018*	
Country	*Score*	*Ranking*	*Score*	*Ranking*	*Score*	*Ranking*
Afghanistan	15	169/177	15	180/183	16	172/180
Bangladesh	26	145	28	143	26	149
Maldives	36	95	33	112	31	124
Nepal	29	131	31	122	31	124
Pakistan	32	116	32	117	33	117
Sri Lanka	36	95	38	91	38	89

Source: Transparency International

million taka ($60,000) in bribe when negotiating the Dhaka-Sylhet expressway expansion project (AFP 2018). Dhaka cancelled the project eventually. China and BRI-related corruption have also rattled Sri Lankan politics. The CHEC was suspected of paying $1.1 million in bribe to Mahinda Rajapaksa's failed election campaign in 2014–2015 after securing a $1.4 billion contract to build the Colombo Port City (Rose 2015). In 2018 amid Sri Lanka's constitutional turmoil that saw a face-off between Ranil Wickremesinghe and Mahinda Rajapaksa vying for the Prime Minister position, China funnelled funds to Mahinda Rajapaksa so that he could bribe parliamentarians for switching allegiance to him from Wickremesinghe who was dismissed earlier by the president (Rasheed and Kuruwita 2018). The shadow of Chinese financial largess also loomed large in the 2018 Sri Lanka local elections (Mushtaq 2018) where Mahinda Rajapaksa's Sri Lanka *Podujana Peramuna* (People's Front) won around 40 per cent of the total votes. In Pakistan, three road projects (Dera Ismail Khan-Zhob, Khuzdar-Basima and Raikot-Thakot roads) have been temporarily suspended (by China) over graft allegations and corruption charges against local officials (Business Line 2017).

5 Conclusion

This chapter has reviewed the implementation of the BRI in South Asia. The overall picture is rather mixed. On the plus side, if projects are well selected and implemented, the BRI benefits the region by strengthening in-country and cross-border connectivity, augmenting electricity production capacity, and promoting industrialisation. However, on the negative side, the BRI heightens the risk of debt distress especially in three BRI countries (namely, Sri Lanka, Maldives, and Pakistan), deepens regional geopolitical risks because of India's hostility to the BRI, and fuels corruption.

Notes

1. A deeper root of CPEC goes back to 2006 when then Pakistani president Pervez Musharraf expressed interest in setting up a 'trade and energy corridor' with China.
2. This is partly because for a number of countries under study, time series data on public external debt is not available.

References

ADB. 2017. *Meeting Asia's Infrastructure Needs.* Manila: Asian Development Bank.

ADB, and ADBI. 2009. *Infrastructure for a Seamless Asia.* Tokyo: Asian Development Bank Institute.

AFP. 2018. Bangladesh Blacklists Chinese Construction Firm, Cancels Highway Deal After Bribe Claim. *Agence France-Presse.* https://www.scmp.com/news/asia/south-asia/article/2129493/bangladesh-blacklists-chinese-construction-firm-cancels-highway. Accessed 1 March 2020.

Ahmed, Faraz. 2019. Coal Share in Electricity Production May Reach 18%. *The Express Tribune.* https://tribune.com.pk/story/1931607/2-coal-share-electricity-production-may-reach-18/. Accessed 9 September.

Andrés, Luis, Dan Biller, and Matías Herrera Dappe. 2014. Infrastructure Gap in South Asia: Infrastructure Needs, Prioritization, and Financing. In *Policy Research Working Paper 7032.* Washington, DC: World Bank.

Aneja, Atul. 2019. Bangladesh-China-India-Myanmar (BCIM) Economic Corridor No Longer Listed Under BRI Umbrella. *The Hindu.* https://www.thehindu.com/news/international/bangladesh-china-india-myanmar-bcim-economic-corridor-no-longer-listed-under-bri-umbrella/article26971613.ece.

Baruah, Darshana M. 2018. India's Answer to the Belt and Road: A Road Map for South Asia. In *Carnegie India Working Paper.* New Delhi: Carnegie Endowment for International Peace.

Basrur, Rajesh. 2019. The BRI and India's Grand Strategy. *Strategic Analysis* 43 (3): 187–198.

Bhandari, Amit, and Chandni Jindal. 2018. *Chinese Investments in India's Neighbourhood*. Mumbai: Gateway House: Indian Council on Global Relations.

Business Line. 2017. China Stops Funding CPEC Road Projects Over Graft Issue: Report. https://www.thehindubusinessline.com/news/world/china-stops-funding-cpec-road-projects-over-graft-issuereport/article9982789.ece. Accessed 20 September 2019.

Contessi, Nicola P. 2019. *China Opens Border Connections to Nepal*. Yale University. https://yaleglobal.yale.edu/content/china-opens-border-connections-nepal.

Custer, Samantha, Tanya Sethi, Jonathan A. Solis, Joyce Jiahui Lin, Siddhartha Ghose, Anubhav Gupta, Rodney Knight, and Austin Baehr. 2019. *Silk Road Diplomacy: Deconstructing Beijing's toolkit to influence South and Central Asia*. Williamsburg: AidData at William & Mary.

Das, Gurudas, and C. Joshua Thomas, eds. 2018. *BCIM Economic Cooperation : Interplay of Geo-economics and Geo-politics*. New Delhi: Routledge.

Dhaka Tribune. 2019. PM Launches Mining Work of Karnaphuli Tunnel in Chittagong. *Dhaka Tribune*. https://www.dhakatribune.com/bangladesh/nation/2019/02/24/pm-launches-mining-work-of-karnaphuli-tunnel-in-chittagong. Accessed 27 September 2019.

Dutta, Prabhash K. 2018. Maldives Election: Who is Ibrahim Mohamed Solih and What Does He Mean to India?. *India Today*. https://www.indiatoday.in/world/story/maldives-election-2018-ibrahim-mohamed-solih-1347563-2018-09-24. Accessed 1 March 2020.

Farole, Thomas, and Gokhan Akinci, eds. 2011. *Special Economic Zones: Progress, Emerging Challenges, and Future Directions*. Washington, DC: World Bank.

Financial Times. 2018. Advantage India in Struggle with China over Maldives. https://www.ft.com/content/24b0bb54-c22d-11e8-95b1-d36dfef1b89a. Accessed 1 March 2020.

GCR. 2019. *Global Construction Review*. http://www.globalconstructionreview.com/news/chinese-firm-starts-16bn-chittagong-road-tunnel-ba/. Accessed 27 September 2019.

Giri, Anil. 2019. *Nepal Trims Projects Under BRI from 35 to 9 at Chinese Call*. https://kathmandupost.com/national/2019/01/18/nepal-trims-projects-under-bri-from-35-to-9-at-chinese-call.

Gokhale, Nitin A. 2017. *Securing India The Modi Way: Pathankot, Surgical Strikes and More*. New Delhi: Bloomsbury.

Grare, Frédéric. 2018. *Along the Road: Gwadar and China's Power Projection*. Paris: European Union Institute for Security Studies.

Hendrix, Cullen. 2016. Rough Patches on the Silk Road? The Security Implications of China's Belt and Road Initiative. In *China's Belt and Road Initiative: Motives, Scope, and Challenges*, ed. Simeon Djankov and Sean Miner. Washington, DC: Peterson Institute for International Economics.

Hull, C. Bryson. 2011. War Crimes Heat on, Sri Lanka's Rajapaksa Goes Back to China. *Reuters*. https://www.reuters.com/article/us-srilanka-china/war-crimes-heat-on-sri-lankas-rajapaksa-goes-back-to-china-idUSTRE77816Z20110809. Accessed 1 March 2020.

Hurley, John, Scott Morris, and Gailyn Portelance. 2018. Examining the Debt Implications of the Belt and Road Initiative from a Policy Perspective. In *CGD Policy Paper 121*. Washington, DC: Center for Global Development.

IMF. 2017. *Maldives: Debt Sustainability Analysis*. Washington, DC: International Monetary Fund.

Khan, Minhas Majeed, Ahmad Rashid Malik, Saira Ijaz, and Ume Farwa, eds. 2017. *China-Pakistan Economic Corridor: A Game Changer*. Islamabad: Institute of Strategic Studies.

Kratz, Agatha, Allen Feng, and Logan Wright. 2019. *New Data on the "Debt Trap" Question*. Rhodium Group. https://rhg.com/research/new-data-on-the-debt-trap-question/. Accessed 5 February 2020.

May, Alexandra. 2019. Greater Integration the Key to Unlocking South Asia's Vast Economic Potential. *World Economic Forum*. https://www.weforum.org/press/2019/10/p-a-b-greater-integration-the-key-to-unlocking-south-asia-s-vast-economic-potential-b-a-p/. Accessed 9 February 2020.

MDTF, Pakistan. 2016. *Industrial Policy 2016*. Islamabad: Multi-Donor Trust Fund for Khyber-Pakhtoonkhwa, FATA and Balochistan.

Ministry of External Affairs. 2017. Official Spokesperson's Response to a Query on Participation of India in OBOR/BRI Forum. https://mea.gov.in/media-briefings.htm?dtl/28463/Official+Spokespersons+response+to+a+query+on+participation+of+India+in+OBORBRI+Forum. Accessed 16 September 2019.

MIT. 2007. *The Future of Coal: Options for a Carbon-Constrained World*. Cambridge, MA: Massachusetts Institute of Technology.

MOEWRI. 2018. *Energy, Water Resources and Irrigation Sector's Current Status and Roadmap for Future*. Kathmandu: Ministry of Energy, Water Resources and Irrigation.

Mushtaq, Munza. 2018. China's Shadow Looms Large in Sri Lanka Local Election. *Nikkei Asian Review*. https://asia.nikkei.com/Politics/China-s-shadow-looms-large-in-Sri-Lanka-local-election2. Accessed 20 September 2019.

NEPRA. 2017. *State of the Industry Report*. Islamabad: National Electric Power Regulatory Authority.

OECD. 2014. *OECD Foreign Bribery Report*. Paris: Organisation for Economic Co-operation and Development.

PCI. 2019. *Energy, Investment & Employment*. Pakistan China Institute. http://www.cpecinfo.com/news/energy-investment-and-employment-statistics-of-cpec-energy-projects.pdf. Accessed 9 September.

People's Daily. 2017. Sri Lanka – China Logistics and Industrial Zone Inaugurated. *People's Daily*. http://en.people.cn/n3/2017/1105/c90000-9288812.html. Accessed 23 September 2019.

Rana, Pradumna B., and Binod Karmacharya. 2016. A Connectivity-Driven Development Strategy for Nepal: From a Landlocked to a Land-Linked State. In *Connecting Asia: Infrastructure for Integrating South and Southeast Asia*, ed. Michael G. Plummer, Peter J. Morgan, and Ganeshan Wignaraja. Cheltenham and Northampton: Edward Elgar and Asian Development Bank Institute.

Ranjan, Amit. 2019. The Making of Bangladesh-China Relations. *Jindal School of International Affairs* 2 (1): 32–44.

Rasheed, Zaheena, and Rathindra Kuruwita. 2018. UN Urges Sri Lanka to Recall Parliament Amid Bribery Claims. *Al Jazeera*. https://www.aljazeera.com/news/2018/11/urges-sri-lanka-recall-parliament-bribery-claims-181102210541175.html. Accessed 20 September 2019.

Rose, Rahul. 2015. Chinese Engineering Company Investigated for Bribery in Sri Lanka. *Global Investigations Review*. https://globalinvestigationsreview.com/article/1017849/chinese-engineering-company-investigated-for-bribery-in-sri-lanka. Accessed 1 March 2020.

Shrestha, Sabita. 2019. "Chinese Investors Interested in Proposed Industrial Park in Chitwan. *Republica*. https://myrepublica.nagariknetwork.com/news/chinese-investors-interested-in-proposed-industrial-park-in-chitwan/. Accessed 23 September 2019.

Siddiqui, Salman. 2017. CPEC Investment Pushed from $55b to $62b. *The Express Tribune*. https://tribune.com.pk/story/1381733/cpec-investment-pushed-55b-62b/.

Singh, Gunjan. 2018. Evolution of China-Sri Lanka Relations. In *VIF Brief*. New Delhi: Vivekananda International Foundation.

Small, Andrew. 2018. The Backlash to Belt and Road: A South Asian Battle Over Chinese Economic Power. *Foreign Affairs*. https://www.foreignaffairs.com/articles/china/2018-02-16/backlash-belt-and-road. Accessed 20 September 2019.

Uberoi, Patricia. 2016. Problems and Prospects of the BCIM Economic Corridor. *China Report* 52 (1): 19–44.

Weerakoon, Dushni, and Sisira Jayasuriya. 2019. Sri Lanka's Debt Problem Isn't Made in China. *East Asia Forum*. https://www.eastasiaforum.org/2019/02/28/sri-lankas-debt-problem-isnt-made-in-china/. Accessed 27 September 2019.

Wijayatunga, Priyantha, D. Chattopadhyay, and P. N. Fernando. 2015. Cross-Border Power Trading in South Asia: A Techno Economic Rationale In *ADB South Asia Working Paper Series No.38*. Manila: Asian Development Bank.

World Bank. 2008. From Periphery to Core (In Two Volumes) Volume II: Full Report. In *Pakistan Balochistan Economic Report*. Washington, DC: World Bank.

Xinhua. 2018. Roundup: China-Funded Bridge Rail Link Contributes to Bangladesh-India Connectivity Project. *Xinhua*. http://www.xinhuanet.com/english/2018-05/09/c_137167483.htm. Accessed 27 September 2019.

Yatsui, Takuma. 2019. China's Belt and Road Initiative in South Asia: Strengths and Issues of Chinese Economic Cooperation Seen in Bangladesh. In *Mitsui & Co. Global Strategic Studies Institute Monthly Report*. Tokyo: Mitsui & Co.

Zhang, Fan. 2019. *In the Dark: How Much Do Power Sector Distortions Cost South Asia?* Washington, DC: World Bank.

CHAPTER 7

BRI and Central Asia

1 Introduction

Central Asia—which includes Armenia, Azerbaijan, Georgia, Kazakhstan, Kyrgyzstan, Turkmenistan, Tajikistan, and Uzbekistan as defined by ADB—has enormous relevance for the BRI. Situated at the heart of the Eurasian continent, Central Asia is where the contemporary Silk Road broadly retraces the ancient Silk Road, and where Chinese President Xi Jinping unveiled his signature Silk Road Economic Belt (SREB) to the world in September 2013.

Central Asian Republics (CARs) are enthusiastic participants in the BRI. In 2014, Kazakhstan took the lead in inking a BRI MOU with China. Armenia, Georgia, Uzbekistan, Tajikistan, and Azerbaijan followed suit successively a year later. In 2018, Kyrgyzstan formally signed onto the BRI cooperative framework. In addition, Azerbaijan, Georgia, Kazakhstan, Kyrgyzstan, Tajikistan, and Uzbekistan are the founding members of the China-initiated AIIB. Because of its foreign policy of permanent neutrality, Turkmenistan is not officially part of the BRI (or AIIB), but it nevertheless is active in pursuing BRI-related infrastructure projects (e.g., the Central Asia-China gas pipeline).

While much has been written about China's multitudinous interest in implementing the BRI in Central Asia (e.g., safeguarding energy security, de-radicalising the restive Xinjiang region through economic development, and securing a stable trade passage to Europe), the geopolitical and economic implications of the BRI for the developing economies from

P. B. Rana, X. Ji, *China's Belt and Road Initiative*,
https://doi.org/10.1007/978-981-15-5171-0_7

Central Asia are relatively under-researched. In this chapter, like Zhang (2015), Inan and Yayloyan (2018), Laruelle (2018) and Linn and Zucker (2019), we investigate major benefits and key risks entailed by the BRI from the perspective of the Central Asian stakeholder countries.

2 BRI Corridors in Central Asia

Two branches of the SREB (the 'Belt') pass through Central Asia. One is the New Eurasian Land Bridge (NELB) linking Asia with Europe and the other is the China-Central Asia-West Asia Economic Corridor (CCAWA) which connects China to the Mediterranean Sea through Central Asia, West Asia, and the Persian Gulf.

As compared to the centuries-old original 'Eurasia Land Bridge' of which Russia's Trans-Siberian railway was the major segment, the NELB provides a shortcut for China to conduct trade with Europe through Kazakhstan. The NELB was first mooted in the mid-1990s but gained traction only after 2011. Now under the BRI, the NELB connects 108 cities in 16 countries from across Asia and Europe (see Appendix 1 for the details of a list newly launched China-Europe railways). Becoming the main overland east-west trading route, 77 per cent of the container traffic between China and Europe went through the NELB in 2018 (Pieriegud 2019). The number of freight trains plying between China and Europe has seen explosive growth in recent years, reaching 6300 in 2018 (Fig. 7.1). In the process, Alashankou/Dostyk and Khorgos/Altynkol crossings on the Chinese-Kazakh border and Małaszewicze/Brest border point on the

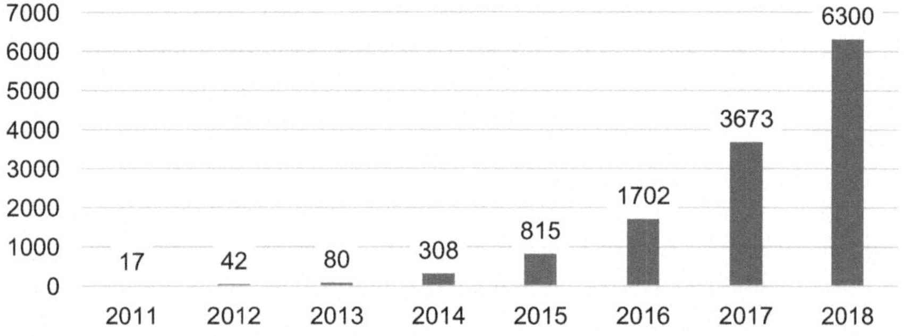

Fig. 7.1 Number of freight trains between China and Europe (2011–2018). Source: Kitade (2019)

Polish-Belarusian border have emerged as the major logistic hubs for trans-Eurasian rail container transport.

The CCAWA corridor for its part enhances transport connectivity within Central Asia and between Central Asia and its neighbourhood regions. Traffic has begun flowing on the China-Kyrgyzstan-Uzbekistan highway since February 2018. The three countries have also signed the 'Intergovernmental Agreement of the Shanghai Cooperation Organisation Member States on the Facilitation of International Road Transport' for unfettered trade and transport facilitation. Similar agreements have been signed for the China-Pakistan-Kazakhstan-Kyrgyzstan, China-Kazakhstan-Russia and China-Kyrgyzstan-Uzbekistan road transport routes. The feasibility study for the China-Kyrgyzstan-Uzbekistan railway is being undertaken with the possibility of extending it southwards to Tajikistan and Afghanistan. In addition, China and several CARs have agreed to reciprocally simplify customs procedures to facilitate cross-border trade. For instance, the newly set up express customs clearance services for agricultural products between China and Kazakhstan, Kyrgyzstan, and Tajikistan have reduced the clearance time required for inspection and quarantine by 90 per cent (Office of the Leading Group for Promoting the Belt and Road Initiative 2019).

In the South Caucasus, the most noteworthy transnational BRI infrastructure project is the Baku-Tbilisi-Kars (BTK) railway, operational since October 2017 between Azerbaijan, Georgia, and Turkey. Two years on, the line had carried 275,000 tonnes of freight (Daily Sabah 2019). More importantly, the BTK rail line is connected north to the Trans-European Rail Network on one hand and forms part of the China-Kyrgyzstan-Uzbekistan-Turkmenistan-Azerbaijan-Georgia-Turkey international multimodal transport corridor on the other. Presently, three trains a week run between Turkey and Kazakhstan, and the block container train services between China and Turkey run once a week. Another promising development is the launch of the container train called the 'Nomad Express' on the China (Shihezi)-Kazakhstan (Dostyk-Aktau)-Azerbaijan (Kishly) route in 2015. The route was made possible by close cooperation between China and the International Association of the Trans-Caspian International Transport Route (Inan and Yayloyan 2018). With respect to bilateral BRI cooperation, Armenia approved a civil aviation agreement with China in April 2019 the pave the way for openining direct flights between the two countries. In a second step, China and Armenia mutually lifted visa requirements in January 2020 to encourage people-to-people exchange. China-led AIIB has a share in the Trans-Anatolian Natural Gas

Pipeline Project in Azerbaijan. In Georgia, Chinese companies are involved in the country's mining, forestry, real estate and hospitality, industrial parks and special economic zones in Kutaisi and Poti.

3 Benefits for Central Asia

3.1 *Economic Renaissance*

To appreciate the BRI's overall significance to Central Asia, it is useful to go back to the history of the region. For much of the bygone era, Central Asia was at the cross-roads of the trans-continental Eurasian trade. This role of Central Asia declined during the Age of Discovery (fifteenth to seventeenth centuries) when alternative sea trading routes between the East and the West were opened and utilised to transport heavier and bulkier goods. By the nineteenth century, the region was mostly conquered by the Russians, becoming the remote border areas of a vast empire ruled from Moscow. During the Soviet era, socio-economic marginalisation and political alienation deepened as the region was relegated to a peripheral position of military base, nuclear weapon test-ground and raw materials supplier. Following the collapse of the Soviet Union, the Central Asian region plunged into protracted economic chaos marked by broken-down public services, disrupted international economic linkages, de-industrialisation and hyperinflation (Jeffries 2003; Batsaikhan and Dabrowski 2017). It took almost a decade for the GDPs of the CARs to bounce back to their pre-independence levels. Growth rates picked up in the early 2000s because of the global commodity boom as many of these countries are resource-rich countries like Kazakhstan (oil and natural gas), Azerbaijan (oil), Turkmenistan (natural gas), and Uzbekistan (gold). Central Asia's growth momentum was, however, interrupted by the 2008 Global Financial Crisis. Economic development of the CARs took a further hit after the sharp fall in international energy prices in 2014.

Against this backdrop, the CARs are hoping to leverage the historic opportunities presented by the BRI to jumpstart a fresh round of economic growth (Pomfret 2019). Indeed since 2013, Central Asia has captured the attention of global investors who had long overlooked the region. A recent report by the consulting firm BCG (2018) notes that Central Asia has become 'a key source of growth [for the global economy that] the world has started to take notice' thanks to the BRI. Various international economic institutions have also become active in the CARs. To give an example, the European Bank for Reconstruction and

Development initiated a biennial Central Asia Investment Forum in 2016 to discuss the practicalities of doing business in Central Asia. The European Investment Bank (EIB) started providing loans to Kyrgyzstan and Uzbekistan in 2013 and 2017, respectively. ADB has also beefed up its financial commitments to Central Asia. Meanwhile, the CARs themselves are keen to capitalise on the investor enthusiasm kindled by the BRI. The biennial Tbilisi Silk Road Forums have been organised by the Georgian government with the support of ADB from 2015 onwards to discuss various trade, investment and connectivity opportunities and challenges under the BRI. Uzbekistan launched a comparable Central Asian Economic Forum in March 2019 in an attempt to attract additional investor interest into Central Asia. Gradually, Central Asia is being transformed by the BRI, and others, from a 'forgotten land' to a 'land of many opportunities' in the words of BCG (2018). The economic revival of Central Asia might well be one of the defining regional economic trends of the twenty-first century.

3.2 *Improved Transport Connectivity*

Apart from Georgia, all CARs are land-locked. Kazakhstan, Kyrgyzstan, Tajikistan, and Uzbekistan are located at least 3500 km away from the nearest maritime port (United Nations 2003). Economic development of Central Asia has, therefore, been retarded by deficient transport connectivity and high transport costs within the region and with the outside world. Coming to their aid, the BRI is addressing CARs' connectivity deficits at the inter-regional, intra-regional and national levels in a number of ways.

3.2.1 CARs Benefit as Transit Countries

First of all, the BRI will increase rail trade between Asia and Europe. While the bulk of Euro-Asian freight is and will be transported via ships (Hillman 2018), Eurasian rail cargo transport has seen steady growth since the advent of the BRI (see Fig. 7.1). A study commissioned by the International Union of Railways estimates that the Eurasian rail transport volume will increase from 141,000 twenty-foot equivalent unit (TEU) in 2016 to 636,000 TEU by 2027, implying a compound annual growth rate of over 16 per cent (Berger 2017). As key transit countries for east-west trade, CARs will benefit from transit fees. For instance, the study by Aitzhanova (2019) suggests that the projected increase in Eurasian container transit would yield $5 billion annually for Kazakhstan.

3.2.2 *CARs Benefit from Enhanced Inter-regional Connectivity*

Improved transport links have also provided CAR with new trading opportunities and export destinations. Kazakhstan offers a case in point. Kazakhstan is a grain producer but in the past it had logistical difficulties reaching markets beyond adjacent countries like Russia; with BRI-related transport infrastructure put into operation, Kazakhstani grains are being transported to new markets inaccessible pre-BRI (Pomfret 2017). The China-Kazakhstan (Lianyungang) Logistics Cooperation Base and Lianyungang SCO International Logistics Park have been developed under the BRI to facilitate Kazakhstan's trade with East and Southeast Asia. In 2017, for example, Kazakhstan exported wheat to Vietnam and Malaysia for the first time by making use of the Khorgos-Lianyungang railway and the logistics facilities in Lianyungang. Elsewhere, Kazakhstan is striving to strengthen trading relations with Georgia, Iran, and Turkey. The BRI is creating the infrastructural facilities for such prospects to materialise. The first west-bound test container train from China arrived in Baku of Azerbaijan through Kazakhstan in August 2015; in January 2016, an east-bound Ukraine-Georgia-Azerbaijan-Kazakhstan-China container train completed a test journey, crossing the Black and Caspian Seas. A key component of the trans-Caspian route is the China-supported construction and development of the Kuryk port in Kazakhstan. The Kuryk port is meant to increase Kazakhstan's trade with neighbouring countries and to increase the all-weather transit potential of the Caspian Sea. The first phase of the project has been completed. In 2017, the port handled 1.5 million tons of goods and reduced travelling time between Kazakhstan and Azerbaijan by up to 10 per cent.

For Kyrgyzstan and Tajikistan, the BRI is delivering results by helping these countries resume their trade with South Asia which had been interrupted by the war in Afghanistan. Instead of transiting via the unstable Afghan territory, Tajik, and Kyrgyz exports are now being transhipped to Xinjiang via the Tajikistan-Kyrgyzstan-China logistics routes before being re-exported to Pakistan through the Karakoram Highway of CPEC. The reverse merchandise traffic flows help bring Pakistani and South Asian cargos to Central Asia.

Turkmenistan has extended its M37 highway up to the Uzbek city of Bukhara, giving Uzbekistan valuable access to the Turkmenbashi International Seaport on the Caspian Sea opened in 2018 (Devonshire-Ellis 2018). In addition to the Turkmen port, another access point for Uzbek international trade is Aktau of Kazakhstan which is undergoing modernisation under the BRI. In May 2019, Uzbekistan railway began transiting cargos through the Aktau port. Having access to two key ports on the Caspian Sea to trade with third countries will greatly re-energise Uzbekistan's international connectivity and trade potential.

3.2.3 CARs Benefit from Internal Connectivity Improvement

Equally important, the BRI is also addressing domestic transport bottlenecks and internal missing links in various CARs. Kazakhstan's existing national railway networks are mostly directed to the north due to Soviet planning. Under the BRI, an east-west trans-Kazakhstan railway is being constructed to connect Khorgos and Aktau. China is investing $3 billion to upgrade the Khorgos dry port to enhance its capacity to inspect containers, handle transhipment and change gauge. At the same time, new BRI railways are being built to connect Zhezkazgan and Beineu, and Arkalyk and Shubarkol, closing critical railway gaps (Samruk-Kazyna 2017).

In Uzbekistan, China Railway Tunnel Group has constructed a 19.2-km-long Kamchiq Tunnel (the longest in Central Asia), opening a direct link between Tashkent and the eastern regions of Namangan, Fergana, and Andijan. The tunnel spares Uzbekistan the need to transit through Tajikistan for reaching those regions which account for nearly a third of the total Uzbek population. The tunnel also saves Tashkent $25 million each year in transit payment to Tajikistan (Sadykov 2013). Ganiev (2019) notes that the tunnel cuts costs by 35 per cent for personal travellers and 50 per cent for transporting oil and oil products. In Kyrgyzstan, China's Exim Bank financed the construction of the country's second north-south road between Balykchy and Jalal-Abad. This line, together with the Bishkek-Naryn-Torugart and Bishkek-Osh-Irkeshtam roads, form the arteries of Kyrgyzstan's road transport network. This will significantly shorten north-south travel time, ease traffic congestion, facilitate the transportation of goods and people along the route, while facilitating the passage of Chinese goods in a win-win situation. In Tajikistan, the China-funded Vahdat-Yovon railway was completed in 2016. From Dushanbe's standpoint, the attraction of this railway lies in its ability to facilitate domestic movement of people and goods between the more densely populated areas in north-central Tajikistan and the resource-rich areas in the south.

As the BRI enhances transport connectivity in Central Asia, new production facilities, distribution networks and industrial areas along the transport routes need to be developed along the corridors. Intra-regional trade in the CARs has improved significantly since 2013, and so has inward foreign direct investment (Fig. 7.2). More significantly, connectivity provides the opportunity for CARs to move away from the hydrocarbon commodity-based growth strategies of the 2000s to a more diversified one

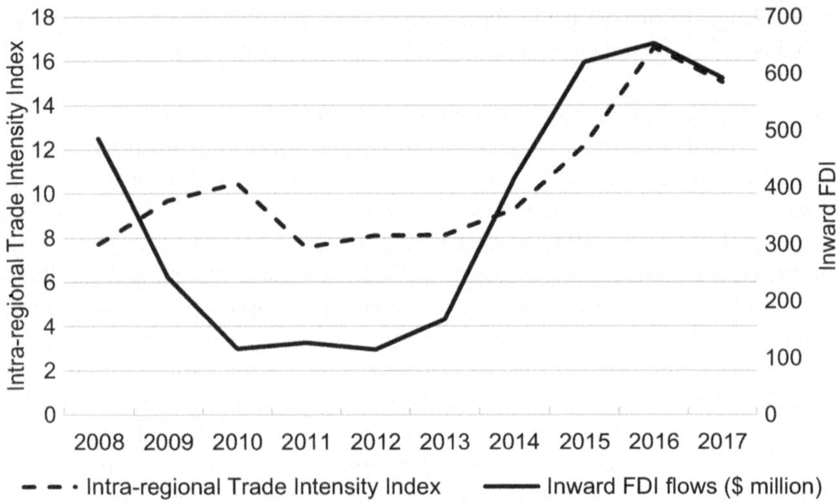

Fig. 7.2 Increasing intra-regional trade and inward FDI in Central Asia. Source: ADB Integration Indicators

that is based on trade- and export-oriented industrialisation and economic modernisation. Multinationals such as General Motors, General Electric, and Toyota have already been incentivised to set up new factories in Central Asia to reap Central Asia's locational and connectivity dividends.

3.3 *Industrialisation and Industrial Parks*

China has deepened industrial cooperation with CARs through the establishment of various industrial parks under the BRI. In 2014, China and Tajikistan signed an MOU to jointly develop a China-Tajikistan Industrial Park, the first such Chinese investment in Tajikistan. The industrial park began operation in 2015 initially to develop Tajikistan's lead-zinc mines. Since September 2017, it has been upgraded to the Tajikistan North Nonferrous Metal Industrial Park. The new park will have an annual processing capacity of 6 million tonnes of non-ferrous raw metal materials with an annual output of around 350,000 tonnes of metals like copper (Xinhua Silk Road 2017). Its output is essential for the industrialisation of Tajikistan. Two other major BRI industrial park projects in the country are the China-Tajikistan New Silk Road Agricultural Textile Industrial Park for cotton planting and textile processing, and the China-Tajikistan Agricultural Processing Park, which cultivates and processes food and vegetables (Feng 2019).

At the 2017 inaugural BRF, China's National Development and Reform Commission and the Ministry of Economic Affairs of Kyrgyzstan signed an MOU on 'Joint Promotion of Industrial Capacity and Key Investment Cooperation Projects'. A flagship cooperation project that flows from the MOU is the Kyrgyzstan Asia Star Agricultural Industry Cooperation Zone, located along the Kyrgyzstan-Kazakhstan highway. The objective of the zone is to develop a vertically integrated, green 'cultivation, production and supply' value chains for meat product, encompassing breeding, rearing, fattening, slaughter, feed processing, food processing. More generally, the park will be a leading logistics centre of frozen products and a centre of international free trade in Central Asia (Xinhua 2017b).

In Kazakhstan, a special logistics and industrial zone, the Khorgos-East Gate Special Economic Zone, is being built, adding to the overall economic value of Khorgos. Samruk-Kazyna (2017), Kazakhstan's sovereign wealth fund, estimates that this SEZ alone will create more than 100,000 jobs. Two other projects, the Sino-Kazakhstan High-tech Industrial Park and the Agricultural Products Processing Logistics Park, are under construction (Feng 2019). With Uzbekistan, besides upgrading a pre-existing Pengsheng Industrial Park in the Sirdaryo state, there is a proposal from the Institute of Bio-organic Chemistry at the Academy of Sciences of Uzbekistan to develop an Uzbek-Chinese industrial park in the Navoi Free Economic Zone of Uzbekistan. The park will host a pharmaceutical complex that produces chemical synthesis of substances necessary for modern pharmaceutical industries, making it the first of its kind in Central Asia. The industrial park, now still in early stage of development, will also train more than 200 qualified scientific and technical personnel and create 500 more local jobs according to the Uzbek news outlet KUN.UZ (2019).

In South Caucuses countries, China's industrial cooperation with Azerbaijan and Georgia has been proceeding steadily with policy support from the BRI. In June 2017, China's Shenzhen city signed an MOU with Azerbaijan to build the China-Azerbaijan Trade and Industrial Park in capital Baku's Qaradağ region. Shenzhen has pledged to invest around $700 million to develop sustainable energy, logistics, industrial manufacturing, modern agriculture, and financial services in the park (Xinhua 2017a). In 2015, China built its first industrial park in Georgia's second-largest industrial city Kutaisi. The $400 million Hualing Free Industrial Zone serves as a linchpin between capital Tbilisi and Black Sea Ports of Poti and Batumi. For now, the zone focuses on developing logging, forestry and wood processing industries to export to neighboring countries. The long-term plan is to establish it as a central Eurasian hub of light industries including a variety of raw materials processing, furniture manufacturing and hardware and construction materials manufacturing activities.

3.4 Development of Financial Sector

Central Asia lags behind East Asia in the area of financial sector development and financial cooperation. Owing to the BRI, Central Asia is starting to press ahead in these two areas.

A showpiece BRI financial project in Central Asia is the Astana International Financial Centre (AIFC), modelled after the Dubai International Financial Centre. In May 2015, kicking off the '100 Concrete Steps National Plan', then Kazakh President Nursultan Nazarbayev issued a decree to commence the development of the AIFC. As to rationale, Kazakhstan wanted to pursue the AIFC project in collaboration with China for three reasons. First, Kazakhstan wanted to position itself as a regional financial hub radiating out to serve its neighbourhood, the EAEU, inner China, Mongolia, and Eastern Europe. Second, the AIFC could play a catalytic role in Kazakhstan's wider economic privatisation and marketisation drive. Third, international capital could be raised to finance BRI projects in Central Asia so as to reduce reliance on CARs' sovereign borrowing. In the words of Kairat Kelimbetov, the governor of the AIFC, Kazakhstan 'plays a strategic role in recreating a trade corridor connecting East and West through China's Belt and Road Initiative. Astana, in particular, has a tremendous opportunity to become a delivery point for the Belt and Road infrastructure financing office' (AIFC 2018).

The AIFC was officially opened in July 2018. In November 2018, the Astana International Exchange (AIX) held its first Initial Public Offering. Within the first year of operation, the AIX had raised more than $70 million in capital equity, and forged financial partnerships with Shanghai Stock Exchange, Silk Road Fund, China Development Bank and China Construction Bank (Kozhanova 2019). To guard against criminal financial activities (e.g., tax evasion and money laundering), an independent AIFC judiciary operating according to English Law has been set up to ensure that individuals and institutions act with integrity in the AIFC. The AIFC has a clear demonstration effect in the reigon, leading for example to the establishment of the Central Asian Stock Exchange (CASE) by Tajikistan in April 2015. In June 2018, CASE signed an MOU with the Uzbek stock exchange Toshkent to strengthen Tajik-Uzbek financial linkage.

CARs and China are also deepening monetary and banking cooperation among themselves. Since 2013, China and CARs have signed four bilateral currency swap agreements (BSAs, see Table 7.1 for details). As noted by McDowell (2019), these BSAs help China internationalise the renminbi. That being the case, the swaps also benefit the CARs. Not only do they provide regional countries with short-term liquidity support to finance balance of payment difficulties and deal with liquidity shocks, but they also facilitate trading and settling contracts in local currencies to avoid exchange risks.

4 Risks Posed by BRI

Regarding the potential downsides of the BRI to the CARS, three main issues have to be considered: public debt risk, Sinophobia, and geopolitical risks.

4.1 Debt Distress

Figure 7.3 shows the evolving public debt situations—as measured by the nominal public and publicly guaranteed debt (PPGD)-to-GDP ratio—in seven BRI countries in Central Asia. The data show that since 2013 debt ratios have increased in all 7 CARs especially in Kyrgyzstan, Armenia, Tajikistan, and Georgia. Presently, the ratios are relatively high—40 to 60 per cent—in Kyrgyzstan, Armenia, Tajikistan, and Georgia. In Azerbaijan,

Table 7.1 China's currency swap arrangements with Central Asian countries

Partner	*Size in renminbi (billion)*	*Size in local currency (billion)*	*Indicative size in USD*[a] *(billion)*	*Initial agreement*	*Validity (years)*
Armenia	1	77	0.14	March 2015	3
Georgia	Undisclosed	Undisclosed	Undisclosed	September 2015	Undisclosed
Kazakhstan[b]	7	200	1	December 2014	3
Tajikistan	3	3	0.43	September 2015	3

Source: Authors' compilations

[a]Calculated using prevailing exchange rate at the time of writing

[b]Kazakhstan and China also renewed an earlier BSA of 1 billion renminbi reached in 2011

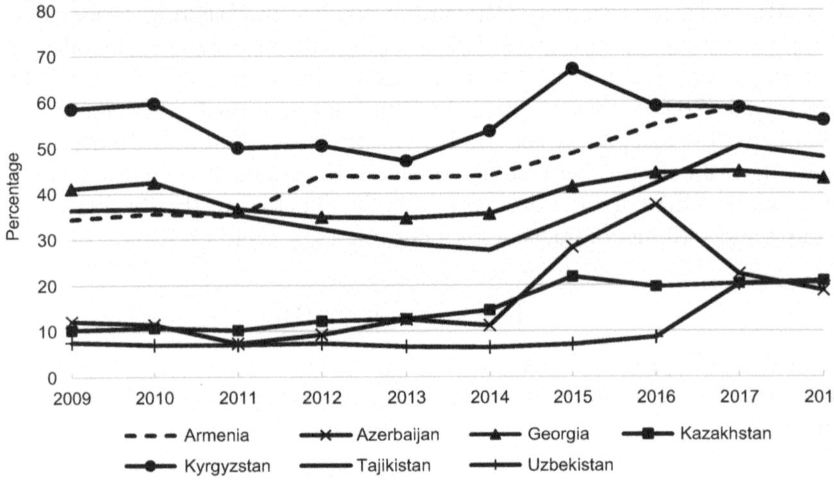

Fig. 7.3 PPGD-to-GDP ratios for seven Central Asian BRI countries. Source: IMF country debt sustainability reports

Kazakhstan, and Uzbekistan, however, they are about 20 per cent well below the 60 per cent threshold as defined by Hurley et al. (2018). Even in the four countries with relatively higher PPGD-to-GDP ratios, with the exception of Tajikistan, the present debt situation appears to be manageable for the following reasons.

Kyrgyzstan has the highest level of PPGD-to-GDP ratio in the region (56% in 2018). The Exim Bank of China is the country's single largest creditor. As of end 2017, the Kyrgyz debt to the Bank made up around 42 per cent of total government external debt and 24 per cent of national GDP (Mogilevskii 2019). In spite of that, almost all BRI projects in Kyrgyzstan have been financed through generous concessional loans with effective interest rates in the range of 1.86–2.5 per cent, to be repaid in 20–25 years' time after grace periods of 5–11 years (Mogilevskii 2019). Therefore, the debt impact of the BRI is likely to be manageable. In fact, Bishkek has been vigilantly monitoring its debt obligations under the BRI (Bhutia 2019). Prudent debt management is paying off—after hitting a high of 67.1 per cent in 2015, the total public debt in Kyrgyzstan has been declining continuously in recent years.

Armenia has the second-highest PPGD-to-GDP ratio among the Central Asian BRI countries (55.8% in 2018). But instead of China, it is the World Bank, IMF, and ADB that are the top international creditors of the country, holding 40 per cent, 12 per cent and 8 per cent of Armenian foreign debt, respectively (Abrahamyan 2015). In addition, a significant chunk of Armenian government debt is associated with the issuance of Eurobonds (World Bank 2019). This broad breakdown of debt sources suggests that the observed upward trend of Armenian public debt has little to do with China or the BRI. Indeed, the study by Hurley et al. (2018) notes that the cost of BRI projects in Armenia 'is not high enough to have an appreciable effect on [the country's] debt levels'.

The public debt of Tajikistan reached 47.9 per cent of GDP in 2018. Between 2007 and 2016, debt to China accounted for almost four-fifths of total increase in Tajikistan's external debt (Hurley et al. 2018). Tajikistan's ability to pay back BRI loans is, however, questionable. Unlike its neighbours that can rely on mineral exports to service foreign debt, Tajikistan as a poor, agriculture state dependent on migrant remittances from Russia needs to take urgent actions to review and deal with the issue of debt accumulation. Otherwise, there is a risk that China might demand access to core Tajik assets as recompense. This is not without precedent. In 2011, Tajikistan handed over 1000 km^2 of (disputed) land in the remote Pamir mountain range to China in exchange for debt forgiveness. On this matter, we concur with the World Bank (2018) and Hurley et al. (2018) that Tajikistan is at a 'high risk' of debt distress, and any further indebtedness due to the BRI could cause sovereignty concerns.

In 2018, Georgia's public debt stood at 43.3 per cent of GDP. The IMF (2019) assesses that Georgia's debt is sustainable, warranting low-level scrutiny under the Fund's Debt Sustainability Analysis framework. Georgia's debt exposure to China remains a small fraction of the country's total debt. As such, it is unlikely that Georgia has or will be beset by BRI-induced debt sustainability problems.

4.2 *Increasing Sinophobia*

Sinophobia poses a serious stumbling block to the BRI in Central Asia. Contemporary Sinophobia was passed on through generations of Central Asians by Soviet anti-China propaganda since the 1960s (Owen 2017). Post-independence, pungent anti-China sentiment has been reinforced by a fear of Chinese territorial and cultural invasions and oppositions to China's alleged repression of Uyghur Muslims in Xinjiang.

As it expands its economic footprint in Central Asia, China has managed to turn around its image in several CARs through soft power campaigns in the form of Confucius Institutes, sister-city initiatives, government scholarships and friendship years, winning public affection and approbation (Custer et al. 2019). In an Armenian public opinion poll carried out in May 2019, 89 per cent of the respondents rated Sino-Armenian relations as 'good' (Alisauskiene 2019). Likewise, in a spring 2016 survey coordinated by the Tajik Academy of Sciences, over 90 per cent of the respondents viewed Chinese engagement with Tajikistan in a positive light (Vakulchuk and Overland 2019). However, an entrenched aversion to China remains problematic in other CARs.

There is a risk that the BRI might generate a new breed of Sinophobia because BRI-related projects offer more tangible and high-profile targets for anti-Chinese wrath. China-backed projects are sometimes also hated as evidence of Chinese economic imperialism that exploits the locals, damages the environment, extorts natural resources while bringing in cheap manufactured goods (Scobell et al. 2014).

In 2016, nation-wide protests broke out in Kazakhstan against proposed changes to Land Code[1] as protestors claimed that reforms would allow China to 'legally' take over scarce arable Kazakh land and displace indigenous farmers. In 2019, Kazakhstan's approval to construct 55 factories to onshore industrial production from China (as agreed to by the BRI MOU) provoked a wide-spread public backlash. Massive anti-China marches swept across six major Kazakh cities, and the construction plans had to be halted as a result. Similarly in Kyrgyzstan, operations at the China-built Junda oil refinery in Kara-Balta was suspended after months of community environment and labour protests in 2014; demonstrators insisted that the refinery had violated national environmental laws and was constructed by imported Chinese workers who impregnated local women (Trilling 2014). The operation of the refinery was suspended once again in 2018 in the aftermath of fresh anti-China protests. In the same year, angry Kyrgyz burned down a Chinese-funded gold-processing plant in Toguz-Toro, ostensibly for environmental reasons. In early 2019, the Kyrgyz capital of Bishkek was overwhelmed by what has been described as 'the biggest public protest to date in Central Asia against Beijing's growing influence' with protestors demanding limits on work permits for Chinese, a reduction in Kyrgyz debt and a ban on Kyrgyz-Chinese interracial marriages (SCMP 2019). A local observer notes that Chinese companies employed almost exclusively Chinese labour, equipment, and materials to implement BRI projects in Kyrgyzstan (Mogilevskii 2019). In the case of Georgia, although organised anti-China public dissent has not yet been staged, Georgians are reportedly holding negative views about

Chinese citizens living in Georgia, accusing them for under-contributing to the local economy (CRRC 2019).

The series of anti-China riots and events mentioned above suggest that the BRI might have increased Sinophobia in Central Asia. If unaddressed, this would only lead to lose-lose situations. For Beijing, it is a public relations hurdle to the BRI's success. For CARs, Sinophobia-related violence is detrimental to their social harmony, economic well-being, public security and political stability. After all, closing Chinese factories and companies reduces public income and result in job losses. The Minister of Economy of Kyrgyzstan Oleg Pankratov, for example, reckoned that the 2018 disruption to the Junda oil refinery meant a loss of 200 million soms in tax revenue for the country (Kostenko 2018). Sinophobia may also agitate fears among local people about possible Chinese ethnic retaliations. And the spectre of potential inter-ethnic worker conflict, production disruption and property damage might deter foreign and Chinese investment in Central Asia, imposing unnecessary economic sacrifice on many other innocent people.

4.3 *Increasing Geopolitical Tensions*[2]

In Central Asia, the implementation of the BRI has to navigate an intimidating geopolitical environment. Central Asia has long been the arena of greater power competition (Brzezinski 1997; Gachechiladze 2002) and is increasingly encircled by geopolitical hotspots. These include the war in Afghanistan, separatist movements in Xinjiang and the North Caucasus, economic sanctions on Iran, the India-Pakistan conflicts in Kashmir and the long-lasting Kurdish-Turkish conflicts.

Within the region itself, inter- and intra-state conflicts are notoriously common. For the east Caspian Sea states, the Kazakh-Uzbek leadership contest has soured regional relations. Notwithstanding the recent bilateral thaw, the two countries remain locked in a tussle for regional primacy. Interwoven border, energy and ethnic struggles are yet another prominent source of regional mistrust and beggar-thy-neighbour economic policies. The disintegration of the Soviet Union is said to have opened 'a Pandora's box of border disputes' (ICG 2002) as it created numerous unmarked territories endowed with rich hydrocarbon resources and fractured transboundary ethnic and religious ties. Provocations of unilateral border demarcation, pre-emptive extraction in contested territories, and making ethnicity-based claims to pieces of land in one another's territorial confines frequently occur. The resulting border skirmishes and ethnic violences further fuel mutual animosity across the region. Water disputes between the upstream (Tajikistan and Kyrgyzstan) and downstream countries (Kazakhstan, Uzbekistan, and Turkmenistan) in Central Asia also add to regional tensions. As a former Uzbek leader, Islam Karimov, once remarked, water-related problems could spark wars in the region.

In South Caucasus, strained regional relations are in part caused by crisscrossing geopolitical alignments and violent secessionism. Armenia looks to Russia as the security guarantor and has fought a war against Azerbaijan over the independence of the self-proclaimed Nagorno-Karabakh region, an Armenian-settled region of Azerbaijan. The pro-Western Georgian government maintains friendly ties with both Armenia and Azerbaijan but is at loggerheads with Russia for Moscow's backing of independence of South Ossetia and Abkhazia. Antagonistic Russo-Georgian relations culminated in a full-blown border war in 2008. Even today, tensions between Armenia and Azerbaijan and those between Russia and Georgia show no sign of abating and will remain as geopolitical obstacles to China's economic and infrastructural engagement in the region.

The BRI will both affect and be affected by the fractious geopolitical situations in Central Asia. Aggressive competition between CARs for Chinese BRI funding could lead to more mistrust while driving up borrowing costs. The execution of BRI transport projects could reignite some of the region's frozen conflicts should they pass through disputed areas, contested energy deposits, and multi-racial communities in frontier territories (e.g., Fergana Valley). For instance, the progress on the China-Kyrgyzstan-Uzbekistan railway is being held back by the Kyrgyz-Uzbek border conflicts. Given the transnational nature of cross-border infrastructure, every country has an effective veto over regional projects. One example is the ill-fated Line D project as the fourth branch of the Central Asia-China gas pipeline. It was designed to deliver Turkmen natural gas to China through Uzbekistan, Tajikistan and Kyrgyzstan. Its construction has been stalled indefinitely after the withdrawal of Uzbek political support. The stance of Uzbekistan dealt a heavy blow to Turkmenistan, which relies on China as a key market for gas export, and to Tajikistan and Kyrgyzstan, which are deprived of millions in potential transit fees.

Even in-country infrastructure development could have profound extra-territorial ramifications, and thus can be met with foreign resistance. In 2012, Uzbekistan issued a threat of war and put Tajikistan under an energy siege for years to deter Dushanbe from constructing the Rogun Dam on the Vakhsh River. Uzbekistan feared that the Tajik dam would endanger irrigation water availability and food security for its population living downstream. The dam project eventually went through in 2018 after a compromise, but the underlying conflicts of interest pitting upstream countries against downstream ones is real. If energy-starving upstream countries brought in Chinese capital to build hydroelectric power stations, the BRI would aggravate the region's pre-existing dispute potential over water. Also, the BRI's energy agenda could intensify regional competition for resources. Such a risk was on display in the EU-led Trans-Caspian Gas Pipeline Project (TCGP) for transporting Caspian natural gas to Europe. Turkmenistan and Azerbaijan both wanted to export gas to Europe, leading to heated disputes on the ownership of some oil and gas fields in the south Caspian basin. To the extent that it also aims to export Caspian Sea resources, the BRI carries the risk of fuelling energy disputes among Caspian Sea countries as the TCGP once did.

5 Conclusion

Given its central and strategic location, Central Asia is critical to the success of China's BRI in promoting integration between China and Europe. From the viewpoint of local stakeholders, however, the BRI implies a number of benefits as well as risks.

On one hand, BRI provides CARs with an opportunity to overcome their land-lockedness and become land-links between China and Europe. This should be beneficial for the economic growth of the CARS as it would mean greater volumes of trade and investment. Indeed, thanks to the BRI, Central Asia is now better integrated with the world economy and better endowed with transport infrastructure that links it with East, South, Southeast and West Asia. Chinese-built and invested industrial parks have turbocharged CARs' industrialisation drive. The AIFC and BSAs developed under the BRI are also seen as mechanisms to promote financial development and connectivity in Central Asia.

At the same time, if BRI funds are not used efficiently and prudently, they could lead to fiscal vulnerability and debt distress especially in the low-income country of Tajikistan. Suspicious attitudes towards China in countries like Kazakhstan and Kyrgyzstan could be worsened by China's BRI. Riots and protests against Chinese investment and projects pose a security risk which could dampen investor confidence. The Central Asia is also geopolitically volatile. Pushing forward the BRI recklessly could add to existing tensions while giving rise to new odious geopolitical frictions. Multilateral coordination and political cooperation and 'soft diplomacy' on the part of the Chinese are required.

Appendix 1 Selected Newly Launched China-Europe Railways

Route	*Frequency (per week)*	*Duration (days)*	*Countries*	*Goods (west bound)*	*Goods (east bound)*
Zhengzhou-Hamburg/Munich	6	15–18	China, Kazakhstan, Russia, Belarus, Poland, Germany	Textiles, auto parts, construction machinery, medical devices, electronic products, tobacco, wine and food	Food, auto parts, complete vehicles, daily necessities
Chengdu-Łódź	3–4	12–15	China, Kazakhstan, Russia, Belarus, Poland	Agricultural products, mechanical equipment, food and alcohol, electrical equipment, automobiles and spare parts	Electronic products, home appliances, auto parts, moulds, clothing, shoes and hats
Chengdu-Nuremberg	1	14–15	China, Kazakhstan, Russia, Belarus, Poland, Germany	Agricultural products, mechanical equipment, food and alcohol, electrical equipment, automobiles and spare parts	Electronic products, home appliances, auto parts, moulds, clothing, shoes and hats
Chengdu-Tilburg	2–3	14–17	China, Kazakhstan, Russia, Belarus, Poland, Germany, Netherlands	Vegetables, fruits, clothing, shoes and hats	Vehicles, auto parts, equipment raw materials, engineering equipment, alcohol
Wuhan-Pardubice/Łódź/Hamburg/Duisburg	2–4	15	China, Kazakhstan, Russia, Belarus, Poland, Czech Republic, Germany	Electronic products, clothing and mechanical accessories	Alcohol, food, drinks, grain and oil
Chongqing-Duisburg	15	15–18	China, Kazakhstan/Mongolia, Russia, Belarus, Poland, Germany	Chemicals, food, clothing, furniture, mechatronics	Daily necessities, milk powder, cosmetics, alcohol

Yiwu-Madrid	1	18–20	China, Kazakhstan, Russia, Belarus, Poland, Germany, France, Spain	Air conditioners, mechanical parts, clothing fabrics, auto parts, power tools	Alcohol, food, cooking oil
Yiwu-London	1	18	China, Kazakhstan, Russia, Belarus, Poland, Germany, Belgium, France, Britain	Maternal and child supplies, soft drinks and vitamin products	–
Yiwu-Prague	–	16	China, Kazakhstan, Russia, Belarus, Poland, Czech	Cloth, clothing, shoes, hats, decorative items	Crystal products, auto parts, beer
Xi'an-Hamburg	3	16–18	China, Kazakhstan, Russia, Belarus, Poland, Czech	Daily goods	–
Xi'an-Kouvola	1	13–15	China, Kazakhstan, Russia, Finland	–	–
Xi'an-Budapest	2	13–15	China, Kazakhstan, Russia, Ukraine, Hungary	Maternal and child supplies, soft drinks and vitamin products	–
Hefei-Hamburg	1	15	China, Kazakhstan, Russia, Belarus, Poland, Germany	–	–
Changsha-Hamburg	1	15	China, Kazakhstan/ Mongolia, Russia, Belarus, Poland, Germany	Electronics, textiles, hardware supplies	–
Xiamen-Hamburg	1	16	China, Kazakhstan, Russia, Belarus, Poland, Germany	Display, printer, LED strip, clothing and shoes	–

Source: Xinhua Silk Road Information Service

Note: – data not available

Notes

1. The proposed land law allowed foreigners to rent agricultural land in Kazakhstan for 25 years. It also allowed land to be sold or leased at auctions.
2. To the extent that Russia's official stance towards the BRI is mildly supportive, in this study Russia's role per se is not considered as a source of geopolitical tension (or geopolitical dividends) as far as China's economic engagement with Central Asian republics is concerned. This is not to argue a structurally diminished role for Russia, whether in terms of security, economics or culture, in this part of the world traditionally under the Russian/Soviet/Russian sphere of influence, but to argue that Russia has so far refrained from pursuing a policy of obstructionism vis-à-vis the BRI and China's economic presence in its backyard. In addition, as this study examines the implications and impacts of the BRI predominately from the perspective of regional countries, the dynamics of greater power competition in which Russia is a major part is not the focus of this chapter.

References

Abrahamyan, Gayane. 2015. Armenia: Like Greece, Too Much Foreign Debt?. *eurasianet*. https://eurasianet.org/armenia-like-greece-too-much-foreign-debt. Accessed 10 October 2019.

AIFC. 2018. *AIFC: The Financial Hub of the Region*. Nur-Sultan: Astana International Financial Centre.

Aitzhanova, Aktoty. 2019. The Belt and Road Initiative : The Case of Kazakhstan. In *China's Belt and Road Initiative: Potential Transformation of Central Asia and the South Caucasus*, ed. Harinder S. Kohli, Johannes F. Linn, and Leo Zucker. New Delhi, Thousand Oaks, London and Singapore: Sage.

Alisauskiene, Rasa. 2019. *Public Opinion Survey: Residents of Armenia*. Center for Insights in Survey Research. https://www.iri.org/sites/default/files/armenia_poll_may_2019_final.pdf. Accessed 1 November 2019.

Batsaikhan, Uuriintuya, and Marek Dabrowski. 2017. Central Asia—Twenty-Five Years After the Breakup of the USSR. *Russian Journal of Economics* 3 (3): 296–320.

BCG. 2018. *Investing in Central Asia: One Region, Many Opportunities*. https://www.bcg.com/Images/BCG-Investing-In-Central-Asia-report-ENG_tcm26-212857.pdf.

Berger, Roland. 2017. *Eurasian Rail Corridors: What Opportunities for Freight Stakeholders?* Paris: International Union of Railways.

Bhutia, Sam. 2019. Data Show Kyrgyzstan Weathering Debt Load. *eurasianet*. https://eurasianet.org/data-show-kyrgyzstan-weathering-debt-load. Accessed 11 October 2019.

Brzezinski, Zbigniew. 1997. *The Grand Chessboard: American Primacy and Its Geostrategic Imperatives.* New York: Basic Books.

CRRC. 2019. *Georgians Have More Negative Attitudes Towards the Chinese than Other Foreigners in Georgia*. Caucasus Research Resource Centers. http://crrc-caucasus.blogspot.com/2019/01/georgians-have-more-negative-attitudes.html. Accessed 11 November 2019.

Custer, Samantha, Tanya Sethi, Jonathan A. Solis, Joyce Jiahui Lin, Siddhartha Ghose, Anubhav Gupta, Rodney Knight, and Austin Baehr. 2019. *Silk Road Diplomacy: Deconstructing Beijing's Toolkit to Influence South and Central Asia.* Williamsburg: AidData at William & Mary.

Daily Sabah. 2019. Two Years on, Baku-Tbilisi-Kars Railway Line Carries 275,000 tons of Freight. *Daily Sabah.* https://www.dailysabah.com/business/2019/10/27/two-years-on-baku-tbilisi-kars-railway-line-carries-275000-tons-of-freight.

Devonshire-Ellis, Chris. 2018. *Uzbekistan Re-Energizing as Central Asia's Traditional Hub for the Silk Belt and Road.* https://www.silkroadbriefing.com/news/2018/07/05/uzbekistan-re-energizing-central-asias-traditional-hub-silk-belt-road/.

Feng, Yujun. 2019. China's Strategy Toward Central Asia: Interests, Principles and Policy Tools. *Вестник СПбГУ. Международные отношения [Bulletin of St. Petersburg State University. International relations]* 12: 23–39.

Gachechiladze, Revaz. 2002. Geopolitics in the South Caucasus: Local and External Players. *Geopolitics* 7 (1): 113–138.

Ganiev, Bahodir. 2019. The Belt and Road Initiative in Uzbekistan. In *China's Belt and Road Initiative: Potential Transformation of Central Asia and the South Caucasus*, ed. Harinder S. Kohli, Johannes F. Linn, and Leo Zucker. New Delhi, Thousand Oaks, London and Singapore: Sage.

Hillman, Jonathan E. 2018. *The Rise of China-Europe Railways.* Washington, DC: Center for Strategic and International Studies.

Hurley, John, Scott Morris, and Gailyn Portelance. 2018. Examining the Debt Implications of the Belt and Road Initiative from a Policy Perspective. In *CGD Policy Paper 121.* Washington, DC: Center for Global Development.

ICG. 2002. Central Asia: Border Disputes and Conflict Potential. In *ICG Asia Report.* Osh and Brussels International Crisis Group.

IMF. 2019. Georgia. In *IMF Country Report.* Washington, DC: International Monetary Fund.

Inan, Feride, and Diana Yayloyan. 2018. *New Economic Corridors in the South Caucasus and the Chinese One Belt One Road.* Ankara: Economic Policy Research Foundation of Turkey.

Jeffries, Ian. 2003. *The Caucasus and Central Asian Republics at the Turn of the Twenty-first Century.* London and New York: Routledge.

Kitade, Daisuke. 2019. *Central Asia Undergoing a Remarkable Transformation.* Tokyo: Mitsui & Co. Global Strategic Studies Institute.

Kostenko, Julia. 2018. *Operation of Junda Oil Refinery Suspended*. https://24.kg/english/100769_Operation_of_Junda_oil_refinery_suspended/.

Kozhanova, Nazira. 2019. AIFC Yearly Report Indicates Key Achievements, Projects. *The Astana Times*. https://astanatimes.com/2019/10/aifc-yearly-report-indicates-key-achievements-projects/.

KUN.UZ. 2019. Uzbek-Chinese Industrial Park to be Created in the Navoi Free Economic Zone. https://kun.uz/en/news/2019/11/02/uzbek-chinese-industrial-park-to-be-created-in-the-navoi-free-economic-zone. Accessed 10 March 2020.

Laruelle, Marlene, ed. 2018. *China's Belt and Road Initiative and Its Impact in Central Asia*. Washington, DC: George Washington University.

Linn, Johannes F., and Leo Zucker. 2019. An "Inside-out" Perspective on the Impact of the Belt and Road Initiative in Central Asia and the South Caucasus: How to Maximize Its Benefits and Manage Its Risks. In *EMF Background Papers*. Gerzensee: Emerging Markets Forum.

Mogilevskii, Roman. 2019. Kyrgyzstan and the Belt and Road Initiative. In *IPPA Working Paper*. Bishkek: University of Central Asia.

Office of the Leading Group for Promoting the Belt and Road Initiative. 2019. *The Belt and Road Initiative: Progress, Contributions and Prospects*. Beijing: Foreign Languages Press.

Owen, Catherine. 2017. "The Sleeping Dragon Is Gathering Strength": Causes of Sinophobia in Central Asia. *China Quarterly of International Strategic Studies* 3 (1): 101–119.

Pieriegud, Jana. 2019. *Analysis of the Potential of the Development of Rail Container Transport Market in Poland*. Brussels: European Commission.

Pomfret, Richard. 2017. Central Asia, Global Value Chains and China's "Silk Road Economic Belt" Initiative. In *The New Silk Road: China Meets Europe in the Baltic Sea Region*, ed. Jean-Paul Larçon. Singapore: World Scientific.

———. 2019. *The Central Asian Economies in the Twenty-First Century: Paving a New Silk Road*. Princeton: Princeton University Press.

Sadykov, Murat. 2013. Uzbekistan: New Ferghana Railway Plan Tweaks Tajikistan. https://eurasianet.org/uzbekistan-new-ferghana-railway-plan-tweaks-tajikistan.

Samruk-Kazyna. 2017. *Railway Infrastructure Upside Transit Potential*. Nur-Sultan: Samruk-Kazyna.

SCMP. 2019. Anti-Chinese Protesters Arrested as Police Break Up Rally in Kyrgyzstan, Where Fear and Anger at Beijing's Influence Grow. *South China Morning Post*. https://www.scmp.com/news/world/russia-central-asia/article/2182604/anti-chinese-protesters-arrested-police-break-rally. Accessed 11 November 2019

Scobell, Andrew, Ely Ratner, and Michael Beckley. 2014. *China's Strategy Toward South and Central Asia: An Empty Fortress*. Santa Monica: RAND Corporation.

Trilling, David. 2014. Kyrgyzstan Suspends Work at New Chinese Refinery. *eurasianet*. https://eurasianet.org/kyrgyzstan-suspends-work-at-new-chinese-refinery. Accessed 11 November 2019.

United Nations. 2003. *Challenges and Opportunities for Further Improving the Transit Systems and Economic Development of Landlocked and Transit Developing Countries*. Geneva: United Nations Conference on Trade and Development.

Vakulchuk, Roman, and Indra Overland. 2019. China's Belt and Road Initiative Through the Lens of Central Asia. In *Regional Connection Under the Belt and Road Initiative: The Prospects for Economic and Financial Cooperation*, ed. Fanny M. Cheung and Ying-Yi Hong. Abingdon, New York: Routledge.

World Bank. 2018. Rogun HPP – Potential Resource for Building Human Capital. In *Country Economic Update*. Washington, DC: World Bank.

———. 2019. Armenia: A Strong Mandate for Change Amid a Global Slowdown. In *Country Economic Update*. Washington, DC: World Bank.

Xinhua. 2017a. China and Azerbaijan to Jointly Build China-Azerbaijan Trade and Industrial Park [中国和阿塞拜疆将共建中阿自由贸易产业园区]. http://www.xinhuanet.com//world/2017-06/29/c_129643499.htm. Accessed 10 March 2020.

———. 2017b. Kyrgyzstan Supports Agro-Industrial Park Built by Chinese Enterprise: Economy Minister. http://www.globaltimes.cn/content/1027648.shtml. Accessed 10 March 2020.

Xinhua Silk Road. 2017. Expansion of Largest China-Tajikistan Cooperation Project on Cards. https://en.imsilkroad.com/p/64333.html. Accessed 10 March 2020.

Zhang, Hongzhou. 2015. Building the Silk Road Economic Belt: Problems and Priorities in Central Asia. In *Policy Report*. Singapore: S. Rajaratnam School of International Studies.

CHAPTER 8

Policy Recommendations

Based on the findings of the preceding chapters, this chapter presents ten key policy recommendations that could be considered by China and Asian BRI stakeholder countries to move towards a mutually beneficial BRI 2.0.[1] Adoption of these policies by China would allow Beijing to strike a balance between pursuing the BRI as an instrument of advancing national objectives while reassuring the BRI partners about its adherence to multilateral norms and rules. The recommendations also suggest ways in which BRI participating countries can best meet their economic and infrastructure needs under the BRI while avoiding the BRI's potential fiscal, socio-economic, and geopolitical pitfalls.

1 Enhance BRI Transparency

(Policy Actions to Be Taken by Both China and BRI Stakeholder Countries)

For China, enhancing transparency of the BRI is the top policy recommendation proposed by Asian opinion leaders in our perception survey (Chap. 4). Transparency is indeed the most fundamental requirement to enhance the short-term effectiveness and long-term success of the BRI. Transparency mitigates governance risks (e.g., rent-seeking, corruption, and embezzlement), promotes corporate social responsibility and

P. B. Rana, X. Ji, *China's Belt and Road Initiative*,
https://doi.org/10.1007/978-981-15-5171-0_8

project financial sustainability, and increases public acceptance of BRI projects.

Specifically, China and BRI stakeholder countries should consider strengthening three broad aspects of procedural, contractual, and informational transparency. First, for any BRI-funded infrastructure project, there should be a transparent project selection, preparation, implementation, and monitoring process covering the entire project cycle. Transparent project selection means conducting participatory consultations with the local community and rigorous impact assessment (IA) on the social, environmental, technical, regulatory, and financial aspects of the project, disclosing the IA reports for public scrutiny, and communicating through the local media about project rationale and justification. Once a bankable and financially viable project is selected, contracts should be awarded through a transparent and competitive tendering process—open to not only Chinese contractors but also those qualified from the host and third countries. Subsequent project procurement decisions should be made in accordance with international best practices (e.g., as enshrined in the WTO Agreement on Government Procurement) and with applicable national laws and regulations. During the operational phase of the project, a monitoring system with transparent performance benchmark indicators should be put in place to make policy-makers, project developers, and operators accountable, and to detect operational irregularities and other unanticipated consequences. When a dispute on investment or labour rights occurs, there should be a transparent and impartial BRI dispute settlement and local grievance mechanism to resolve the issues as promptly and amicably as possible.

Second, given that many BRI contracts feature opaque terms, there is need for China and BRI stakeholder countries to collectively enhance contractual transparency. The terms and conditions of BRI projects should be publicly disclosed, avoiding confidentiality clauses wherever possible. In keeping with this recommendation, Russel and Berger (2019) have called on Beijing to develop a standardised and transparent BRI contract template based on the International Federation of Consulting Engineers standard contracts. China may, alternatively, seek to make greater use of its own 'Model Conditions on Contract for Works of Building Construction' in foreign BRI projects. To be sure, such standardised BRI contract templates will have to be negotiated and adapted to the circumstances of specific projects. But the baseline transparency afforded by a reference contract will enhance clarity and help manage expectations on contractual obligations including inter alia financing terms, Chinese labour requirement, quality control measures, and debt restructuring options.

Third, international contractors often complain about information asymmetry that places them at a significant disadvantage when competing for projects vis-a-vis their Chinese competitors. Foreign leaders and the global research community also complain about being under-informed about the details of the initiative and individual BRI projects. A comprehensive BRI project database could be a remedy for this information gap. Presently, major think tanks and knowledge platforms (e.g., Center for Strategic and International Studies, Mercator Institute for China Studies, American Enterprise Institute with The Heritage Foundation, the Council on Foreign Relations and China Africa Research Initiative) and various Chinese provincial authorities such as the Hong Kong Trade Development Council maintain BRI-related databases. But these databases are necessarily partial and incomplete. The Chinese central government should, therefore, establish an exhaustive, bilingual (Chinese and English) and internationally searchable database detailing BRI project's location, status, design, costs, funders, contractors, and operators alongside with all the relevant pre- and post-project legal documents like IA reports. The proposed database should cover not only on-going and completed projects but also the proposed ones so that potential bidders can have up-to-date information about commercial opportunities that could arise.

2 Strengthen Economic and Infrastructure Governance

(Policy Actions to Be Taken by Both China and BRI Stakeholder Countries)

Promoting good governance is the number one policy recommendation for BRI host countries to enact as offered by the over one thousand Asian opinion leaders who participated in our perception survey (Chap. 4). Since the 1990s, many institutions including the World Bank have established an unambiguous causal link between good governance and economic performance, asserting that '[g]ood governance is synonymous with sound development management' (World Bank 1992). An empirical cross-country analysis of developing Asian countries by economists at ADB has also confirmed that 'good governance, while important in and of itself, can also help in improving a country's economic prospects' (Han et al. 2014).

Infrastructure development is a public good and cannot be supplied by private sector in sufficient amounts on its own. The public sector has to step in. Also, infrastructure development in an environment where governance is poor and the regulatory and legal framework is weak has often delivered corruption, delays, cost overruns, poor quality, accelerated physical deterioration, and inadequate coverage especially of the poorest and rural citizens (World Bank 2002; OECD 2017).

The World Bank's Worldwide Governance Indicators, published annually since 1998, provide an overview of the governance situation in countries. Six indicators are provided: Voice and Accountability, Political Stability/Lack of Violence, Government Effectiveness, Regulatory Quality, Rule of Law, and Control of Corruption. Figure 8.1 presents the simple average governance scores for East and Southeast Asian, South Asian, and Central Asian BRI countries. The average scores for high-income Organisation for Economic Co-operation and Development

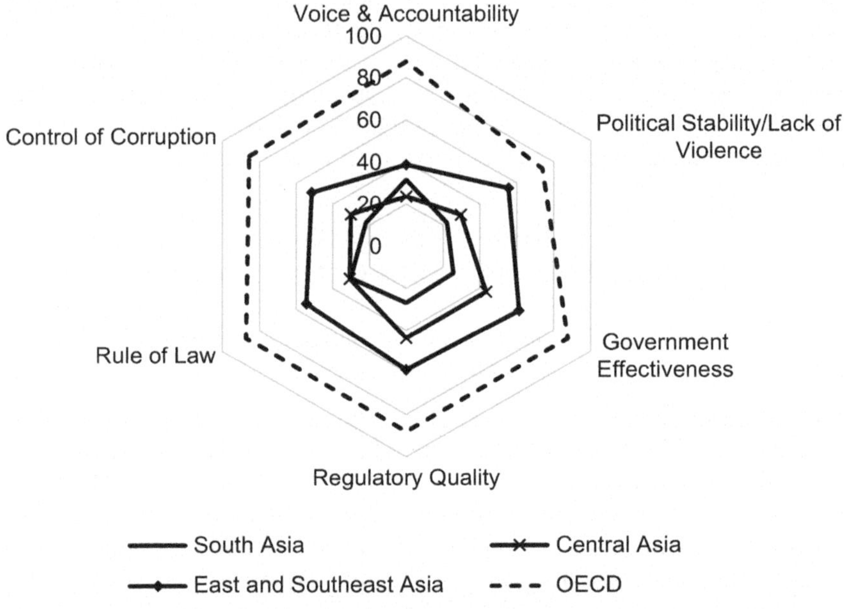

Fig. 8.1 Average governance scores of OECD and Asian sub-regions in 2018. Note: Asian scores correspond to countries that participate in the BRI
Source: Author's calculations based on Worldwide Governance Indicators

(OECD) countries are also provided as the comparator. The data show that among the Asian BRI countries, the East and Southeast Asian countries rank the highest for all six indicators. Central Asian BRI countries rank higher than South Asian BRI countries in all indicators except on Voice and Accountability. This is because South Asian BRI countries are democracies and have greater civil liberty and freedom of speech. As such, in order to maximise the benefit from the BRI, South Asian and Central Asian stakeholder countries must strengthen their governance considerably across all six indicators. South and East Asian BRI countries must also strive to improve governance as they still have to catch up with the high-income OECD countries.

At the project level, reflecting the relationship between good governance and quality infrastructure, the OECD has championed the concept of 'Governance of Infrastructure'. A policy framework for public governance and delivery of infrastructure is developed by the organisation with the aim to 'make the right projects happen in a manner that is cost-efficient, affordable and trusted by users and citizens' (OECD 2017). In particular, the framework emphasises that effective governance of infrastructure hinges on (1) coherent national strategic planning, (2) a transparent project prioritisation mechanism, (3) a decision-making process that focuses on project affordability, (4) regulatory transparency, (5) robust coordination across government bureaucracies, and (6) a clearly defined asset performance evaluation protocol (OECD 2017). This OECD framework will be helpful for Asian BRI countries to scout, prioritise, plan, budget, deliver, evaluate, and regulate their BRI infrastructures. China should also follow this framework wherever applicable. Among others, China needs to tighten up internal control of corruption, level up auditing standards, step up regulatory oversight over the operation of state-owned enterprises abroad, and refrain from signing contracts with inflated prices. Evidence of BRI-fuelled corruption scandals has already been uncovered in many countries.

3 Secure the Buy-in of Major Powers

(Policy Actions to Be Taken by China)

While BRI projects are designed and built chiefly to serve the infrastructure needs of participating countries, they are oftentimes seen as a form of Chinese economic power projection, thereby creating uneasiness among major powers unsympathetic to China's actions (e.g., the United States) and those who see the BRI as a Chinese intrusion into their traditional spheres of influence (e.g., India in South Asia). As the region-focused chapters have shown, there is a risk of Asian countries being caught in the cross-fire between world powers, particularly when implementing the so-called 'geopolitically risky infrastructure projects' with perceived military-civilian dual-use potential (e.g., Hambantota port). Therefore, it is in the best interest of Asian BRI participating countries to hedge their bets across available connectivity and infrastructure development initiatives (Chap. 2) in order to mitigate geopolitical risks. For China, it is imperative to secure the buy-in of other major powers. Chinese diplomacy should concentrate on winning over the support of the European Union (EU) and Japan which have shown a conditional willingness to engage with the BRI.

The BRI is in many aspects China's 'Pivot to Europe' in response to Obama's 'Pivot to Asia', but the EU did not take China's initiative seriously until 2015 when about one-half of the EU member states joined the AIIB without consultations with the European Commission. Brussels was taken further aback by the '16+1' mechanism (now '17+1' with the addition of Greece in 2019) through which China institutionalises economic and BRI cooperation with Central and Eastern European countries. The EU then gradually adjusted its China policy, becaming more cautiously receptive to the BRI. At the time of this writing, 18 EU members and all 5 EU candidate countries (including Turkey) have signed a BRI MOU/document with China. In addition, Austria, Belgium, Britain, France, Italy, the Netherlands, Portugal, and Spain have agreed separately to cooperate with China in third-party markets in fulfilment of the 'triple-win', or what China terms '1+1+1>3' situation (NDRC 2019). Exemplary cases include Sino-Italian cooperation in Greater Beirut Water Supply Project (Lebanon), Gilgel Gibe III Dam (Ethiopia) and the Integrated Steel Mill Complex Project (Azerbaijan); and Sino-Spanish joint construction of the Los Ceibos hospital in Ecuador (NDRC 2019).

Regionally, in 2015, the EU and China established an EU-China Connectivity Platform, aiming to shape the BRI into an 'open platform which adheres to market rules and international norms'. China was also the first and largest non-EU contributor to the EU's €315 billion 'Juncker Plan' for boosting investment in Europe in the aftermath of the global financial and the eurozone crises. China should remain financially engaged in the EU's successor initiative, the InvestEU Programme for 2021–2027. In 2018, the EU announced its own Eurasian connectivity initiative

(Chap. 2). Synergies should be sought between the BRI and the EU strategy by concluding a formal EU-China MOU on connectivity and infrastructure development. Jointly addressing infrastructural bottlenecks that constrain east-west trade flows across the Eurasian landmass is a promising area of China-EU cooperation.

Apart from Europe, China should try to win over the support of Japan whose Expanded Partnership for Quality Infrastructure represents a genuine challenge and credible alternative to the BRI. Like the EU, Japan initially adopted a passive stance towards the BRI. Tokyo refused to join the AIIB and turned down China's invitations to attend the Belt and Road Forum (BRF) twice. But a thaw in bilateral relations in 2018 witnessed China and Japan moving from competition to cooperation on matters related to infrastructure. As with Europe, through the modality of third-party market cooperation, China and Japan are working side-by-side on a few foreign infrastructure projects (NDRC 2019). For example, China General Technology Group collaborated with Japan's Sumitomo and Mitsubishi Heavy Industries to build a coal-fired power station in Central Java, Indonesia. Oil companies from China, Japan and France co-invested in Russia's Yamal liquefied natural gas project. In Vietnam, China's Exim Bank and Japan Bank for International Cooperation co-financed the Hai Phong power station (Phase II). Such cooperative cases should be promoted and the scope of Sino-Japanese cooperation expanded to cover a wider spectrum of economic activities and infrastructural sectors.

4 Multilateralise the BRI

(Policy Actions to Be Taken by China)

The international community has long called for the multilateralisation of the BRI to dilute the image of it being overly China-oriented. China has shown eagerness to multilateralise the BRI and taken a number of actions to this end, but more needs to be done.

First, at the 2019 BRF, President Xi pledged to adopt a multi-participatory approach to partnering with key international institutions including the United Nations, ASEAN, African Union, EU, and Eurasian Economic Union (EAEU). In fact, just before the 2019 BRF, China's Ministry of Finance signed an MOU with the World Bank, the International Fund for Agricultural Development and six regional development banks from Asia, Europe and the Americas to establish a Multilateral Cooperation

Centre for Development Finance (MCDF). The MCDF's mandate is to assist BRI countries in information sharing, capacity building and project preparation. In January 2019, China Council for the Promotion of International Trade and Singapore International Mediation Centre signed an MOU for jointly establishing a multilateral mediators' panel to settle commercial disputes arising from the BRI. The panel will be staffed by experienced legal professionals from countries involved in the BRI. To meet the low-cost, small to medium-value dispute resolution needs of ASEAN countries, the Beihai Asia International Arbitration Centre opened in Singapore in August 2019. The multilateral arbitration centre is headed by a Singaporean national and draws mediators from China, India, Indonesia and Sri Lanka. These actions will alleviate the suspicion that BRI-related commercial disputes will be settled invariably in China's favour.

Second, the BRI has created or will construct multi-country transport networks (e.g., China-Europe railway network), at-the-border assets (e.g., Khorgos dry port), in-country infrastructure with strong spill over effects (e.g., hydropower dams in Central Asia), and infrastructure physically located in-country but economically dependent on transit or consumption by another country (e.g., China-Central Asia gas pipeline). In those cases, the merits of individual projects are inseparable from their wider externalities. As such, multilateral planning, construction, management, and maintenance of transnational BRI infrastructure projects should be promoted. Consider the China-Central Asia gas pipelines as a negative example. Far from being an entity that is implemented multilaterally, the project is split into three separate enterprises each based on a 50–50 arrangement between China and Kazakhstan, China and Uzbekistan and China and Turkmenistan. A fragmented management model of this type tends to inhibit optimal risks, costs, and revenue sharing; invite politically motivated operation interruptions; expose divergence in national regulatory, technical and construction standards; and create confusion about project timeline, contract enforcement, and country-specific responsibilities.

Given the BRI's network and cross-border nature, China and Asian stakeholder countries could employ the 'Best-practice Framework for Managing Transnational Infrastructure Programmes' developed by the World Economic Forum (WEF) (WEF and BCG 2014). The WEF model divides a project's life-cycle into several phases. During the *origination* phase, the emphasis is on carrying out regional planning. In the *preparation* phase, it is crucial to allocate costs and benefits fairly while seeking to harmonise regulations across participating countries. The priority of the *implementation* phase, on the other hand, is to regionally align construction, operation and maintenance processes and standards. For the framework to deliver results to its best, countries have to move away from the current practice of separate planning without coordination, to separate planning with coordination, and finally towards an institutionally integrated planning process. Recasting this readily available WEF model to fit the BRI will help structure BRI infrastructure projects on a multilateral basis and enhance country-ownership. Evidence suggests that countries are increasingly aware of such a necessity of horizontal cooperation. Multilateral management of transnational project is on the upswing of late. For example, Kazakhstan, Azerbaijan, and Georgia signed a tri-partite Cross-sea Transport Channel Agreement in April 2017, coordinating the construction of transport infrastructure in the Caspian Sea region. Under the China-Mongolia-Russia Economic Corridor, the three countries have established a joint venture railway company and a Joint Centre for Investment Planning for effective infrastructure investment coordination.

Third, so far, it has not happened but eventually China should use BRI funds to co-finance with the World Bank and other MDBs including regional MDBs. The new MDBs, namely the AIIB and the New Development Bank have signed MOUs with the traditional MDBs, the World Bank and the ADB, to enhance cooperation in various functional areas such as knowledge and information sharing, staff secondment, operational procedures, and co-financing arrangements. Co-financing operations and cooperation between the traditional and new MDBs have been mutually beneficial to the institutions and the client countries (Rana and Pardo 2018). These good practices should be adopted in the context of the BRI.

5 Liberalise and Facilitate International Trade

(Policy Actions to Be Taken by Both China and BRI Stakeholder Countries)

Simulations of a CGE model in Chap. 3 have shown that trade liberalisation may generate higher economic benefits than reduction in transport cost. It is, therefore, appropriate that the BRI has incorporated 'unimpeded trade' as one of the five official goals along with improved infrastructure connectivity and others.

Despite decades of multilateral and regional efforts to liberalise trade, the simple average applied tariffs in several Asian BRI countries remain high compared to the global average (of 5.2%): Iran (20.9%), Uzbekistan (13.7%), Bangladesh (13%), Nepal (12.7%), Pakistan (12.6%), Cambodia (12.4%), Maldives (11.1%), and Sri Lanka (10.3%). The BRI should, therefore, seek to reduce tariffs further in these stakeholder countries. In this regard, China has in recent years signed or upgraded its free trade agreements (FTAs) with ASEAN, Georgia, Singapore, and Pakistan. China's FTA with the EAEU also went into effect in October 2019. Signed trade trade treaties with Maldives and Mauritius await ratifications before taking effect. These FTAs are steps in the right direction. Going forward, signing more FTAs that reduce non-tariff measures and protect investment should be high on the BRI's trade agenda. China should also open up its domestic market to its BRI partners so that they can earn foreign exchange reserves to repay their loans owed to China.

While trans-Pacific and transatlantic economic ties have been advancing rapidly, ties among the Eurasian countries have long lagged behind. With the BRI and its continental coverage, the case for enhancing economic ties among Asian and European countries has strengthened. One such proposal is to establish an 'ASEM Open and Fair Trade Agreement' (Yeo 2018). The agreement will not only deepen Asia-Europe commercial relations but also support the liberal rules-based economic order.

Besides reducing tariffs, Asian BRI participating countries also need to improve their customs performance and border management. According to the World Bank's Doing Business indicators, in Bangladesh, for example, it can take more than five months (168 days) to comply with all the procedures to export goods. Mismanagement, bureaucratic delays, understaffing, excessive formalities, insufficient digitalisation and lack of coordination between border agencies are among the contributing factors to the inefficient border crossing in some BRI countries, resulting in uncertainties about goods release, corruption scandals, long border compliance time, and additional fees.

A World Bank study (Johns et al. 2018) finds that traders have to face more time than the global average to import on all BRI corridors except the New Eurasian Land Bridge (NELB), and take above-global-average time to export on all corridors with the exception of the NELB and CPEC. To improve the regulatory environment, Shanghai Cooperation Organisation in 2018 issued a statement aimed at facilitating trade across its members' borders. China has also implemented the 'Agreement for the Facilitation of Cross-Border Transport of Goods and People in the Greater

Mekong Sub-region' to streamline border practices in collaboration with Southeast Asian countries. For the BRI as a whole, there is a compelling case for all signatory countries to adhere to the WTO's Trade Facilitation Agreement (TFA) which took effect in 2017. The WTO TFA provides for a set of globally acceptable best practices in relation to the simplification, modernisation, and harmonisation of border processes.

6 Manage Risk of Public Debt Distress

(Policy Actions to Be Taken by Both China and BRI Stakeholder Countries)

Chapters 5–7 of the book have found that the BRI has, so far, not caused wide-spread debt distress in Asian participating countries. Nevertheless, prudent debt management is a pre-condition for the success and sustainability of the BRI. BRI-related infrastructure loans could lead to public debt distress because of (1) pre-existing fiscal vulnerability, (2) inappropriate selection of infrastructure projects, and (3) the fact that China's lending behaviour is not bound by international best practices in terms of lending transparency, procurement standards, and financial concessionality. Accordingly, the following steps could be taken.

First, BRI countries should stabilise and consolidate their fiscal positions so that they can either pursue an independent infrastructure development course (see below) or engage with the BRI in a good fiscal shape. While infrastructure projects implemented properly are productive assets that can pay for themselves over a long horizon, not all projects will turn out to be self-sustaining especially when there are unanticipated shocks to their revenue flows. Thus, government should have the fiscal space to absorb potentially bad infrastructure borrowings or short-term disruptions to the profitability of otherwise financially sound infrastructure projects. There is clearly awareness among some BRI countries of what went and could go wrong in their borrowing approach. Even before concerns about debt sustainability came to a head, a number of countries in Southeast and South Asia (e.g., Malaysia, Thailand, Nepal, and Indonesia) had begun to have second thoughts on the terms of the contracts signed with China, leading to cancellation, scaling-down, or renegotiation of BRI commitments. Highly indebted countries like Tajikistan should follow in their footsteps, and refrain from taking additional collateralised loans to prevent sovereignty risks.

Second, both BRI countries and Chinese funding agencies must perform thorough and transparent due diligence to ensure the bankability and financial viability of proposed infrastructure projects. China has formulated the 'Guiding Principles on Financing the Development of the Belt and Road' and published the 'Debt Sustainability Framework for Participating Countries of the Belt and Road Initiative' to advise on disciplined and market-conforming BRI borrowing. Yet, the BRI Guiding Principles and debt sustainability framework are for voluntary adoption and reference. This non-mandatory practice contrasts with the World Bank's International Development Association where the amount, the proportion of grant versus loan, and the overall concessionality of the assistance package are determined in part by the results of a debtor country's debt sustainability analysis.

The BRI debt sustainability test should similarly be made a compulsory component of the pre-project appraisal process. Those countries without ability to gather evidence and assess the debt implications of interested BRI projects could turn to capacity-building programmes of other major donors and the newly established multilateral MCDF for assistance. Another platform that such countries could use is the Infrastructure Transaction and Assistance Network's Transaction Advisory Fund, through which the United States government provides subsidised professional and legal services to partner countries in the Indo-Pacific region. The Singapore-based Asian Infrastructure Centre of Excellence also performs similar functions. Private professional, consulting, management and financing companies can also help countries identify the most suitable projects.

Third, China should seek associate membership of the OECD Development Assistance Committee (DAC) and full membership of the Paris Club. The former is a forum for coordinating official development assistance among major lending countries, whereas the latter structures sustainable solutions to debt repayment difficulties experienced by borrowing countries. Joining the two reputable international institutions will help China align its lending and debt relief behaviours under the BRI with the prevailing multilateral rules and norms. These actions will also signal Beijing's commitment to transparent and collective creditor actions which in turn can bolster the general credibility of the BRI undertaking. In 2015, China joined the OECD Development Centre.

China is also moving closer to joining the Paris Club. The 2016 Hangzhou G20 Summit Leaders' Communiqué stated: 'We welcome China's continued regular participation in Paris Club meetings and intention to play a more constructive role, including further discussions on potential membership.' In recent years, other emerging creditors such as South Korea and Brazil have joined the Paris Club and China should follow suit sooner rather than later. In the meantime, China like the AIIB it leads should adhere to international best practices and multilateral sovereign debt restructuring rules upheld by the DAC and the Paris Club on a voluntary basis.

7 Prepare a National Infrastructure Strategy

(Policy Actions to Be Taken by BRI Stakeholder Countries)

One of the important recommendations of Asian opinion leaders in our survey is that countries should have a national infrastructure development strategy in place before or while seeking funding for projects from available sources including the BRI. Such an infrastructure strategy should take into account existing infrastructure, medium and long-term needs, and sectoral priorities. The strategy should also identify infrastructure development policies including financing policies and the role of various development partners such as China and the BRI. Projects selected for possible BRI financing should flow from the strategy to ensure full country-ownership. Otherwise there is a risk that projects pushed by Chinese banks and construction companies may have their own agenda and the recipient country could end up with paying for 'white elephant' projects and 'bridges to nowhere'.

Several Asian BRI countries already have drawn up such dedicated infrastructure strategies or action plans (Table 8.1). However, a majority of Asian BRI countries still do not have stand-alone national infrastructure development plans, although infrastructure development tends to feature prominently in their broader multi-year national development plans. Drafting a dedicated national infrastructure strategy with a whole-of-government vision for the use of BRI infrastructure and funding could be considered for countries to better seize the opportunities and meet related challenges under the BRI.

Table 8.1 National infrastructure plans in Asian BRI countries

Country	*Budget*	*Period*	*Priority sector(s)*
Afghanistan	$800 million	2017–2021	Energy, transport, water, urban development, telecom, regional connectivity
Indonesia	5957 trillion rupiah ($412 billion)	2020–2024	Transport (60% of spending), energy (17%), irrigation (10%), information and communications (8%), water (5%)
Kazakhstan (Nurly Zhol)	5559 billion tenge ($14.79 billion)	2020–2025	Road, railway, civil aviation, industrial infrastructure and tourism infrastructure
Kyrgyzstan	Unspecified	2018–2040	Energy, transport, water, environment and climate change
Mongolia	Unspecified	2016–2020	Urban development, energy, transport
New Zealand	$110 billion (2016–2025)	2016–2045	Transport, telecom, energy, water, social infrastructure
Pakistan	Unspecified	2014–2025	Transportation, communications, water, energy
Philippines (Build, Build, Build)	8–9 trillion pesos ($157–177 billion)	2017–2022	Transport, civil aviation, water, irrigation, flood management
South Korea (9-BRIDGE Strategy)	Unspecified	Unspecified	Gas, railways, ports, power generation, North Pole Route, shipbuilding, agriculture, fisheries, industrial complex
Thailand	$49.6 billion	2015–2022	Transport
Tajikistan	$118.1 billion	2016–2030	Transport, telecom, social infrastructure

Source: Authors' compilations based on government documents

8 Empower and Protect Local Communities

(Policy Actions to Be Taken by Both China and BRI Stakeholder Countries)

For various practical reasons, Chinese companies prefer importing Chinese labour, construction materials and engineering equipment to BRI host countries to execute BRI infrastructure projects. The influx of Chinese migrant workers was rated as the second most salient risk by Asian opinion leaders in our survey (Chap. 4) and this has also stirred up some local resentments against the BRI. Without local support, good infrastructure projects can falter. In the future, BRI-supported infrastructure projects should maximise local employment; and this requires concerted efforts from both sides.

The BRI host countries should reform restrictive labour laws to give contractors the legal flexibility of hiring and firing workers, so that their willingness to source labour locally will increase. Employment opportunities in upcoming BRI infrastructure projects should be advertised on time and widely including through local media and recruitment agencies for a minimum period of time in order to maximise the participation of the local labour force. In the event that foreign workers have to be brought in to meet labour or skill shortages, importing companies should conduct local stakeholder consultation; justify the need and size of the on-shoring foreign workforce; screen all the potential social, economic and environmental implications of the temporary labour inflow; strengthen the management of foreign workers' camps; and make contractually binding contingency plans to prevent or cope with potential adverse consequences to indigenous peoples (World Bank 2016; Russel and Berger 2019). Using local goods and services in procurement and project delivery is yet another forceful way to provide a boost to the local economy. Setting up a vehicle to provide preferential funding to infrastructure projects that employ local content beyond a reasonable threshold value could be considered. In fact, both the World Bank's and ADB's procurement policies provide for 'Domestic Preference' to incentivise contractors to use local goods and services and to catalyse the development of local consulting, construction and manufacturing industries in project host countries.

As much as they offer benefits from reducing barriers to international trade, BRI-supported infrastructure projects and free trade deals could also bring heightened foreign competition to previously sheltered local communities, possibly resulting in involuntary job losses. Therefore, China and BRI participating governments should introduce a multilateral Belt and Road Adjustment Assistance Fund to assist adversely affected local communities in various re-adjustment areas such as vocational education, re-skilling, re-employment, relocation, wage insurance, and healthcare credit. In addition, the BRI may entail physical relocation of inhabitants living on, near or along the construction sites to make way for BRI infrastructure projects. In the past, infrastructure-related asset dispossessions and human displacements (e.g., involuntary resettlement, stealth land grabbing, and non-existent relocation assistance) were rampant in China to meet rapid modernisation and economic development needs. As it reflects on its infrastructure development policies and land acquisition laws of the past, China has gradually taken corrective actions to avoid involuntary resettlement; and where involuntary resettlement is inevitable, the government makes sure that the lost assets are compensated according to their market value. As far as the BRI is concerned, China should not backslide on its improving resettlement standards just because the projects are located not at home but on foreign soils. On the contrary, a further Chinese convergence towards globally leading resettlement and safeguard policies should be encouraged. Resettlement outlays should be fully factored into project budgets. This should be the case irrespective of infrastructure types, but particular attention ought be devoted to transport projects because past experience of ADB (2006) shows that transport projects tend to affect many more people than other types of infrastructure.

Once or shortly before BRI infrastructure projects pass the initial construction stage, the policy focus should shift to cultivating a local talent pool to perform day-to-day operation and maintenance (O&M) duties. Well-maintained BRI infrastructure stock will increase utilisation and value for money, but a sufficient number of qualified technical and managerial professionals are required to perform O&M functions. Many developing BRI countries, however, lack skilled O&M staff. As such, training local residents to be engineers and managers through BRI-sponsored capacity-building and up-skilling programmes is important. It will also create high-quality jobs and facilitate technology transfer from project developers to host countries. The Alliance of International Science Organisations in the Belt and Road Region was established in 2018, charged with building a technology transfer platform to serve developing countries' needs. A bright spot can be found in Kenya. China Road and Bridge Corporation has set up a railway training institute near Nairobi to train local youths into rail-tech specialists, preparing them for operating the China-built Mombasa-Nairobi railway on their own.

9 Address Chokepoints and Missing Links in BRI Transport Networks

(Policy Actions to Be Taken by Both China and BRI Stakeholder Countries)

The effectiveness of a transport network is only as good as its weakest link. The BRI corridors examined in this book are of no exception. Achieving seamless transport connectivity across the vast Eurasian continent requires China and BRI stakeholder countries to also focus on relieving transport chokepoints and filling key missing links as discussed below.

The main transport bottleneck of the NELB is at the Polish-Belarusian border, where a shift from broad to standard track gauge width has to be made for trains. The Terespol-Małaszewicze (Poland)/Brest (Belarus) border crossing is the most heavily used for Asia-Europe freight traffic. The Małaszewicze station is the largest transhipment terminal on the European side, but its capacity is limited to just 12 to 14 train pairs per day. The rapid surge in the train trips between China and Europe (Chap. 7) has caused severe capacity constraints and congestions on both sides of the crossing. As a result, in some cases, rail shipments experience delays lasting over ten days in Małaszewicze. With a view to achieving a daily capacity of up to 55 pairs of trains, the EU is currently funding the expansion, modernisation and electrification programme for Małaszewicze (Pieriegud 2019). China should join forces with the EU to upgrade Małaszewicze or explore alternative crossing points (e.g. Vysoka/Litousk, Siemianówka-Cisówka/Swislocz, Kuźnica Białostocka/Bruzgi, Czeremcha/Wysokolitowsk and Włodawa/Tomaszówka) that can be used for Eurasian rail traffic.

The weakest transport link along the China-Central Asia-West Asia Economic Corridor is in the Caspian Sea. Due to bad weather, there are no large-scale container vessels crossing the sea. Alternative types of commercial ferry and feeder services are not regularly scheduled and are not available for 90 days a year on average (Mukhtarov 2018). As China strives to upgrade the railway infrastructure around the Caspian Sea (Chap. 7), the maritime transport chokepoint and the containerisation of goods transport in the Caspian Sea should also be addressed to make the corridor genuinely multi-modal and efficient. However, given the intimidating geopolitics in the Caspian Sea region and China's intimate political relations with Russia, it appears that cross-Caspian maritime connectivity is low on Beijing's priority list (Mardell 2019).

Along CPEC, the Karakoram Highway is a seasonal bottleneck constraining trade between China and Pakistan. Of particular concern is the Khunjerab pass, the highest point of the highway with an elevation of around 4700 meters. Covered in snow in winter, the pass is generally closed from 1 December to 31 March. To expand bilateral and transit trade via the Karakoram Highway, China and Pakistan need to find solutions to ensure all-weather, year-round opening of the Khunjerab pass. A comparable case that may offer hope and inspiration is the Karasu pass on the Sino-Tajik border which first opened in 2004. Like Khunjerab, Karasu was normally closed due to high elevation (of around 4400 meter) and the threatening weather conditions from 1 December to mid-April. In 2016, China and Tajikistan managed to open the Karasu pass to business all year round to facilitate trade. If the Khunjerab pass could see a similar breakthrough, China-Pakistan trade as well as their trade with Central Asia would receive a major boost.

There are also missing rail links in the China-Indochina Peninsula Economic Corridor which deserve policy attention (Ganjanakhundee 2018). The construction of the railway between the southern Vietnamese Ho Chi Minh City and the Cambodian capital of Phnom Penh has still not begun despite years of bargaining over relative funding contribution. The governments of Laos and Vietnam have not yet secured funding for constructing a rail road from Vientiane to the central Vietnamese port of Vung Ang. China could consider funding the two railways within the scope of the BRI. Moreover, the BRI should seek to regionalise and harmonise national railway standards in ASEAN. This is important because national railway systems in Southeast Asian countries follow different technical standards (e.g., metre gauge in Cambodia, Laos and Vietnam versus standard gauge in Malaysia, Singapore and Thailand), making cross-border freight and passenger operations costly and time-consuming. In an encouraging sign, greenfield investments in the region's high-speed railway have uniformly adopted relevant Chinese standards to promote intra-ASEAN high-speed rail inter-connectivity.

10 Transform Transport Corridors to Economic Corridors

(Policy Actions to Be Taken by Both China and BRI Stakeholder Countries)

Although the BRI corridors have been officially labelled economic corridors, at present they focus mainly on building transport (or transit) corridors, except for CPEC which also has associated energy projects and industrial parks (Chap. 6). In other words, the BRI to date is building *transport* corridors, rather than *economic* corridors that have been implied by their official names. To maximise the long-term economic benefits of the BRI, it is necessary to transform these connectivity-improving transport corridors into growth-enhancing economic corridors.

According to an ADB study (Mitra et al. 2016), an economic corridor comprises three main components that are complementary: an industrial production base, an urban centre, and a transport corridor, all located within a specific spatial area. In general terms, the industrial production base produces goods and relies on the transport corridor for distribution and trade; the urban centre is a source of labour, consumption, services, and technologies feeding into industrial production; and the transport corridor reduces the effect of distance, allows for labour mobility and represents a cost-effective way for companies to do business and organise production fragmentation. Going forward, it is logical for BRI stakeholder countries to transform various BRI trade and transport corridors into integrated economic corridors for achieving sustained economic prosperity.

One possible roadmap for BRI transport-to-economic corridor transformation is shown in Fig. 8.2. First, countries should ensure that BRI transport infrastructure is constructed (or retrofitted) to serve major existing industrial, economic or urban centres, rather than investing in stranded roads, railways or pipelines in the middle of nowhere. The BRI host countries should also be prepared to build new industrial facilities, special economic zones and logistic hubs along planned or exisiting BRI transport infrastructures, so that the BRI can be a stepping stone towards industrialisation, diversification and modernisation. Second, infrastructure must be improved to attract investment and secure industrial production input provision within each of the connected industrial enclaves. Ramping up digital connectivity is also vital for producers to optimise their supply chain management. Complementing hard infrastructure development, investment in soft infrastructure such as health care, social security, research and development, and technological innovation is equally critical for human development, job creation, technology transfer and productivity increment along the economic corridors. Concurrently, countries should embrace smart city initiatives (Chap. 5). This is to ensure that nodal cities and industrial hubs along BRI economic corridors are liveable and socially sustainable.

Third, it is incumbent on national governments to create an enabling policy and commercial environment to make it easier for BRI economic corridors to flourish and thrive. The World Bank's Doing Business Report is particularly well suited to guide BRI countries when it comes to pursuing pro-market policy reforms. Among others, BRI governments should be encouraged to simplify regulations for business, protect property rights, adopt an open-door trade policy, withhold over-intervention in the labour and financial markets, and lower taxes (World Bank 2004).

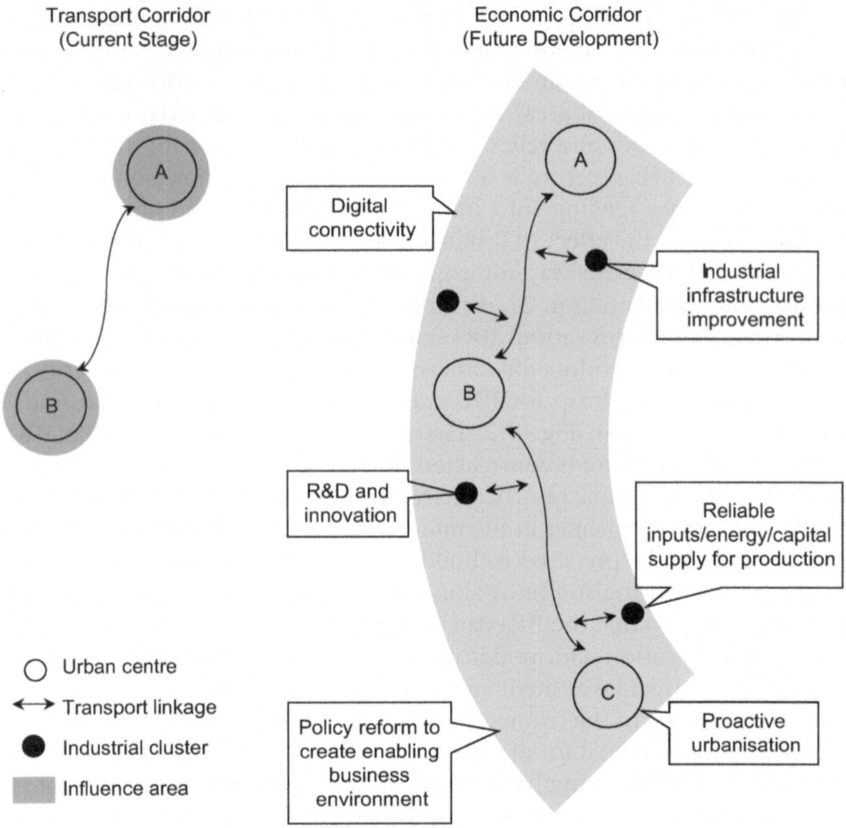

Fig. 8.2 Transformation of BRI transport corridors into economic corridors. Source: Adapted from Petrella (2018) and Mitra et al. (2016)

Note

1. Other policy recommendations proposed by opinion leaders surveyed are highlighted in Chap. 4.

References

ADB. 2006. Involuntary Resettlement Safeguards. In *ADB Evaluation Study*. Manila: Asian Development Bank.

Ganjanakhundee, Supalak. 2018. Completion of High-Speed Southeast Asian Rail Link Is Still Far Down the Track. *The Nation*. https://www.nationthailand.com/ann/30336801.

Han, Xuehui, Haider Khan, and Juzhong Zhuang. 2014. Do Governance Indicators Explain Development Performance? A Cross-Country Analysis. In *ADB Economics Working Paper Series*. Manila: Asian Development Bank.

Johns, Marcus Bartley, Julian Latimer Clarke, Clay Kerswell, and Gerard McLinden. 2018. Trade Facilitation Challenges and Reform Priorities for Maximizing the Impact of the Belt and Road Initiative. In *MTI Discussion Papers*. Washington, DC: World Bank.

Mardell, Jacob. 2019. On the "Middle Corridor," China Is Largely Absent. *Berlin Policy Journal*. https://berlinpolicyjournal.com/on-the-middle-corridor-china-is-largely-absent/.

Mitra, Sabyasachi, Rana Hasan, Manoj Sharma, Hoe Yun Jeong, Manish Sharma, and Arindam Guha. 2016. *Scaling New Heights: Vizag-Chennai Industrial Corridor, India's First Coastal Corridor*. Manila: Asian Development Bank.

Mukhtarov, Agshin. 2018. *A Case Study: Feasibility Analysis of Container Feeder Vessel as a Short Sea Shipping Service in the Caspian Sea*. MSc Programme in Maritime Affairs, Shipping Management & Logistics, World Maritime University.

NDRC. 2019. *1+1+1>3: Third-Party Market Cooperation Guidelines and Cases*. Beijing: National Development and Reform Commission.

OECD. 2017. *Getting Infrastructure Right: A Framework for Better Governance*. Paris: Organisation for Economic Co-operation and Development.

Petrella, Stephanie. 2018. *What Is an Economic Corridor?*. CSIS. https://reconnectingasia.csis.org/analysis/entries/what-economic-corridor/.

Pieriegud, Jana. 2019. *Analysis of the Potential of the Development of Rail Container Transport Market in Poland*. Brussels: European Commission.

Rana, Pradumna B., and Ramon Pacheco Pardo. 2018. Rise of Complementarity Between Global and Regional Financial Institutions: Perspectives from Asia. *Global Policy* 9 (2): 231–243.

Russel, Daniel R., and Blake Berger. 2019. *Navigating the Belt and Road Initiative*. New York and Washington, DC: Asia Society Policy Institute.

WEF, and BCG. 2014. *African Strategic Infrastructure Initiative Managing Transnational Infrastructure Programmes in Africa – Challenges and Best Practices*. Geneva: World Economic Forum.

World Bank. 1992. *Governance and Development*. Washington, DC: World Bank.

———. 2002. *Building Institutions for Markets*. Washington, DC: World Bank.

———. 2004. *Doing Business in 2004: Understanding Regulation*. Washington, DC: World Bank.

———. 2016. *2016 Labor Influx Guidance Note*. Washington, DC: World Bank.

Yeo, Lay Hwee. 2018. ASEM Open and Fair Trade Area – From Vision to Reality. In *My ASEM Wishlist: How Asia and Europe Should Really Be Working Together*. Brussels: Friends of Europe.

Index[1]

[1] Note: Page numbers followed by 'n' refer to notes.

P. B. Rana, X. Ji, *China's Belt and Road Initiative*,
https://doi.org/10.1007/978-981-15-5171-0

The manufacturer's authorised representative in the EU is Springer Nature Customer Service Centre GmbH, Europaplatz 3, 69115 Heidelberg, Germany. If you have any concerns regarding our products, please contact ProductSafety@springernature.com

Printed and bound by CPI Group (UK) Ltd, Croydon, CR0 4YY
05/10/2026
02228121-0001